TAYLC

AND PHILOSOPHY

The Blackwell Philosophy and Pop Culture Series

Series editor: William Irwin

A spoonful of sugar helps the medicine go down, and a healthy helping of popular culture clears the cobwebs from Kant. Philosophy has had a public relations problem for a few centuries now. This series aims to change that, showing that philosophy is relevant to your life—and not just for answering the big questions like "To be or not to be?" but for answering the little questions: "To watch or not to watch South Park?" Thinking deeply about TV, movies, and music doesn't make you a "complete idiot." In fact, it might make you a philosopher, someone who believes the unexamined life is not worth living and the unexamined cartoon is not worth watching.

Already published in the series:

Alien and Philosophy: I Infest, Therefore I Am
Edited by Jeffery A. Ewing and Kevin S. Decker

Avatar: The Last Airbender and Philosophy
Edited by Helen De Cruz and Johan De Smedt

Batman and Philosophy: The Dark Knight of the Soul
Edited by Mark D. White and Robert Arp

The Big Bang Theory and Philosophy:
Rock, Paper, Scissors, Aristotle, Locke
Edited by Dean A. Kowalski

BioShock and Philosophy: Irrational Game,
Rational Book
Edited by Luke Cuddy

Black Mirror and Philosophy
Edited by David Kyle Johnson

Black Panther and Philosophy
Edited by Edwardo Pérez and Timothy Brown

Disney and Philosophy: Truth, Trust, and a Little Bit
of Pixie Dust
Edited by Richard B. Davis

Dune and Philosophy
Edited by Kevin S. Decker

Dungeons and Dragons and Philosophy: Read and
Gain Advantage on All Wisdom Checks
Edited by Christopher Robichaud

Game of Thrones and Philosophy: Logic Cuts Deeper
Than Swords
Edited by Henry Jacoby

The Good Place and Philosophy: Everything is Fine!
Edited by Kimberly S. Engels

Star Wars and Philosophy Strikes Back
Edited by Jason T. Eberl and Kevin S. Decker

The Ultimate Harry Potter and Philosophy:
Hogwarts for Muggles
Edited by Gregory Bassham

The Hobbit and Philosophy: For When You've Lost
Your Dwarves, Your Wizard, and Your Way
Edited by Gregory Bassham and Eric Bronson

Inception and Philosophy: Because It's Never
Just a Dream
Edited by David Kyle Johnson

LEGO and Philosophy: Constructing Reality
Brick By Brick
Edited by Roy T. Cook and Sondra Bacharach

Metallica and Philosophy: A Crash Course in
Brain Surgery
Edited by William Irwin

The Ultimate South Park and Philosophy:
Respect My Philosophah!
Edited by Robert Arp and Kevin S. Decker

The Ultimate Star Trek and Philosophy:
The Search for Socrates
Edited by Jason T. Eberl and Kevin S. Decker

The Ultimate Star Wars and Philosophy:
You Must Unlearn What You Have Learned
Edited by Jason T. Eberl and Kevin S. Decker

Terminator and Philosophy: I'll Be Back, Therefore I Am
Edited by Richard Brown and Kevin S. Decker

Watchmen and Philosophy: A Rorschach Test
Edited by Mark D. White

Westworld and Philosophy: If You Go Looking
for the Truth, Get the Whole Thing
Edited by James B. South and Kimberly S. Engels

Ted Lasso and Philosophy
Edited by Marybeth Baggett and David Baggett

Mad Max and Philosophy
Edited by Matthew P. Meyer and David Koepsell

Taylor Swift and Philosophy: Essays from the Tortured
Philosophers Department
Edited by Catherine M. Robb and Georgie Mills

Joker and Philosophy
Edited by Massimiliano L. Cappuccio, George A. Dunn,
and Jason T. Eberl

The Witcher and Philosophy
Edited by Matthew Brake and Kevin S. Decker

The Last of Us and Philosophy
Edited by Charles Joshua Horn

For the full list of titles in the series see
www.and philosophy.com

TAYLOR SWIFT AND PHILOSOPHY

ESSAYS FROM THE TORTURED PHILOSOPHERS DEPARTMENT

Edited by

Catherine M. Robb
Georgie Mills

WILEY Blackwell

Library of Congress Cataloging-in-Publication Data

Names: Robb, Catherine M., editor. | Mills, Georgie, editor.
Title: Taylor Swift and philosophy: Essays from the Tortured Philosophers Department / edited by Georgie Mills, Catherine M. Robb.
Description: Hoboken, New Jersey: Wiley-Blackwell, [2025] | Includes bibliographical references and index.
Identifiers: LCCN 2024014116 (print) | LCCN 2024014117 (ebook) | ISBN 9781394238590 (paperback) | ISBN 9781394238613 (adobe pdf) | ISBN 9781394238606 (epub)
Subjects: LCSH: Swift, Taylor, 1989—Philosophy. | Swift, Taylor, 1989—Criticism and interpretation. | Music and philosophy.
Classification: LCC ML420.S968 T38 2024 (print) | LCC ML420.S968 (ebook) | DDC 782.421642092–dc23/eng/20240405
LC record available at https://lccn.loc.gov/2024014116
LC ebook record available at https://lccn.loc.gov/2024014117

Cover Design: Wiley
Cover Images: © Eleonora Grigorjeva/Getty Images, © ChiccoDodiFC/Getty Images, © chachamp/Adobe Stock

Set in 10/12pt SabonLTStd by Straive, Pondicherry, India

SKY10087568_101124

Contents

Contributors

Agnès Baehni is a PhD candidate in philosophy at the University of Geneva. She divides her time between moral philosophy and listening to Taylor Swift's music, and often does both at the same time. She is currently writing a doctoral thesis on the topic of the moral relationship to the self.

Tom Beevers is eagerly awaiting an invite on tour as Swift's traveling philosophical adviser. In the meantime, he whiles away his hours as an Assistant Professor in Philosophy at Northeastern University London. He writes on philosophy of language and epistemology, and also enjoys running and cooking (does Taylor need a chef?).

Erica Bigelow is a PhD candidate in philosophy at the University of Washington. Her dissertation asks about our ethical obligations to others' emotions, particularly against the backdrop of vast structural injustice. Erica is also a precollege philosophy facilitator with PLATO. She attended Taylor Swift's infamous Gillette Stadium "rain show" in 2011, and hasn't missed a tour since.

Jonathan Birch is Professor of Philosophy at the London School of Economics and Political Science, where he is best known for his work on animal consciousness and the origins of altruism. He once confused his students by giving "a bad Taylor Swift album" as an example of something that is conceivable but not metaphysically possible.

Brian Britt is Professor of Religion and Cultural Theory in the Department of Religion and Culture at Virginia Tech, where he also serves as Director of the ASPECT PhD program. He writes and teaches about biblical tradition, modern religious thought, literature, and popular culture. The present collaboration with Lucy Britt is the latest in a series of projects informed by his children, including essays on TikTok and the Teletubbies.

Lucy Britt is an Assistant Professor of Politics at Bates College, where she teaches and researches the politics of race and ethnicity, the politics of memory, and African American political theory. She also teaches feminist political theory and writes about feminism and popular culture, from Taylor Swift to trauma-dumping on *The Bachelor*. She is excited that the discourse surrounding Taylor Swift has become an opportunity to engage in critical feminist, queer, and intersectional interventions in "Swiftiedom."

Christopher Buford is Professor of Instruction at The University of Akron. His research interests include external world skepticism, personal identity, and advance directives. When not working on philosophy, he enjoys listening to metal, jazz, and EDM. More Swiftie-adjacent than Swiftie, he does admit that the algorithms have started working Taylor's songs into his playlists.

Jana Alvara Carstens obtained her PhD in philosophy at the University of Pretoria. She once arrogantly proclaimed that she doesn't listen to Taylor Swift. Not long after making this statement, she borrowed a friend's car and a *1989* CD was in the stereo. She didn't turn down the volume. Instead, she realized she was a snob like the guy from "We Are Never Ever Getting Back Together." She wanted to contribute to this book to atone for publicly bashing Swift. Perhaps she's also a little bit afraid of karma.

Alba Curry is a Lecturer in Philosophy at the University of Leeds, UK. Currently her work defends the positive value of anger in ancient Chinese and Greek ethics, individually and comparatively, and its value to contemporary philosophies of emotions, feminism, and artificial intelligence. Despite having been one of those who said, "Who is Taylor Swift anyway?," she became a fan because she loves to investigate phenomena she doesn't immediately like (much like how she started her research on anger).

Amanda Cercas Curry is a postdoctoral researcher at MilaNLP at Bocconi University, Italy. Her research interests are broad and as a computer scientist working on AI, she loves to spend time working with philosophers. She believes that multidisciplinary approaches involving diverse teams and feminist design methods are key in solving today's ethical and technical challenges. As a woman in STEM, she often feels she has had to prove there is more to her than meets the eye, and has found great solace in Taylor Swift's takes on life (she even slept at an airport for her).

Patrick Dawson was, to confess, a bit of a Taylor Swift hater in his younger days. Then he got an education, traveled the world, and took up his current fellowship at University College Dublin. Now, Patrick tries to prove that the past doesn't exist. All that's real is the present, Swift-appreciating Patrick of today. He's also dabbled in debate and stand-up comedy. Given these interests in the present, and the spoken word, you'd think *Speak Now* would be his favorite album. But Patrick's more of a *folklore* guy, reflecting his other loves: nature, cardigans, and that "single thread of gold" from him to his daughter, Idun.

Shoshannah Diehl is an English instructor at Marshall University, where she uses her Swiftie abilities to teach textual analysis to the next generation. Her scholarship interests include linguistics, philosophy, sci-fi and fantasy literature, and deciphering the difference between Quill Lyrics, Fountain Pen Lyrics, and Glitter Gel Pen Lyrics. She spends her spare time writing fiction and cultivating the persona of an argumentative, antithetical dream girl.

Joshua Fagan is a graduate student at the University of St Andrews, Scotland. Like Taylor Swift, he fantasizes about disappearing into the greenery of the Lake District and never returning. When not debating whether *folklore* is better than *evermore*, he specializes in nineteenth-century British and American literature, with a particular focus on the intersection of literature and science in response to the upheaval and malaise created by industrialization.

David Hahn is an adjunct at SUNY Geneseo. He has been called Treacherous, Trouble, and an Anti-Hero; but rarely because of his Dress. If you have a Getaway Car, he knows places in Buffalo NY where he can see you standing in Snow on the Beach.

Rebecca Keddie works as an archivist, and recently graduated with an MA in archives and record management. Her master's dissertation looked at how place can function as archive and was inspired by her obsession with Taylor Swift's song "Cornelia Street." Post-graduation, she's put her degree to good use by continuing to relate it back to Taylor Swift, as with just about everything else in her life.

Sarah Köglsperger is a PhD candidate in philosophy at the University of Fribourg. When she was young and reckless, studying philosophy at LMU Munich, she was immediately enchanted with Taylor Swift's music. Currently, Sarah is working on the influence of personal relationships on blame and forgiveness. She enjoys listening to Taylor Swift's songs, as they vividly capture the intricate nature of relationships and the moral challenges they may pose. Now midnights become her afternoons, as she writes her dissertation while her cat is purring in her lap 'cause it loves her.

Eline Kuipers is a PhD candidate in philosophy of mind at Ruhr University Bochum, Germany, as well as a long-time Swiftie. For her dissertation, she gives her blood, sweat, and tears to investigate how we plan, control, and execute our actions. In her free time, she loves to make sparkling friend-ship bracelets, cuddle with her red cat and bearded dragon, have the time of her life in theme parks with her partner in crime, annoy her friends with marvelous Easter egg interpretations, and proudly sing Taylor Swift songs as if she was the loudest woman the town has ever seen.

Urja Lakhani recently completed her graduate education in philosophy from Birkbeck, University of London. Her research is focused on political epistemology and feminist philosophy. Currently working as a policy analyst, Urja also serves on the editorial board of *The Philosopher*, the UK's longest-running public philosophy journal. Urja has been a lifelong Swiftie. Her childhood in India was accompanied by the sounds of Taylor Swift's earlier albums. Despite never owning a guitar, she found herself shedding tears over teenage heartaches to the tunes of "Teardrops on My Guitar." Later, she moved to New York, where the bright lights never blinded her. Now, she resides in London with her own London boy.

Gah-Kai Leung is a PhD candidate in the Department of Politics and International Studies, University of Warwick, UK. Like Taylor Swift's back catalogue, his philosophical interests are wide and eclectic, including social and political philosophy, applied ethics, the philosophy of social science, and the philosophy of art. His current karaoke song of choice is "Anti-Hero" and someday he hopes to be just as talented at lip syncing as Emma Stone, only with Swift songs rather than tracks by DJ Khaled.

King-Ho Leung is Lecturer (Assistant Professor) in Theology, Philosophy, and the Arts at King's College London, UK. The lingering questions that keep him up—and sometimes wonderstruck—include the relation between philosophy and religion, what it means to exist spiritually or authentically, and whether Taylor Swift will ever return to writing pop-country ballads.

Georgie Mills is a philosopher, nap enthusiast, and songwriter living in the Netherlands. Her philosophical work spans topics such as personality, emotion, disability, fandom, and punk rock. She has been furious with Taylor Swift since a sixteen-year-old Georgie heard the first album of a sixteen-year-old Swift, and she couldn't believe someone her own age had the audacity to be such an accomplished songwriter. Her fandom has Swiftly increased with each subsequent album release. She lives in hope that one day beaded bodysuits will count as acceptable work attire for phi-losophers as well as pop superstars.

Neil Mussett has written philosophy and pop culture chapters on *Spider-Man, Dungeons and Dragons*, and *The X-Files*, so obviously his life grav-itates toward being edgy, sexy, and cool. This did not earn him any points with his daughters Ausra and Ollie or niece Christina, so he jumped at the chance to write about our common love of Taylor Swift. Neil is frustrated that the CIA is getting credit for all the work he has put into making sure that Taylor's boyfriend Travis made it to the Super Bowl.

Glen Pettigrove is Professor of Philosophy at the University of Glasgow. According to Spotify, he spent more time listening to Taylor Swift's music in 2023 than 96 percent of UK listeners. Even so, he cannot compete with his daughters, one of whom was in the top 2 percent and the other in the top 1 percent of listeners. He has published a book, two edited collections, and more than forty papers on philosophical topics, but this is the first time he's gotten to co-author something with one of his children. He is already looking forward to the next time.

Sophia Pettigrove is a philosophy student at the University of Glasgow. Both philosophy and Taylor Swift have been central elements of her life since she was a child, the former due to her father's influence, the latter due to impeccable taste. She is very excited to have convinced her father to write a paper on Taylor Swift with her, and even more excited to share it with other fans.

Lottie Pike is a third-year undergraduate student studying Philosophy with Art History at Northeastern University London. Lottie is the co-chair of POLIS, an inter-university network for philosophy students across London, and is also the President of her university's Philosophy Society. She loves philosophy *almost* as much as she loves Taylor Swift, and has been searching for a way to combine the two. She hopes to pursue a career in academia, with a focus on the intersection between the philosophy of mind and art.

Catherine M. Robb is an Assistant Professor of Philosophy at Tilburg University, Netherlands. She was born in the same year as Taylor Swift, so naturally *1989 (Taylor's Version)* is her favorite album, with "Out of the Woods (Taylor's Version)" often played on repeat. She has happy memories of dancing around the room with her dad to "Shake It Off," and listening to *folklore* during the hard times of the COVID-19 lockdowns.

Macy Salzberger is an Assistant Professor of Philosophy at San Francisco State University. Like Swift, she often writes about relationships and their dynamics. On occasion, she dabbles in songwriting and performance to serenade her dog, Benny (whose favorite Swift song is "Shake It Off").

Eric Scarffe is an Assistant Professor of Philosophy at Florida International University, and earned his PhD in philosophy from Boston University in 2020. He believes that philosophy is not something reserved for academic journals and university classrooms, but is found everywhere. An avid bar-room defender of the thesis that Taylor Swift is as thoughtful a poet as Bob Dylan, the number one song on his Spotify for the past year has been "marjorie."

Kate C.S. Schmidt is happily "living in a big old city," working at Metropolitan State University of Denver. Being an Associate Professor of Philosophy can be "miserable and magical," but she keeps "cruising," just like Taylor Swift. It is pretty standard at her house to "leave the Christmas lights up until January."

Roos Slegers in an Assistant Professor of Philosophy at Tilburg University, Netherlands. She is interested in themes at the intersection between philosophy, literature and (pop) culture. One of her research projects focuses on eighteenth-century conceptions of vanity, and another on the philosophical importance of fantasy and science-fiction stories about cyborgs. Roos struggled to find a way to unite these two projects until she saw Taylor's video for "… Ready for It" and now has no further questions.

Katherine Valde is an Assistant Professor of Philosophy at Wofford College in Spartanburg, South Carolina. She received her PhD in philosophy from Boston University in 2019. As a proud millennial, and just a few months Swift's junior, Katherine has grown up with Swift (and listening to Swift's music). Lately she's been jamming in the *Midnights* (2022) era, and her favorite track is "Karma."

Introducing ... Taylor Swift's Philosophy Era

Catherine M. Robb and Georgie Mills

What if we told you Taylor Swift was a mastermind? Not just when it comes to being "cryptic" and "Machiavellian" in relationships, as she tells us in *Midnights*. And she's not just a musical mastermind, with her record-breaking songwriting and international stadium tours. Taylor is also a *philosophical* mastermind. Since the release of her debut album, Taylor has been writing about themes, ideas, and questions that have kept philosophers busy for millennia.

Have you ever wondered whether you should forgive your ex for breaking up with you, or why your reputation is so important? Have you ever wondered what is so threatening about an angry woman, or whether you really know nothing when you're seventeen? Have you ever considered why Taylor's "Easter eggs" are so fascinating? Or what you would do if you found yourself on an imaginary Christmas tree farm? Have you ever asked yourself what it means to go back to December, or love someone in August? These are all philosophical questions that touch on the nature of heartbreak, forgiveness, time, love, imagination and memory, emotion, feminism, and knowledge.

In this book, we've assembled a team of Swifties who also happen to be philosophy professors and scholars, proving that philosophy isn't just for bespectacled old men behind ivy-covered walls. A philosopher can also be a bejeweled young woman with a guitar and talent for writing lyrics, or anyone who lives their life with curiosity and reflection. With the help of Taylor's lyrics, interviews, and speeches, we will delve into the philosophy that is scattered throughout her discography, like the Easter eggs that she loves to hide. Together we can take pride in the wisdom that comes from Taylor's songs and the ideas that they inspire in you.

Taylor has declared herself to be the "Chairman of the Tortured Poets Department." But with this book a new Era is dawning—Taylor is now in her "Philosophy Era." In fact, as the pages ahead will show, Taylor and her fans have been in this Era all along. It is only fitting then that we now declare Taylor Swift the honorary Chairman of the "Tortured Philosophers Department."

"WHO IS TAYLOR SWIFT ANYWAY? EW"

Is Taylor Swift a Philosopher?

Catherine M. Robb

After being awarded an honorary doctorate by New York University (NYU) in 2022, Taylor Swift gave a commencement speech for the graduates. During her speech Taylor spoke of the exciting challenge of figuring out who we are and who we want to be: "… we are so many things, all the time. And I know it can be really overwhelming figuring out who to be, and when."[1] Taylor tells us that we all play different roles, and our identity is not defined by just one of them. Taylor, for example, is not only a singer and songwriter, but also a film director, actress, celebrity, honorary academic doctor, and the self-appointed Chair of the "Tortured Poets Department."[2]

Many cultural commentators have added the role of "philosopher" to the list that defines Taylor. The journalists Kayla Bartsch, Peter M. Juul, and Clare McCarthy have all claimed or reported that Taylor is a philosopher.[3] Scott Hershovitz, a philosopher and writer for the *New York Times*, has claimed that Taylor is a philosopher of "forgiveness,"[4] and others have stated that Taylor has a philosophy of "writing,"[5] "dating,"[6] and "music."[7]

Although Taylor has spoken openly about many aspects of her life, and has also name-dropped the ancient philosopher Aristotle (384–322 BCE) in *The Tortured Poets Department* ("So High School"), as far as we know she has never called herself or identified as a philosopher. Taylor's music, career, and life as a celebrity are philosophically interesting, raising philosophical questions that are worthy of further discussion and exploration. But it is a much stronger claim to say that Taylor is, herself, a philosopher. So, how can we decide if Taylor really is a philosopher?

The Answer Is Not That Simple

You might think that the answer to this question is easy—all we need to do is figure out what being a philosopher is or what philosophers do, and then see if Taylor fits this description. So, how do we define what it is to be a philosopher? It seems obvious that philosophers do philosophy, and so if Taylor is doing philosophy then she is a philosopher, and if not, then she's not a philosopher—simple, right? Well, as you've probably guessed given the number of pages left in this chapter, finding a definition of what

Taylor Swift and Philosophy: Essays from the Tortured Philosophers Department, First Edition. Edited by Catherine M. Robb and Georgie Mills.

philosophy is and what philosophers do is not that simple. Philosophers disagree about this so much that some even think it is impossible or useless to define what philosophy is.[8] There are good reasons for this difficulty.

First, philosophy is difficult to define because it is pluralistic—hard to pin down as being about just one thing. It is possible to study the philosophy *of* almost anything, including many of the themes that Taylor explores in her lyrics, such as friendship, love, heartbreak, gender, reputation, and knowledge. The way that we can *do* philosophy is also highly varied. Some philosophers will approach a particular topic, like heartbreak, by focusing on how it is experienced from a first-person point of view, and others will try to define heartbreak as accurately and consistently as possible. Still other philosophers might do philosophy by considering the role that heartbreak plays in our well-being and interactions with others, and some might analyze how heartbreak is felt differently depending on one's gender. All these methods count as philosophy.

It is so difficult to pin philosophy down as being about just one thing or method because making decisions about the *right* way to do philosophy is itself a philosophical issue.[9] After all, we can do philosophy *of* anything— even of philosophy itself. Because philosophers have different theories, ideas, and arguments about what philosophy is, answers to the question, "What is philosophy?" are hotly debated and controversial. If it is just a part of philosophy that we cannot agree about what it is, then how can we figure out whether Taylor is a philosopher?

Life Hacks and Embracing Cringe

One way to get out of this stalemate is to forget that professional philosophers argue about what philosophy is, and just use the everyday understanding of philosophy that most people agree on. One popular assumption about philosophy is that it consists in words of wisdom, guiding principles, and values that provide advice about how to live and what to do.[10] If you've ever given anyone general life advice—"never go to sleep angry" or "never trust someone who lets you down twice"—then on this definition you are a philosopher.

This way of understanding what philosophy is certainly makes Taylor Swift a philosopher. All of her albums include song lyrics scattered with pieces of wisdom and guiding principles for how to live and what to do. Beginning with her debut album, Taylor gives us wisdom about how to deal with an uncertain future ("A Place in This World"), and advice against cheating on your partner and asking for forgiveness retrospectively ("Should've Said No"). Fast forward eighteen years to the release of *The Tortured Poets Department*, and Taylor continues to impart philosophical wisdom. In "The Black Dog" she tells us how hard it is to give up old habits (they "die screaming"), and in "I Can Do It With a Broken Heart" she explains that you know you're good at your job "when you can even do it / With a broken heart."

Taylor has also expressed her philosophical views in interviews and speeches. In her 2023 *TIME* Person of the Year interview, she supplies wisdom on how to deal with our enemies, recommends that we take time to celebrate ourselves in the present, and reminds us that "Life is short."[11] In her 2022 NYU commencement speech, Taylor shares a number of "life hacks" that she hopes will be helpful to us "navigating life, love, pressure, choices, shame, hope and friendship."[12] If we take a "life hack" to be the same as a piece of wisdom about how to live a good life, then we can see Taylor as offering us quite a few pieces of philosophical wisdom. She tells us that we ought to embrace cringe, embrace the mistakes that we've made because these often lead to the best things in our lives, and leaves us with a message of resilience and empowerment: "... hard things will happen to us. We will recover. We will learn from it. We will grow more resilient because of it." One of my favorite guiding principles that Taylor has shared came after the Superbowl game in 2024, when she told Travis Kelce that "jet lag is a choice."[13]

And so, if philosophy is defined as being able to articulate and live by guiding principles and pieces of wisdom, offering life hacks and suggestions for how to live a good life, then Taylor is definitely a philosopher. This is also what some journalists and media reports have in mind when they claim that Taylor is a philosopher, because her lyrics contain "words of wisdom" and "valuable life lessons,"[14] because she reminds us "of the things that truly matter in life,"[15] and "offers genuine insight."[16]

Unsolicited Advice

There is a problem, though, with labeling Taylor as a philosopher in this way. If philosophy just means sharing words of wisdom, then not only is Taylor a philosopher but so is almost everyone else. I'm sure we've all been at the receiving end of unsolicited advice given to us by friends and family, co-workers, taxi drivers, people standing in line next to us at the store or coffee-house, or even people sitting next to us on public transport. All these people too would have to count as philosophers. This just seems implausible—as the contemporary philosopher Edward Craig has claimed, understanding philosophy in this way means it is "so broad as to be close to meaningless."[17] There must be something more that Taylor does if she is a philosopher.

Philosophy has to do with how we critically reflect on and scrutinize our beliefs, figuring out whether they stand the test of time. As philosopher Julian Baggini writes, doing philosophy is not blindly accepting a piece of wisdom, but involves a "systematic investigation of the nature of the world"—this entails providing reasons for our ideas and beliefs that can be "scrutinized, judged, assessed, accepted or rejected."[18] It is not enough to just state your life hack; you must also provide a systematic or methodical way of critically reflecting on it, considering more carefully how you arrived at your belief, and providing reasons to support your view. Taylor has given us many different life hacks throughout the years, but does she critically reflect and methodically scrutinize these life hacks, giving us reasons for why we ought to believe them?

Simple Existential Questions

Contemporary philosophers have already begun to do this critical reflection on Taylor's behalf, taking her views on topics she's written about in her lyrics, and highlighting how these touch on already-existing philosophical ideas and questions. For example, Keshav Singh has shown how Taylor's lyrics about the relationship between love and madness track the different theories of historical philosophers such as Nietzsche (1844–1900) and Plato (c. 427–347 BCE).[19] Luke Russell highlights the philosophical assumptions that Taylor makes about forgiveness, clarifying these ideas and asking us further questions to reflect on.[20] And Lindsay Brainard has offered a philosophical analysis of "Champagne Problems" as a way to think more critically about the ethics of making good decisions.[21]

In these examples the philosophers are the ones doing the heavy lifting when it comes to the critical reflection and scrutiny of the ideas that Taylor expresses in her lyrics. This only goes to show that Swift is being *philosophical*—offering up ideas, thoughts, and questions that have the potential to be philosophically analyzed by "real" philosophers. Maybe this isn't such a problem. Taylor herself acknowledges that some of her lyrics are philosophical. When describing the chorus of "Lover" she says, "I wanted the chorus to be these really simply existential questions that we ask ourselves when we're in love."[22] Here, Taylor expresses the philosophical idea that being in love alters our identity and sense of who we are. Stating this idea is certainly philosophical. But on the definition of philosophy we've been exploring, to be a philosopher Swift would need to critically reflect on and provide a methodical analysis of the reasons for believing the idea. But who is to say that Taylor *does not* critically reflect on the pieces of wisdom and philosophical questions she raises in her lyrics, interviews, and speeches?

A Narrow Operation

The philosopher Iris Murdoch (1919–1999) claimed that because philosophy involves "the critical analysis of beliefs," it must be "discursive" (providing reasons and justification for the claims that you make), "direct" (clearly and explicitly getting to the point), and "abstract" (only dealing with general theories and ideas rather than particular personal experiences).[23] And as the contemporary philosopher Susan L. Anderson has summarized, according to the standard idea of philosophical method, we do philosophy when we express our "views as clearly as possible, in an unemotional fashion, defending them with arguments, defining crucial terms, and considering all possible objections to one's view."[24] This would mean that only a limited selection of texts would count as philosophy, usually only written by those who are trained in university philosophy departments and publish in professional philosophy journals. Songs definitely would not count.

However, this concept of philosophy is too narrow and restrictive. Many famous philosophers were not philosophy professors or even students in philosophy departments, such as René Descartes (1596–1650) who studied law and mathematics, and David Hume (1711–1776) who studied Latin and Greek. And many well-respected works of philosophy take other forms than a direct and abstract piece of writing—for example Plato's famous dialogues, Mary Wollstonecraft's (1797–1851) letters, or the way in which African philosophers have used oral traditions to pass down their work without the use of a written text at all. As the philosopher Edward Craig argues, to think that philosophy is a "narrow operation that only occurs in universities" is "restrictive and misleading."[25] Philosophical analysis can take different forms depending on the culture and historical time period, and it is more than just an abstract written text authored by a philosophy professor at a university. So, in what way do Taylor's songs, speeches, and other works count as philosophy?

Double Standards and Personal Experience

Taylor actually does critically analyze her life hacks, words of wisdom, and ideas. How? By reflecting on her own personal experiences and that of fictional characters. As an example, let's take Taylor's analysis of gender stereotypes and discrimination. In her acceptance speech as the first ever recipient of *Billboard*'s Woman of the Decade award in 2019, Taylor tells us that "people love to explain away a woman's success."[26] On its own, this would be a mere nugget of wisdom. But in that same speech, Taylor offers many different personal examples that support her statement: people claimed that her record label, male producer, or male co-writer were the reason for her success, and people accused her of lying about writing her own songs. Ultimately, Swift argues that she was held to higher standards than male artists. In an interview for *CBS News* in 2019, Taylor gives further support for her claim that women are subjected to double standards: "A man does something, it's strategic. A woman does the same thing, it's calculated. A man is allowed to react. A woman can only overreact."[27]

Throughout her discography, Taylor systematically examines the different aspects and experiences of the discrimination experienced by women—from the perspective of one's emotions not being taken seriously ("mad woman"), double standards ("The Man"), being cast as a homewrecker (in the *folklore* love triangle), the difficult tension between being in a steady relationship and pursuing one's own career ("Midnight Rain"), and the social pressure to have a reputation of being a "good girl" and a "dutiful daughter" ("Bejeweled" and "But Daddy I Love Him").

Looking at Taylor's body of work as a whole, we see that her method is to state standard stereotypes that women are subjected to, and at the same time consider how and why they ought to be subverted. For example, in "mad woman" she highlights the typical stereotype that "no one likes a mad woman," in "Vigilante Shit" it is the fact that "Ladies" are always expected to play nice and "always rise above," and in "Lavander Haze," Taylor writes of the idea that women are either thought of as "a one-night" stand or a "wife," with there being no middle ground. Yet at the same time, Taylor sings of how these stereotypes ought to be challenged: "If a man talks shit, then I owe him nothing" ("I Did Something Bad"); "I'm so sick of running as fast I can / Wondering if I'd get there quicker / If I was a man" ("The Man"); "I'm damned if I do give a damn what people say / No deal, the 1950s shit they want from me" ("Lavander Haze"); and "I'll tell you something 'bout my good name / It's mine alone to disgrace" ("But Daddy I Love Him").

Rather than offering an abstract written discussion exploring the reasons for challenging each stereotype, Taylor provides an account of what it is like to *experience* these double standards, from either a personal point of view or from the point of view of an imagined character as part of a fictional narrative. In "The Man," Taylor wonders what it would feel like for her if she was not subjected to the double standards thrown at her, and in "Miss Americana and the Heartbreak Prince" she sings about what it feels like for her to be labeled a "bad, bad girl." But in "the last great american dynasty" Taylor sings of Rebakah's experiences of being labeled as a mad, chaotic, and sad woman, and in "august" she sings of Augustine's experiences of being cast as the "other woman."

As Taylor explains during her *Billboard* acceptance speech, her albums are an account of how she attempts to subvert the sexist labels put on her: "Whatever they decided I couldn't do is exactly what I did. Whatever they criticized about me became material for musical satires or inspirational anthems."[28] What makes this approach powerful is that it does not analyze the sexist stereotypes from an abstract and detached point of view. The harm that these stereotypes can inflict on women is real and experienced as part of everyday life. The way women challenge these stereotypes is not theoretical, but performed by acting in ways that subvert expectations and question the status quo. This is messy, and not something that can always be abstractly and directly explained without emotional weight.

The value of Taylor's contribution to feminist philosophy is the way she uses her own personal experiences and fictional characters to explore, challenge, and subvert negative gender stereotypes that have caused harmful discrimination against woman. In doing so, Taylor doesn't merely state a life hack or piece of wisdom. Instead, she critically and systematically reflects on and critiques gender stereotypes.

The Accidental Philosopher

"But, Taylor Swift writes songs," the skeptic might proclaim, "how can this be philosophy?" Taylor isn't doing philosophy in any of the standard ways that we would teach philosophy students when they take a philosophy course in high school or university. But if doing philosophy involves critically reflecting and systematically analyzing our worldviews and beliefs, then Taylor is doing that by offering a first-personal and fictional analysis in her songs, interviews, and speeches.

The contemporary philosopher Martha Nussbaum claims that poetry, fiction, and storytelling can be powerful tools for philosophers to express certain philosophical truths about how to live a good life. Nussbaum argues that when Western philosophy first emerged in ancient Greece, it was the poets who were the "central ethical teachers and thinkers" because their works allowed for a "process of inquiry, reflection."[29] This makes sense because philosophical inquiry often requires "the perception of particular people and situations rather than abstract rules."[30] And so, doing philosophy is not just about providing an abstract theory that has nothing to do with emotions or our own personal lives. Instead, Nussbaum implies that we can also be philosophers by providing stories of our own personal experiences, or the experiences of fictional characters and circumstances, using these to methodically reflect on and analyze our beliefs and ideas about how to navigate the challenges of living a good life. And this is the way that Taylor Swift is a philosopher.

Of course, even if we think Swift is a philosopher, it doesn't mean that all her work counts as philosophy, or that she is a philosopher *all the time*. And we don't know whether she ever intended to be a philosopher—maybe it's a label that she doesn't even want. But being a philosopher is something that Taylor should be proud of, using her work to systematically reflect on the big questions in life. There are good and bad ways to do philosophy. After all, philosophers train for years to sharpen their thinking skills and analyze systems of thought and different forms of argumentation. Without this training, Taylor is an accidental philosopher. But just think of the philosophical wisdom that will leave us enchanted when, like she sings in "Bejeweled," her philosophical skills "polish up real nice."

Notes

1. Hannah Dailey, "Taylor Swift's NYU Commencement Speech: Read the Full Transcript," *Billboard*, May 18, 2022, at https://www.billboard.com/music/music-news/taylor-swift-nyu-commencement-speech-full-transcript-1235072824.
2. Taylor Swift, "All's Fair in Love and Poetry …," Instagram, February 5, 2024, at https://www.instagram.com/p/C28vsIzO_bL/?utm_source=ig_web_copy_link&igsh=MzRlODBiNWFlZA==.
3. Kayla Bartsch, "Taylor Swift: Empress of the Zeitgeist," National Review, September 24, 2023, at https://www.nationalreview.com/2023/09/taylor-swift-empress-of-the-zeitgeist; Peter M. Juul, "Reflections on Taylor Swift, or the Pop Star as Philosopher," Peter M. Juul: Writer, Researcher, Policy Analyst, December 31, 2019, at https://pmjuul.com/2019/12/31/reflections-on-taylor-swift-or-the-pop-star-as-philosopher; Clare McCarthy, "Taylor Swift the Great Philosopher: Headteacher Says She Should Be Viewed alongside Shakespeare and He Uses Her Lyrics for Inspiration in School Assemblies," *Daily Mail*, April 10, 2021, at https://www.dailymail.co.uk/news/article-9455857/Headteacher-praises-Taylor-Swift-great-philosopher-quotes-lyrics-school-assemblies.html.
4. Scott Hershovitz, "Taylor Swift, Philosopher of Forgiveness," *The New York Times*, September 7, 2019, at https://www.nytimes.com/2019/09/07/opinion/sunday/taylor-swift-lover.html?action=click&module=Opinion&pgtype=Homepage.
5. Marcus Chan, "Taylor Swift and Ed Sheeran's Writing Philosophies," Medium, October 31, 2021, at https://writingcooperative.com/taylor-swift-and-ed-sheerans-writing-philosophies-905305ac1574.
6. Zach Seemayer, "Taylor Swift Gets Personal About Friends & Romances: 'I Don't Make the Same Mistake Twice,'" ET, August 3, 2015, at https://www.etonline.com/music/169265_taylor_swift_gets_personal_about_friends_romances_i_don_t_make_the_same_mistake_twice.
7. Jocelyn Vena, "You Will Never Believe Who Taylor Swift Just Called Her 'Friend,'" *Billboard*, April 24, 2015, at https://www.billboard.com/music/music-news/taylor-swift-glamour-uk-interview-6545767.
8. Edward Craig, *Philosophy: A Very Short Introduction* (Oxford: Oxford University Press, 2002), 5; Stephen J.E. Norrie, "What Is Philosophy? Prolegomena to a Sociological Metaphilosophy," *Metaphilosophy* 49 (2018), 649.
9. Graham Priest, "What Is Philosophy?" *Philosophy* 81 (2006), 189; Søren Overgaard, Paul Gilbert, and Stephen Burwood, *An Introduction to Metaphilosophy* (Cambridge: Cambridge University Press, 2013), 3.
10. Overgaard, Gilbert, and Burwood, *An Introduction to Metaphilosophy*, 2.
11. Sam Lansky, "2023 Person of the Year: Taylor Swift," *TIME*, December 6, 2023, at https://time.com/6342806/person-of-the-year-2023-taylor-swift.
12. Dailey, "Taylor Swift's NYU Commencement Speech."
13. Hilary Hanson, "Taylor Swift's 5-Word Take on Jet Lag Will Have You Go, 'Hmmm,'" *Huffington Post*, February 17, 2024, at https://www.huffpost.com/entry/taylor-swift-jet-lag_n_65d0d71de4b0f7fbe7b2d130.
14. McCarthy, "Taylor Swift the Great Philosopher."
15. Juul, "Reflections on Taylor Swift."

16. Hershovitz, "Taylor Swift, Philosopher of Forgiveness."

17. Craig, *Philosophy*, 8.

18. Julian Baggini, *How the World Thinks: A Global History of Philosophy* (London: Granta Publications, 2018), xxx.

19. Keshav Singh, "Swift on Love and Madness," Daily Nous, April 7, 2023, at https://dailynous.com/2023/04/07/philosophers-on-taylor-swift/#singh.

20. Luke Russell, "Taylor Swift Is Never Ever Going to Forgive You," Daily Nous, April 7, 2023, at https://dailynous.com/2023/04/07/philosophers-on-taylor-swift/#russell.

21. Lindsay Brainard, "Can Gut Feelings Solve 'Champagne Problems'?" Daily Nous, April 7, 2023, at https://dailynous.com/2023/04/07/philosophers-on-taylor-swift/#brainard.

22. The New York Times, "Taylor Swift Tells Us How She Wrote 'Lover' | Diary of a Song," YouTube, December 24, 2014, at https://www.youtube.com/watch?v=UEeWmItgdxA.

23. Iris Murdoch, "Philosophy and Literature," in Brian Magee ed., *Men of Ideas* (Oxford: Oxford University Press, 1982), 233–236.

24. Susan L. Anderson, "Philosophy and Fiction," *Metaphilosophy* 23 (1992), 204.

25. Craig, *Philosophy*, 9.

26. Rebecca Schiller, "Taylor Swift Accepts Woman of the Decade Award at Billboard's Women in Music: Read Her Full Speech," *Billboard*, December 13, 2019, at https://www.billboard.com/music/awards/taylor-swift-woman-of-the-decade-speech-billboard-women-in-music-8546156.

27. David Morgan, "Taylor Swift: 'There's a Different Vocabulary for Men and Women in the Music Industry,'" *CBS News*, August 25, 2019, at https://www.cbsnews.com/news/taylor-swift-preview-sexist-labels-in-the-music-industry/?ftag=CNM-00-10aab6i&linkId=72505330&fbclid=IwAR0Tu6eR1hHvOgN7gbB10UfIAfOJHfucfWpI5BF7ZVpzcsb-khuCOIe_L9A

28. Schiller, "Taylor Swift Accepts Woman of the Decade Award."

29. Martha Nussbaum, *Love's Knowledge: Essays on Philosophy and Literature* (New York: Oxford University Press, 1990), 22.

30. Nussbaum, *Love's Knowledge*, ix.

2

"You Should Find Another Guiding Light"

Is Taylor Swift Admirable?

Kate C.S. Schmidt

Taylor Swift is wildly talented, rich, and successful, yet in the final song of the *Midnights (3am)* album, she cautions her listeners against admiring her. Addressing the listener or "reader" directly, in "Dear Reader" Swift advises against using her as a beacon of light or inspiration on the path toward a good life: "You should find another guiding light / Guiding light / But I shine so bright / You should find / Another guiding light / Guiding light / But I shine so bright." We should be careful with our feelings of admiration because of the impact on our emotional and moral lives. So maybe Swift has a point. How should we decide whether or not to admire her?

Taylor Swift Is Inspiring, But Is She Admirable?

Admiration is a way to acknowledge the things we find valuable, whether it's an attitude, a song, or an artist herself. Admiration can be an intuitive and natural response to meaningful art, and Taylor Swift certainly creates music with widespread appeal. Her songs are not only commercially successful but also deeply meaningful to many of her listeners. When we sing along to a song, we can get more in touch with our own emotions and lives by inserting ourselves into the lyrics. Singing along to "Bejeweled" reminds us of our worth, while dancing around after a tough day might help us to "Shake It Off." It seems natural to admire the music and the artist who can generate so much joy.

Admiration is not just a feeling, but an emotion: it offers a specific appraisal of the world. To see something as admirable is to view the object as good, and worthy of the attention and praise that come along with admiration. This means we need to consider the proper limits of admiration. It's risky to end up admiring the wrong things because your whole life

Taylor Swift and Philosophy: Essays from the Tortured Philosophers Department,
First Edition. Edited by Catherine M. Robb and Georgie Mills.
© 2025 John Wiley & Sons, Inc. Published 2025 by John Wiley & Sons, Inc.

could be transformed. Swift herself reminds us that chasing "the wrong guy" can leave you vulnerable as "a moth to the flame" ("long story short" and "Better Than Revenge (Taylor's Version)"). How can we properly appreciate what is truly admirable while minimizing the chances of making a mistake?

Taylor Swift Is Divisive

One way to answer this question is to advise everyone to trust their own feelings. Admiration is a positive emotion, a sort of overall appraisal that someone or something is excellent. Some people naturally have no emotional reaction to Taylor Swift, while others have strong reactions in response to her music and popularity, some positive and some negative—along with the praise there has also been a backlash against her music as superficial and annoying. Perhaps the question of admiration is a personal one: Does Taylor Swift make you feel admiration? Admiration as an emotion presents its object as valuable, and involves "distinct physical feelings, including the feeling of dilation or opening in the chest, combined with the feeling that one has been uplifted or 'elevated.'"[1]

While this approach affirms the listener's feelings, it doesn't seem like a reliable way to assess one's emotions or to understand the world. We want our emotions to reflect the world, not just ourselves. Emotions are combined with action tendencies, and so ideally, people will be able to adjust their emotional responses to "feel better."[2] It is possible to trust one's emotional appraisal of the world, while also thinking that it is a good idea to revise emotional habits over time.[3] Contemporary philosopher Linda Zagzebski advocates trusting the emotion of admiration, but still advises individuals to reflect upon their own judgments of what is admirable in order to avoid mistakes. She writes that the "emotion of admiration is generally trustworthy when we have it after reflection and when it withstands critique by others."[4] So we should reflect on the value of Taylor Swift and consider the critique others may have of her.

Admire the Art, Not the Artist

Popular assessments of Swift's personal characteristics diverge—some see her as a role model, while others see her as a rich, out-of-touch celebrity. Perhaps Swift's art and artistic abilities are admirable. If so, we as listeners can admire her music, without making a judgment about her admirability as a person. It seems easier to judge her songs as excellent, without needing to make a moral judgment about Swift herself. This notion of admiration is close to the notions of "wonder" or "awe." The contemporary philosopher Wojciech Kaftanski describes this type of admiration as "oriented toward beauty; it is produced in us when encountering, for instance, objects of art."[5] So an object is admirable when it is good, excellent, or morally valuable. If Swift's songs express moral ideals or beauty, perhaps admiration is fitting.

However, this type of admiration is very different from what Zagzebski and other philosophers have in mind. According to many definitions of admiration, it is only fitting in response to people, not to art or objects. Specifically, Zagzebski says that admiration helps us to identify people who are exemplary and worth imitating. Zagzebski argues that admiration is an especially powerful emotion, and has a central role to play in healthy ethical development.[6] Admiration is a tool that helps us to become better people because the emotion is characterized by a motivation to imitate the admirable. Zagzebski claims: "Admiration is an emotion in which the object is 'seen as admirable,' and which motivates us to emulate the admired person in the relevant respect."[7] We all naturally admire people who we think are morally good, and that admiration helps to motivate us to imitate our admirable exemplar. Over time, this makes admiration a powerful tool for moral development in which we become the best versions of ourselves. It also means that admiration is appropriate when it targets people, not works of art. It's possible to imitate Swift the person, but not your favorite song.

Another problem with admiring Swift's songs rather than her as a person is that this approach artificially separates Swift, the artist, from her own work. Swift says, "when it comes to my songwriting and my life, they are one in the same."[8] Importantly, there is a person behind the music: when Swift sings "Shake It Off," it's not just the notes that matter, it's the idea of a person who refuses to be discouraged. If admiration narrowly focuses on the song, we miss the wider context of why resilience is important not just in art, but in the context of a person's life. Songwriting is a deeply personal activity, and so perhaps art and the artist are necessarily connected. Swift writes about personal struggles and triumphs in her music. It matters that her songs aren't just fantasy, because when she says, "long story short, I survived," we feel invested in a success story ("long story short").

Taylor Swift May Not Be Virtuous

If admiration is meant to guide us toward self-improvement, it's important to only admire people who are morally good. Admirable people need to represent the kinds of actions and intentions that are morally excellent. Creating beautiful art isn't enough—it's a person's character that makes them admirable. Swift clearly inspires her fans. In fact, adolescents who are asked who they take as a role model list entertainers like Swift more often than any other category.[9]

However, Swift tells us explicitly that we shouldn't take her advice, in light of her personal failings. She seems to argue in "Dear Reader" that she lacks the necessary qualities of excellence, and that her life is walking "to a house not a home." She cautions the listener to "never take advice from someone who's falling apart." So, she doesn't seem to endorse her actions as those of a role model. Speaking during her NYU commencement speech, she said: "Please bear in mind that I, in no way, feel qualified to tell you what to do. You've worked and struggled and sacrificed and studied and dreamed your way here today and so, you know what you're doing."[10] In truth, Swift hasn't always acted morally. While her songs represent many ideals, she has been criticized for failing to uphold those ideals in her own life. Consider for example the controversy over her dating (and giving stage space to) Matty Healy, who has been criticized for saying racist and misogynistic things.[11] Although the two broke up, the events still raised questions for fans. But is it fair to have an opinion on Swift's love life? If her love life shows us things about Swift's characteristic moral intentions and actions, then the answer is yes.

Other fans have criticized Swift for not speaking up for women's rights and LGBTQ rights, despite the supportive attitudes in songs like "The Man" and "You Need to Calm Down." Swift sings "I'm so sick of running as fast as I can" in the face of a sexist society, but has failed to use her significant wealth or influence to comment on the issues when they arise politically. Some conscientious listeners might worry about whether it's important to determine the facts about Swift's character and beliefs before supporting her. Perhaps we need to know her motivation in writing the songs, as Ted Nannicelli argues.[12] None of us have perfect behavior, so looking at Swift's motivation might seem like the best strategy. However, making these determinations about Swift's character may be impossible because of her level of celebrity. Swifties can claim to know something about Swift as an artist or a celebrity, but none of us can claim to know her as a person—we're very badly positioned to comment on any of her motivations or intent.

Is Swift an admirable person? As listeners, we know the art, but we don't know the artist fully, and it is hard to argue that she exemplifies a virtuous life. In particular, she seems suspect in light of her enormous wealth, and the relatively little she has done with it. Likewise, Swift has been criticized for overusing her private jet and ignoring the environmental impact of her actions.[13]

The Ideal of Taylor Swift

Contemporary philosophers Alfred Archer and Benjamin Matheson argue that admiration is closely connected to our ideals.[14] This means that admiration is connected to the ideals that an admired person or action represents: "In other words, a person becomes admirable for an action to the extent that she manifests an ideal in so acting."[15] This is not just an overall character assessment, as a person's behavior need not be good overall in order to be admired. Not all moral errors will make someone an unfitting object of admiration—once someone is admired, they only cease to be admirable if they act in a way that violates the admirable ideal.

This focus on "ideals" explains how part, but not all, of a person can be admirable. Listening to Swift can inspire imitation not of her whole life, but of the moral ideals represented in her songs. Some of these Swiftian ideals are loving with an open heart, living a joyful life, standing up for yourself, and persevering through challenges. This type of admiration still targets morally relevant traits and habits, and engaging with these habits can facilitate self-reflection and self-growth.

Another benefit of this type of admiration is that it seems more realistic. If I only admire people who are morally excellent, and I'm not morally excellent, it will be harder for me to know how to emulate them. It's far easier to imitate someone who has some good traits (like a hero) without being morally perfect (like a saint).[16] It ends up being more morally beneficial to admire someone who can inspire us to change ourselves.

In this case, the emotion of admiration isn't aimed at Taylor Swift the person, but at the ideal of someone who perseveres through hardship, who can live joyfully after heartbreak, and who celebrates the significance of love. When I admire these values, I am also driven to imitate the ideals in my own life. I recognize that it would be good for me to be joyful and persistent. As Zagzebski says, "The admired person in this case is not a competitor, but is more like an ideal self."[17] So, I am not admiring Swift the person, but the type of person I could be in the emotional context of the song.

This admiration helps each of us envision a future where we better exemplify moral ideals, and admiration helps us to stay connected to our ideals over time. Archer and Matheson point out that admiration depends upon telling a good story about living up to an ideal over time:

> When we admire a person for acting a particular way, we desire to emulate them. We do not just try to emulate how she acts at a particular time but how she acts over time. So it not only matters that she manifests an ideal at a particular time but also how she subsequently lives with respect to that ideal – that is, it matters that she lives within the range of acceptable narratives associated with that ideal.[18]

Swift's music consistently highlights the importance of persistence, resilience, and a commitment to living a good life despite any challenge or heartbreak. These traits don't have to belong to Taylor Swift the person, because they belong to the ideal protagonist of her songs. The ideal woman in Swift's songs reminds us not to give up on what matters, by telling the stories of her challenges framed as obstacles to be overcome, rather than reasons to give up. As listeners, we can imagine how our ideal selves rebuff those who tell us to quit by singing "all you're ever gonna be is mean," as we "shake it off," "shine so bright," and then look back to say, "long story short, I survived" ("Mean," "Shake It Off," "Bejeweled," and "long story short"). It doesn't matter if the song, or Taylor Swift herself, is admirable—what's worth admiring and pursuing is the ideal character we envision for ourselves. We can engage with this kind of optimism and determination about the challenges in our own lives through Swift's songs.

The Good News

We often feel like we "get older but just never wiser" ("Anti-Hero"), but the good news is that music can help us to stay grounded in our lives and push ourselves toward self-improvement. Or in other words: "Everything you lose is a step you take / So make the friendship bracelets / Take the moment and / Taste it / You've got no reason to be afraid / You're on your own, kid / Yeah, you can face this" ("You're on Your Own, Kid").

Notes

1. Linda Zagzebski, "I—Admiration and the Admirable," *Aristotelian Society Supplementary Volume* 89 (2015), 208.
2. Charlie Kurth, "Inappropriate Emotions, Marginalization, and Feeling Better," *Synthese* 200 (2022), 155.
3. Christine Tappolet, *Emotions, Values, and Agency* (Oxford: Oxford University Press, 2016).
4. Linda Zagzebski, "Exemplarist Virtue Theory," *Metaphilosophy* 41 (2010), 41–57.
5. Wojciech Kaftanski, "Admiration, Affectivity, and Value: Critical Remarks on Exemplarity," *The Journal of Value Inquiry* (2022), 1–18.
6. Zagzebski lays out her view in several works. See Zagzebski, "Exemplarist Virtue Theory"; Zagzebski, "I—Admiration and the Admirable"; and Linda Zagzebski, *Exemplarist Moral Theory* (Oxford: Oxford University Press, 2017).
7. Zagzebski, "I—Admiration and the Admirable," 205.
8. Abid Rahman, "Taylor Swift Reveals Her Writing Process in Nashville Songwriter Awards Speech," *The Hollywood Reporter*, September 21, 2022, at https://www.hollywoodreporter.com/news/music-news/taylor-swift-songwriting-process-nashville-speech-1235224700.
9. Alison B. Hammond, Sara K. Johnson, Michelle B. Weiner, and Jacqueline V. Lerner, "From Taylor Swift to MLK: Understanding Adolescents' Famous Character Role Models," *Journal of Moral Education* (2022), 1–19.

10. Hannah Dalley, "Taylor Swift's NYU Commencement Speech: Read the Full Transcript," *Billboard*, May 18, 2022, at https://www.billboard.com/music/music-news/taylor-swift-nyu-commencement-speech-full-transcript-1235072824.

11. Chiara Giovanni, "Taylor Swift and Matty Healy Relationship Backlash Reveals the Hypocrisy of Political Critique of Celebrities," *Teen Vogue*, May 30, 2023, at https://www.teenvogue.com/story/taylor-swift-matty-healy-relationship-backlash-hypocrisy-political-critique-celebrities-op-ed.

12. Ted Nannicelli, *Artistic Creation and Ethical Criticism* (Oxford: Oxford University Press, 2020).

13. Isabella O'Malley, "Why Taylor Swift's Globe-Trotting in Private Jets Is Getting Scrutinized," *AP NEWS*, February 2, 2024, at https://apnews.com/article/taylor-swift-climate-jet-carbon-emissions kelce-chiefs-02ac425d24281 bd26d73bfdf4590bc82.

14. Alfred Archer and Benjamin Matheson, "Admiration over Time," *Pacific Philosophical Quarterly* 101 (2020), 669–689.

15. Archer and Matheson, "Admiration over Time," 675.

16. Michel Croce and Maria Silvia Vaccarezza, "Educating through Exemplars: Alternative Paths to Virtue," *Theory and Research in Education* 15 (2017), 5–19.

17. Zagzebski, "I—Admiration and the Admirable," 214.

18. Archer and Matheson, "Admiration over Time," 684.

3

Eyes Open
Taylor Swift and the Philosophy of Easter Eggs

Eline Kuipers

I love that they like the cryptic hint-dropping. Because as long as they like it, I'll keep doing it. It's fun. It feels mischievous and playful.

—Taylor Swift[1]

It started with secret messages hidden within song lyrics in album booklets. Fans who took the time to follow the breadcrumbs of capital letters left by Taylor Swift could find secret messages like "you are not alone" ("The Outside") and "I cried while recording this" ("Fearless") hidden within her albums. Although Swift stopped hiding messages in her printed song lyrics after her 1989 era, it was the start of an age of "Easter eggs." Easter eggs are hidden surprises that are included in media, such as games, movies, and music videos.[2] Taylor Swift has mastered the art of Easter eggs, and is known to hide clues and references in almost everything she does and creates. Think, for example, of her song "Invisible String" referring to "Bad Blood (Taylor's Version)," with the line "Bad was the blood of the song in the cab / On your first trip to LA." Or remember the neon letters featured in her music video for "ME!," revealing the title of her then-upcoming album *Lover*. Another example of Swift's use of Easter eggs is her announcement of *Red (Taylor's Version)*, which contained song titles from her album *Speak Now*, hinting that this would be the next rerecorded album to be released. Similarly, her music video for "I Can See You (Taylor's Version) (From The Vault)" is full of outfits and details that can be recognized from earlier music videos. Swift knows all too well that the devil is in the details, so she packs her work with as many cryptic clues as she possibly can.

Not only is Taylor Swift famous for her ingenious way of hiding announcements and references, but her fanbase is renowned for thoroughly unraveling and discussing these shrouded mysteries. Numerous blogs, YouTube channels, and Instagram and TikTok accounts are dedicated to analyzing everything she does for the hint of an Easter egg. When she uploads a post on social media or makes a surprising remark during a

Taylor Swift and Philosophy: Essays from the Tortured Philosophers Department,
First Edition. Edited by Catherine M. Robb and Georgie Mills.
© 2025 John Wiley & Sons, Inc. Published 2025 by John Wiley & Sons, Inc.

concert, just like clockwork, the investigations of possible Easter eggs begin. Why are Easter eggs so intriguing? What causes Swifties to spend hours trying to find and interpret them?

Enchanted by Puzzles

We can understand Taylor Swift's Easter eggs as a type of puzzle—mysterious clues and references that need to be found and deciphered. Humans have always been enchanted by puzzles.[3] From riddles to jigsaw puzzles, and from mathematical problems to anagrams, people of all ages enjoy finding creative solutions. Puzzles are entertaining and surprising, but also thought-provoking. They make us look at the world from different perspectives, make us think in ways we have never thought before, and guide our attention to novel things. Precisely because working on a puzzle requires mental effort from curious minds, the most satisfying part of the experience happens when our pondering is abruptly stopped by the solution presenting itself to us. We have all experienced the "Aha!" moment that elicits a rush of excitement and relief.[4] Feeling wonderstruck is what makes us come back to the timeless, mind-bending world of puzzles, including the hunt for Easter eggs.

Humans are not alone in their love for puzzles; animals of all kinds are known to enjoy engaging with puzzles, suggesting that our interest in them might be a deep-rooted evolutionary trait. For example, cats love playing with food puzzles, which reward them with treats if they interact with them in the right way. These puzzles do not just entertain; they can actually reduce stress, anxiety, and aggression.[5] So, if you want a cat purring in your lap because it loves you, like Swift suggests in "Karma," you should probably present them stimulating and tasty puzzles. Remarkably, many animals (although, ironically, not cats) would rather solve a puzzle for food than get their food for free. From giraffes to rats, and from chickens to humans, many animals prefer to work for their food even when similar food is freely available to them.[6] Long story short, the love for puzzles is widespread throughout the animal kingdom.

Her Best Laid Plan

By hiding Easter eggs in her work, Taylor Swift makes good use of this deep-rooted love for puzzles. Searching for an Easter egg is as much a puzzle as figuring out the meaning of the cryptic egg itself, which causes twice the excitement. Of course, the solutions to both sides of the puzzle are intertwined, since it is much harder to find an Easter egg if you do not know its meaning.

For example, it is easier to notice that Swift is sending a message with her outfit, if you recognize it from one of her music videos or can see its significance, such as when she wore snake boots and fans were convinced this heralded the release of the rerecording of *reputation*. Similarly, once you know that her lucky number is thirteen, you notice it reappearing in release dates, shows, songs, and videos. Likewise, knowing the order of her album releases and the colors that are associated with each album makes it easier to spot Easter eggs, such as the elevator buttons in her music video for "Bejeweled." Unraveling Swift's clues requires detailed and up-to-date knowledge of both her oeuvre and her personal life, as well as some strong detective skills and a lot of imagination.

Swift is famous for hiding secret messages in almost everything she creates, which means that every aspect of her life generates a feeling of suspense among Swifties. She even plays with this suspense by planting Easter eggs that cannot be unraveled at the time of their release.[7] These second-tier Easter eggs can only be found once other songs or the full albums are released. For instance, in the second scene of the "ME!" music video, Brandon Urie mentions the title of Taylor Swift's next single, "You Need To Calm Down," in French, but Swifties could only decipher this after the single was released months later. The same goes for understanding the meaning of the Christmas tree standing in the living room, which refers to the first line of the title track of her then-upcoming album *Lover*, which states "We could leave the Christmas lights up 'till January." When it comes to Swift's Easter eggs, there is an invisible string that ties everything together over time. Consequently, fans need to keep returning to her work and life to fully engage in the scavenger hunt.

By weaving her little webs of clues and hints, Swift makes fans engage with her work in a profound and active way. Finding and understanding an Easter egg creates a strong connection between the creator and the audience. Swift has left the eggs especially for her fans to uncover, which signals to them that they are important and seen. Easter eggs can often only be found and unraveled by committed fans, which makes them feel as though they are part of her inner circle. Acing her tests rewards fans for their loyalty by giving them a secret message.[8] As she has pointed out, Easter eggs are a form of communication between her and her fans.[9] Figuring out whether she has sent them a message might be one of the main reasons why fans try to notice everything she does or does not do.

'Cause She's a Mastermind

This strong connection between Swift and her fans is a "parasocial relationship." Within this kind of relationship, someone experiences an intimate and familiar connection with an artist or celebrity, as if they know them personally, while their relationship is actually non-reciprocated.[10]

Parasocial relationships are formed through parasocial interactions, which are interactions that are experienced as personal and shared, while in fact, they are not. For instance, a video in which Swift looks straight into the camera and says "It's me. Hi!" may be experienced as if she is talking to a fan personally, even though fans know this cannot be the case. Similarly, when she posts something about her personal life on social media—for example when she posted behind the scenes footage of the Superbowl afterparty on TikTok in February 2024—this gives fans insight into her life and makes them feel even more personally connected to her. These parasocial interactions are a little like the kind of optical illusion in which an image appears to move even though we know it is not actually moving. Fans know that their interactions with Taylor Swift are not reciprocal interactions, but they still experience them as such.[11]

Parasocial relationships are common in all sorts of fandoms, which is why philosophers are becoming increasingly interested in them. For instance, contemporary philosophers Catherine Robb and Alfred Archer have argued that cultivating and maintaining parasocial relationships with fans is a skill, which some celebrities have mastered better than others. When a celebrity can make their fans experience an intimate and emotional connection, even though this connection is only illusionary, they can create loyalty among their fans and generate more, and continuous, public visibility.[12] Hence, celebrities can become more famous and successful when they know how to play their fans like a violin and keep the illusion alive.

Taylor Swift is an expert in fostering parasocial relationships, but so are many other celebrities. What distinguishes Swift from other celebrities is that she provides her fans with an abundance of parasocial interactions through her Easter eggs, with each of these secret messages strengthening their parasocial relationship. The Easter eggs provide a way for fans to actively engage with and pay close attention to Swift's work and other aspects of her personal life. The mere possibility of a coded clue keeps fans hooked on Taylor Swift. The fact that she has made it clear that she reads and watches some of her fans' theories on Easter eggs, makes Swifties feel seen and heard while they publicly interpret her hints and references.[13] Clearly, like Swift herself beautifully described in "mirrorball," she is trying everything to keep fans looking at her.

Trying to Know Somebody You Never Met

Fans engage in parasocial relationships because they want to experience a strong connection and feel like they belong. Humans have a fundamental desire to belong, which expresses itself in our innate yearning to form and maintain social bonds. After all, humans are social animals that thrive by living in societies and for whom loneliness causes distress and pain.

Social bonds provide us with much-needed comfort, reassurance, and guidance.[14] As contemporary philosopher Gen Eickers puts it: "Feelings of belonging involve an emotional sense of security, a sense of feeling at home with others, and a sense that one can reach out for support."[15] Like other kinds of relationships, parasocial relationships can deliver such a sense of belonging.

Interestingly, parasocial relationships can generate this sense of belonging without some of the negativities that come with regular social relationships. Making friends can be scary and risky, as there is always a chance of rejection or bad blood. However, there is very little risk of rejection in parasocial relationships, as they are one-sided, making them less delicate than regular social relationships. So, parasocial relationships can provide the benefits of a social relationship, such as a sense of belonging, in a more reliable and predictable way.[16] Research shows that parasocial relationships can even have benefits for fans' well-being. For instance, parasocial relationships have been found to make people with low self-esteem see themselves in a more positive light, whereas this was not the case for regular relationships.[17] Importantly, fans do not become less social or forget about their other relationships when they invest time and energy in a parasocial relationship, which means that they can maintain other forms of social relationships at the same time.[18] So, through her Easter eggs, which generate parasocial relationships, Swift provides her fans with a sense of belonging.

Nevertheless, there are some less positive aspects related to the one-sidedness of parasocial relationships. Philosophers Archer and Robb fruitfully interpret parasocial relationships as being constituted by three structural asymmetries.[19] The first asymmetry is one of "attention," as Swifties pay more attention to Taylor than Taylor does to them. Although Swift does spend time with some individual fans, she will usually only communicate with her fandom as a whole, for example through social media posts, or by talking to the audience at a concert. There is also a "communication" asymmetry, as Swift decides which information about her work and personal life gets shared and when this is communicated, while fans are mainly the receivers of this information. Swifties can, of course, also initiate communication with her by messaging her via social media, but she does not often interact with these messages. Lastly, there is an "epistemic" asymmetry—an asymmetry regarding knowledge. This arises because fans, especially those who hunt for and decode Easter eggs, know a lot about Swift's work and life, while she knows very little if anything about the lives of her individual fans. Thus, while Swifties put a lot of time and energy into getting to know more about Taylor Swift, this is unreciprocated by Swift herself.

According to Archer and Robb, these three asymmetries give rise to a more substantial asymmetry in the way that fans and celebrities can influence each other's identities.[20] We all need to find our place in this world, as Swift sings in "A Place in This World (Taylor's Version)," but we are definitely not alone and on our own in doing so. Our human desire to belong reflects how important social relationships are to us, which makes it not at all surprising that our connections to others play a key role in defining who we are. As pointed out by contemporary philosopher Charles Taylor, we can only define ourselves, form our own opinions, aspirations, and ideals, when we have acquired rich languages for expressing ourselves. These languages do not always have to involve words; they can also include acts of love and expressions of art. Importantly, such languages of self-expression can only be acquired through exchanges with people who are important to us. Even when we have acquired the languages to express ourselves, the dialogue with the people we love continues, as we define our identities, according to Charles Taylor, "always in dialogue with, sometimes in struggle against, the identities our significant others want to recognize in us."[21] The people that we are connected to help us develop and express our identity by interpreting our identity.

However, because parasocial relationships are mainly non-reciprocal, it seems unlikely that such a dialogue is possible. This is why Archer and Robb speak of a more substantial asymmetry in the influence on identity in parasocial relationships.[22] Celebrities, such as Taylor Swift, mainly play a directive role in the identity formation of fans. Because many Swifties see Taylor as a friend or a mother figure, she has a great influence on their beliefs, desires, and interests. Many fans look up to Swift and see her as an exemplar of what one should strive for in life, which can strongly shape their identity. The fans, on the other hand, do not have such a directive influence on Taylor Swift. Rather, Swifties interpret her public identity, like they interpret Easter eggs, by expressing judgments about the ways she behaves and presents herself. However, Swift cannot interpret the identities of her fans, as she cannot get to know all of them individually.

Because such interpretations are key to developing and expressing our identities, no meaningful dialogue about identity can take place within a parasocial relationship. While Taylor Swift can shape the identities of fans, Swifties can in this relationship not really explore what they find important themselves or define their own identity. So, can being a Swiftie help Taylor Swift fans figure out who they are and who they want to be?

It's Nice to Have a Friend

While their parasocial relationship with Taylor Swift already makes fans experience a sense of belonging, their investment in this relationship can provide them with a community to belong to and in which they can explore their identity. Fans of an artist like to discuss the artist's work and share interesting facts and opinions. Swift's Easter egg mayhem has created a bond between fans that goes further than just the search for secret messages.

The lively discussion of her Easter eggs among fans is what transforms them from a group of individuals into a community characterized by shared interests, understanding, and camaraderie. Members of the Taylor Swift fandom feel connected through their love for the singer and her work, but it is their interaction with each other that really brings them together. As Taylor Swift puts it in "You're On Your Own, Kid," they "make the friendship bracelets, take the moment, and taste it."

Belonging to a community allows fans to shape their own identity through dialogue that consists of both interpretation and direction. The sense of belonging itself is also important, as it provides a safe place to be vulnerable and initiate fearless dialogue. Within the community, Swifties can express themselves and explore what is important to them in conversation with other fans. For fans who are highly engaged in the Taylor Swift fandom, their connection to the community can become part of their identity. But even less-dedicated members of the fandom can profit from the dialogue with and between other Swifties when exploring their own personalities.

Swift herself encourages this search for identity in relation to the fandom, for example by providing empty diary pages among fragments of her own diary published with the deluxe edition of *Lover*. These empty pages allow fans to relive their own experiences through Swift's self-narrative, exploring their own identity in relation to her and the fandom. Swift again asks her fans to actively engage with her and her work. By sharing these explorations online with Swift and other fans, Swifties become even more connected to the community.[23]

Enjoying and engaging with Swift's work can best be done within the Taylor Swift community. As the philosopher Charles Taylor argues, some good things in life can only be accessed and fully understood if they are enjoyed with other people, especially with the people we love.[24] Hence, Swift does not just enchant her fans with musical masterpieces and mercurial music videos, but also provides the basis for a community to which Swifties can belong and in which they can explore their own identities.

You Belong with Me

Call it what you want, but Taylor Swift takes her own advice very seriously: "If you fail to plan, you plan to fail" ("Mastermind"). Like an architect, she draws up the plan ("I Think He Knows") and plants Easter eggs in everything she does and creates. By hiding Easter eggs, Swift taps the deep-rooted human love for puzzles and fosters strong parasocial relationships with her fans. These relationships can provide fans with a sense of belonging but are, due to their fundamental asymmetries, not good ground for developing an identity. Nevertheless, through these parasocial relationships, Taylor Swift has also created a passionate community to which her fans can belong. She invites her fans to actively engage with her work and with each other, enabling them to create and explore their own identities as members of her fanbase. Even when she says that there is not a lot going on at the moment, fans need to keep their eyes open, as there is definitely an Easter egg hidden somewhere, waiting to be found. This makes her fans stay connected to her, and puts them in continuous dialogue with each other, developing their identity along the way. Swift's fans will forever and always worry their "pretty little minds" about whether they have found all of her encrypted secret messages, but that is what makes them Swifties for evermore. Easter eggs can come in all shapes and sizes and can be hidden anywhere, from music videos to social media posts, and from live shows, to phrases, words, and sentences within this chapter. Did you find them all?[25]

Notes

1. Alex Suskind, "New Reputation: Taylor Swift Shares Intel on TS7, Fan Theories, and Her Next Era," *Entertainment Weekly*, May 9, 2019, at https://ew.com/music/2019/05/09/taylor-swift-cover-story.
2. "Easter Egg," in *Cambridge Advanced Learner's Dictionary & Thesaurus*, at https://dictionary.cambridge.org/dictionary/english/easter-egg (accessed April 17, 2024).
3. Marcel Danesi, *The Puzzle Instinct: The Meaning of Puzzles in Human Life* (Bloomington: Indiana University Press, 2002), 3–5.
4. Martin Tik, Ronal Sladky, Caroline Di Bernardi Luft, David Willinger, Andre Hoffmann, Michael J. Banissy, Joydeep Bhattacharya, and Christian Windischberger, "Ultra-High-Field fMRI Insights on Insight: Neural Correlates of the Aha!-Moment," *Human Brain Mapping* 39 (2018), 3241.
5. Letitcia M.S. Dantas, Mikel M. Delgado, Ingrid Johnson, and C.A. Tony Buffington, "Food Puzzles for Cats: Feeding for Physical and Emotional Wellbeing," *Journal of Feline Medicine and Surgery* 18 (2016), 724–727.
6. Mikel M. Delgado, Brandon Sang Gyu Han, and Melissa J. Bain, "Domestic Cats (*Felis Catus*) Prefer Freely Available Food over Food That Requires Effort," *Animal Cognition* 25 (2022), 96–101.
7. Capital FM, "Taylor Swift Reveals More Clues to Find in 'ME!' Music Video 🦋 | FULL INTERVIEW | Capital," YouTube, May 7, 2019, at https://www.youtube.com/watch?v=72g_jwnJrZg.
8. Matthew Lakier and Daniel Vogel, "More Than Just Software Surprises: Purposes, Processes, and Directions for Software Application Easter Eggs," *Proceedings of the ACM on Human–Computer Interaction* 6, no. CSCW1 (2022), art. 102, 3.
9. Seija Rankin, "Taylor Swift Divulges the Secrets to Her Album Easter Eggs in EW's Exclusive Video," *Entertainment Weekly*, May 9, 2019, at https://ew.com/music/2019/05/09/taylor-swift-secrets-album-easter-eggs.
10. Donald Horton and R. Richard Wohl, "Mass Communication and Para-Social Interaction," *Psychiatry* 19 (1956), 215–217.

11. Tilo Hartmann, "Parasocial Interaction, Parasocial Relationships, and Well-Being," in Leonard Reinecke and Mary Beth Oliver eds., *The Routledge Handbook of Media Use and Well-Being* (New York: Routledge, 2017), 131–132.
12. Catherine M. Robb and Alfred Archer, "Talent, Skill, and Celebrity," *Ethical Perspectives* 29 (2022), 47–49.
13. Carolina Graciela Montes Herrera, "Swifties e Easter Eggs: Interacción entre fans de Taylor Swift a través de Easter Eggs," *Figshare* (2022), at https://doi.org/10.6084/m9.figshare.21587112.v1.
14. Roy F. Baumeister and Mark R. Leary, "The Need to Belong: Desire for Interpersonal Attachment as a Fundamental Human Motivation," *Psychological Bulletin* 117 (1995), 47–49.
15. Gen Eickers, "Social Media Experiences of LGBTQ+ People: Enabling Feelings of Belonging," *Topoi* (2024), 4.
16. Jaye L. Derrick, Shira Gabriel, and Kurt Hugenberg, "Social Surrogacy: How Favored Television Programs Provide the Experience of Belonging," *Journal of Experimental Social Psychology* 45 (2009), 353–354.
17. Jaye L. Derrick, Shira Gabriel, and Brooke Tippin, "Parasocial Relationships and Self-Discrepancies: Faux Relationships Have Benefits for Low Self-Esteem Individuals," *Personal Relationships* 15 (2008), 275–276.
18. Hartmann, "Parasocial Interaction," 138–139.
19. Alfred Archer and Catherine M. Robb, "Ethics of Parasocial Relationships," in Monika Betzler and Jörg Löschke eds., *The Ethics of Relationships: Broadening the Scope* (Oxford: Oxford University Press, 2024).
20. Archer and Robb, "Ethics of Parasocial Relationships."
21. Charles Taylor, *The Ethics of Authenticity* (Cambridge, MA: Harvard University Press, 1991), 31–34.
22. Archer and Robb, "Ethics of Parasocial Relationships."
23. Margaret Rossman, "Taylor Swift, Remediating the Self, and Nostalgic Girlhood in Tween Music Fandom," *Transformative Works and Cultures* 38 (2022), 3.1–3.3.
24. Taylor, *The Ethics of Authenticity*, 14.
25. The author would like to thank her fellow Swifties Stella Kuipers, Lea Franz, and Jonathan Birch for discussing all things Taylor Swift and philosophy, as well as Maja Griem, Ludmila Reimer, and Leonard Dung for giving helpful feedback from an outsider's perspective, becoming Taylor Swift enthusiasts in the process.

4

Taylor Swift and the Ethics of Body Image

Gah-Kai Leung

Taylor Swift's body is constantly (and literally) on display at her concerts, on album covers, in music videos, and in memorabilia. The visibility of her body goes hand in hand with her high public profile, and her physical appearance is often the subject of intense scrutiny. Much of this scrutiny is negative. Swift has been both publicly fat-shamed, criticized for supposed excessive weight gain, and skinny-shamed, admonished for not weighing *enough*.[1]

In the Netflix documentary *Miss Americana*, Swift briefly addresses how public criticism has affected her relationship with her body, and hints that she has struggled with some form of disordered eating. In response to concerns that she wasn't eating enough, Swift states, "I was like, 'What are you talking about? Of course I eat, it's perfectly normal, I just exercise a lot.' And I did exercise a lot, but I wasn't eating."[2] Many commentators have interpreted this as Swift admitting to having an eating disorder, although Swift does not explicitly say so.[3] Swift also alludes to this aspect of her life in the initial edit of the music video for "Anti-Hero," which depicted her stepping on a scale labeled "FAT." This triggered accusations of fatphobia and fat-shaming, which ultimately led to the scene being deleted. But some have argued that the scene was actually Swift objecting to body image standards imposed upon herself and women more generally.[4]

You might think that body image and beauty norms are quite trivial things. However, as you'll see in this chapter, Taylor Swift's apparent experience of eating disorder, and her relationship to her body image, can highlight the ways that current beauty ideals are harmful to society. Before we dive in, it's important to note that philosophy cannot offer a psychological assessment of any kind of eating disorder that Swift may or may not have. What philosophy can do is provide a deeper understanding of the body shaming that Swift has been subjected to, and the influence that this has had on her. This point is particularly important because of how women's bodies have been, and are still being, written about. They have often been subject to vilification, critique, and shame by commentators who make unfair and unjustified assumptions. We shouldn't add to this historical pile-on—quite the opposite.[5]

The Demand to Be Beautiful

In *Miss Americana*, Swift suggests one reason why she may have been exercising a lot and not eating enough—the incessant pressures placed upon female celebrities to live up to unattainable and often contradictory body image standards. As she says, "if you're thin enough then you don't have that ass that everybody wants. But if you have enough weight on you to have an ass, then your stomach isn't flat enough."[6] Swift makes clear the pernicious and pervasive beauty norms which set expectations about how bodies ought to look, and the intense social pressure to conform to these norms. Given that these body image standards are in tension with each other, it becomes impossible to conform to them.

The contemporary philosopher Heather Widdows has argued that the demand to be beautiful and conform to social beauty norms is not just an aesthetic matter—not just about what is beautiful and ugly. It has become an ethical demand—about what is good and bad, right and wrong. Widdows claims that it is now unfortunately perceived as a moral failing if you do not live up to the relevant beauty ideals.[7] This is all further amplified by our *hypervisual* culture, where images are central to how we communicate in the public sphere, especially on social media.[8]

According to Widdows, the contemporary ethical beauty ideal consists of four components. First, we are told that we have to be *thin* and *slim*. While there are different versions of thinness (from being catwalk thin to athletically thin), it is almost always preferred to fatness. Swift alludes to this thinness ideal in *Miss Americana*, when she discusses the manipulation of fitness norms to conceal restricted eating. It is also this ideal that Swift may be satirizing in the now-deleted "FAT" scene from "Anti-Hero."

Second, Widdows claims that we are told to be *firm* and *buff*. In a hypervisual culture, there is an increasing emphasis on the naked body and this naked body must appear young, firm, and buff in terms of body shape and tone, as well as skin texture and tone. Swift herself tells us that thinness is not enough: the ideal (or idealized) woman must have "that ass that everybody wants," which is firm, pert, and curvaceous.[9]

Third, the beauty ideal consists of being *smooth* and *luminous*. We are told that the ideal face and body must be smooth, without blemishes or pockmarks, or uneven pigments. A smooth body implies a hairless body (at least for women). It also implies a body with a certain skin tone, ideally golden or bronze, which hints at the way beauty norms often have a racial character. An article in *Lifestyle Asia*, for example, claims to give readers the secrets behind Taylor Swift's beauty routine, so they can achieve the same "striking glow" that she has.[10]

Finally, the beauty ideal tells us that we must be *youthful*. The ideal face and body should appear youthful, and the proliferation of anti-ageing treatments cater to this demand. "Ageing gracefully" is the exception rather than the rule. In the words of the *Lifestyle Asia* article, if readers follow Swift's beauty routine they will always be "feeling 22!"[11]

Why Beauty Is Ethical

For Widdows, the contemporary beauty ideal has become an ethical demand in the sense that it is supposed to give us a value framework by which we live, and by which we judge others as being good or bad. Beauty success is *moral* success and, by contrast, beauty failures are seen as a kind of *moral* vice. We praise ourselves and punish ourselves for how much we live up to the ideal. We also morally praise or condemn others depending on how far their bodies are keeping up with the ideal, even if it's totally impossible.[12]

For example, when your friend says, "I feel bad for not going swimming today, I put on too much weight over Christmas," he's not just commenting on how he looks. He's making a moral claim that it's bad not to go swimming after a festive season when he's eaten too much. Similarly, when your friend says, "Taylor Swift doesn't look as good as she should," he's not just making an aesthetic claim about Swift's appearance. He's actually saying that Swift has acted badly or done something wrong by failing to meet beauty standards. This is passing moral judgment on Swift.

The idea that appearance-based claims are moral claims and not just aesthetic ones might seem weird at first. But Widdows thinks this is exactly what's happening every time someone says, "You look good today," or "I feel bad for not going to the gym." Notice the language of "good" and "bad"—that's moral language hidden in plain sight. For Widdows, this kind of moral talk shows how contemporary beauty standards are quite different from previous beauty norms, which were mostly based on aesthetics alone and had very few ethical implications.

Beauty Norms Are Really Bad for Us

Widdows claims that our fixation on beauty, and particularly the way in which beauty has taken on an ethical role in society, is incredibly morally damaging for us. The beauty ideal has become *dominant*, because it applies almost everywhere, to all types of women, in situations where it previously did not, and because beauty has become an ethical matter in a way we haven't seen before. In a hypervisual culture, we are expected to be camera-ready, and so beauty norms affect ordinary people just as much as celebrities, whose bodies and faces are constantly on display. We could try to undermine the ideal, but how much we can do so is limited by the fact that the ideal is everywhere.[13]

The beauty ideal has also become *global*. There may be pockets of resistance, but the overwhelming dominance of the current ideal means there are few genuine alternatives.[14] As an international superstar, Taylor Swift is not just a beauty icon for the West, but a beauty icon for women the world over. Everyone wants to be just as thin, firm, smooth, and youthful as she is. The fact that many people want to be as beautiful as Taylor Swift reinforces the pressures that Swift herself feels to look as good as everyone expects her to.

The global beauty norms have also become *demanding*, as the standard of "normal" is rising upwards, and the range of acceptable faces and bodies is becoming vanishingly small.[15] Practices we think of as "routine" or "normal" are increasingly burdensome for many women. For example, the average UK woman in 2016 used twenty-seven different products in her makeup routine, taking forty minutes a day, compared to just eight items a decade earlier.[16] The language of "normal" can be manipulated to conceal the extent to which beauty norms have become more demanding. "Normal" is not a neutral category—ever more onerous practices are becoming *normalized* as a result of the beauty ideal.

The fact that Taylor Swift has been both fat-shamed *and* skinny-shamed demonstrates the contradictions of the dominant beauty ideal. Swift can aim to get thinner to avoid being criticized for gaining weight, but then as she attempts to comply with increasingly demanding beauty standards, her thinness comes to represent this increasing demandingness. Consequently, she is vilified for making things apparently too demanding for everybody else. The skinny-shaming can be read as a backlash against rising beauty standards in the media, which are symbolized and indeed normalized by Swift's own thin youthful appearance.

Swift's disordered eating can be seen as a response to the pressure to maintain both the dominance and demandingness of the contemporary beauty ideal. As Swift tells us in *Miss Americana*:

I tend to get triggered by something, whether it's a picture of me where I feel like my tummy was too big or ... or, like, someone said that I looked pregnant or something, and that'll just trigger me to just ... s-starve a little bit, just stop eating.... You don't ever say to yourself, "Look, I've got an eating disorder," but you know you're, like, making a list of everything you put in your mouth that day, and you know that's probably not right, but then again there's so many diet blogs that tell you that that's what you should do.[17]

Today, everyone seems to be an expert or critic on health, beauty, and dieting, especially on social media—from tabloid photographers, to gossip columnists, to food writers. In the quote above, Swift points to the implicit moral messages around beauty which are communicated by paparazzi photos or diet blogs, showing that her conception of the beauty ideal is not just aesthetic, but also ethical.

Celebrity and Gossip

Although Widdows claims that the effects of the beauty ideal are being felt by individuals across society, the burdens of this ideal are not distributed equally. Celebrities like Taylor Swift may be particularly badly affected, given their prominence in public life.

The contemporary philosophers Alfred Archer and Maureen Sie suggest that celebrities play the role of enabling gossip, which has moral advantages and disadvantages.[18] We gossip about celebrities all the time—it is through gossip that we can weigh up and discuss with others which lifestyles are morally better than others. Archer and Sie discuss the example of Jamie Lynn Spears, whose pregnancy announcement at age 16 prompted widespread media debate around teenage pregnancy. Celebrities additionally have *epistemic* power, which is the power to influence people's beliefs and knowledge, which they can use to draw attention to social issues, like #MeToo or COVID-19 guidelines.[19]

While gossiping about celebrities can have these moral and epistemic benefits, it also has its downsides for celebrities themselves. Celebrities lose their privacy, because strangers start talking about them as if they were their own friends. Gossip also means that celebrities' moral lives are up for grabs and widespread public discussion. For celebrities from minority or oppressed backgrounds, this often includes a touch of stereotyping, prejudice, and discrimination. Fame can also lead to what Archer and Sie call "moral disorientation." This means that celebrities become unable to rely on the values that had structured their lives, because fame has either corrupted them, or caused them to exploit and neglect significant personal relationships.[20]

So, due to the nature of their celebrity, people like Taylor Swift deal with certain negative experiences that ordinary citizens don't have to face. Gossiping about Swift's health and her relationship to food puts her life under a moral microscope and invades her privacy. Whatever she says and does comes up for public discussion and is the topic of moral praise or blame. Swift faces sexist stereotypes about dieting and exercise. Moreover, she has told us that she experiences moral disorientation, as fame taints her perception of her body and her sense of self-worth:

I thought that I was, like, supposed to feel like I was gonna pass out at the end of a show or in the middle of it. I thought that was how it was, and now I realize: no, if you eat food, have energy, get stronger, you can do all these shows and not feel [exhausted]. Which is ... [sighs] a really good revelation, because I'm a lot happier with who I am ... and I don't care as much if, like, somebody points out that I have gained weight.[21]

Swift reveals how the lack of energy caused by restricted dieting, shaped by beauty norms of thinness, and coupled with the physical toll of lengthy concert tours, can be dangerously draining. She has had to work to reclaim her self-worth, in order to be comfortable with eating a more plentiful diet that helps her perform successfully, and yet not feel bad about her weight.

Resisting the "Hate Spiral"

Swift tells us that unlearning the harmful beauty norms so prevalent in society has been a constant process of challenging negative thoughts. As she says in *Miss Americana*:

This [unflattering picture] would cause me to go into a real shame, like, hate spiral. And, like, I caught myself yesterday starting to do it, and I was like, "Nope, we don't do that anymore, ... because it's better to think you look fat than to look sick.... We're changing the channel in our brain, and we're not ... doing that anymore. That didn't end us up in a good place.[22]

Swift suggests that unhealthy beauty standards can continue to influence a person even when that person recognizes how unhealthy they really are. The prospect of falling back into a negative body image—what Swift calls a "hate spiral"—is always lurking. So, to what extent is resistance really possible?

Maybe Swift just has to get in the right mindset. This individual approach to resistance might initially be tempting, because it reflects the idea of what Widdows calls the "malleable self."[23] This means that you are able to change and control your sense of self under the influence of your own willpower. If only we could wish away the bad thoughts, "change the channel in our brain" in Swift's words, then everything would be alright. But this fails to recognize just how powerful the dominant beauty ideal is. As Widdows makes clear, resistance to the beauty ideal is limited by the fact that the ideal is everywhere and oppresses everyone. An individual-level approach ignores the very real challenges to how our sense of self is influenced by others in the public sphere.

Oppressive beauty norms are a *communal* harm because the harm falls on women as a group, rather than on any one person.[24] The injustice of beauty norms is also *structural* because it arises as a result of how society is structured and organized. This occurs for three reasons.[25] First, beauty ideals are not freely chosen by people, but rather come about through social norms. Second, the harms that come from these beauty norms cannot be traced to any one person, but are part of a beauty culture more generally. Third, the harms that come from the beauty norms are not the result of a wrongful action, or a wrongful law or policy, but social pressure. Because the injustice is communal and structural, an individual-level approach will at best only change the consciousness of a few people here and there. Perhaps Swift can change her own mindset, and be a good role model to help her fans do the same, but this will not change the beauty culture as a whole.

That being said, Taylor Swift is in a special position to challenge oppressive beauty norms, because of the considerable power that comes from her celebrity status. Because of Swift's public visibility, she has the power to influence what people believe and know about beauty norms simply by drawing attention to them, in much the same way as the celebrities behind #MeToo galvanized a popular movement to combat sexual assault and harassment.

Importantly, #MeToo succeeded because it involved a group of celebrities who used their power together to influence social norms. They were united in their objectives and didn't let individual conflicts distract from the overall goal. As the saying goes, there is strength in numbers. The lesson here is that the more that prominent individuals call attention to oppressive beauty standards, the more likely it is that their collective power will succeed in challenging the injustice of beauty norms. This is *organized collective resistance*, where a group come together to fight against the prevailing and dominant social norms.[26]

Taylor Swift is a celebrity with one of the biggest and most supportive fanbases, but she is also a woman who is held to the same beauty standards as many other women in society. Is she in a more powerful position to change unjust beauty norms, or is she in fact *more* vulnerable to these norms given her status as a celebrity? Perhaps she is best placed to resist unjust beauty norms when she does so with a team of other celebrities who work alongside her in a common collective pursuit of transformation. This happened to some extent after the release of *Miss Americana*. For example, fellow celebrity Lady Gaga supported Swift and praised her for opening up about her experience. Gaga has previously shared her own past struggles with eating disorders as a teenager, and has taken quite a clear stand against beauty oppression. Both Swift and Gaga have sent powerful messages to the world about the real harms of modern beauty norms. Given their profile and popularity, hopefully this will translate into meaningful social change.

If you or someone you know may be struggling with an eating disorder, please reach out for help. You can contact your local eating disorder helpline for free, or visit their website.

Notes

1. Amanda Ross, "After a Fan Asked How Taylor Swift Got Fat, Someone Made a Twitter Account Dedicated to Her Weight Gain," Babe, May 17, 2018, at https://babe.net/2018/05/17/after-a-fan-asked-taylor-swift-how-she-got-fat-someone-made-a-twitter-account-dedicated-to-her-weight-gain-57212;

Sarah Larimer, "The Skinny-Shaming of Taylor Swift," *The Washington Post*, November 14, 2014, at https://web.archive.org/web/20141117181346/https://www.washingtonpost.com/news/to-your-health/wp/2014/11/14/the-skinny-shaming-of-taylor-swift.
2. *Miss Americana*, dir. Lana Wilson (Tremolo Productions, 2020).
3. Laura Snapes, "Taylor Swift Discloses Fight with Eating Disorder in New Documentary," *The Guardian*, January 24, 2020, at https://www.theguardian.com/music/2020/jan/24/taylor-swift-eating-disorder-miss-americana-documentary-sundance-film-festival-lana-wilson; Mark Savage, "Taylor Swift Reveals Eating Disorder in Netflix Documentary," *BBC News*, January 24, 2020, at https://www.bbc.com/news/entertainment-arts-51234055.
4. Olivia Truffaut-Wong, "Taylor Swift, Fatphobia, and Me," The Cut, October 25, 2022, at https://www.thecut.com/2022/10/taylor-swifts-anti-hero-video-sparks-fatphobia-debate.html.
5. I thank Heather Widdows for pressing me to clarify this point.
6. *Miss Americana*.
7. Heather Widdows, *Perfect Me: Beauty as an Ethical Ideal* (Princeton, NJ, and Oxford: Princeton University Press, 2018), 1–16.
8. Sally M. Promey, "Situating Visual Culture," in Karen Halttunen ed., *A Companion to American Cultural History* (Malden, MA, and Oxford: Blackwell, 2008), 286–288.
9. *Miss Americana*.
10. Kriti Nayyar, "Emulate Taylor Swift's Skincare and Beauty Tips for That Striking Glow!" *Lifestyle Asia*, August 23, 2023, at https://www.lifestyleasia.com/hk/beauty-grooming/skin/taylor-swift-skincare-diet-and-beauty-tips.
11. Nayyar, "Emulate Taylor Swift's Skincare."
12. Widdows, *Perfect Me*, 26–35.
13. Widdows, *Perfect Me*, 26–35.
14. Widdows, *Perfect Me*, 70.
15. Widdows, *Perfect Me*, 97–98.
16. Francesca Rice, "Women Now Have 27 Steps in Their Make-Routine," *Prima*, November 14, 2016, at https://www.prima.co.uk/fashion-and-beauty/beauty-news/news/a36603/women-27-steps-make-routine. This statistic is also cited in Widdows, *Perfect Me*, 99–100.
17. *Miss Americana*.
18. Alfred Archer and Maureen Sie, "Using Stars for Moral Navigation: An Ethical Exploration into Celebrity," *Journal of Applied Philosophy* 40 (2023), 340–357.
19. Archer and Sie, "Using Stars for Moral Navigation, 344–345.
20. Archer and Sie, "Using Stars for Moral Navigation, 350–352.
21. *Miss Americana*.
22. *Miss Americana*.
23. See Widdows, *Perfect Me*, 42–43.
24. Widdows, *Perfect Me*, 139–140.
25. This discussion draws on Heather Widdows, "Structural Injustice and the Requirements of Beauty," *Journal of Social Philosophy* 52 (2021), 251–269, especially section 3. For the classic account of structural injustice, see Iris Marion Young, Responsibility for Justice (Oxford: Oxford University Press, 2011), 45–52.
26. Steven Klein, "Democracy Requires Organized Collective Power," *Journal of Political Philosophy* 30 (2022), 26–47.

5

So Mother for That
Taylor Swift and Childless Mothering

Lucy Britt and Brian Britt

Music critic Ann Powers explained Taylor Swift's public image as follows: "Taylor doesn't have a child. And in our patriarchal society, when does a woman change? When she becomes a mother ... maybe one of the main reasons why we don't accept Taylor as an adult is because the childless woman remains a strange figure in our society."[1] Childless in a society that identifies female maturity with maternity, Swift does not conform to the popular image of a fully adult woman. Yet fans of Swift have adapted the term "mother" from Black and queer ballroom culture of the 1980s and 1990s to signify her as a mother figure to her fandom, including a subculture of fans, called "Gaylors," who believe that Swift herself is lesbian or bi/pansexual. While this might point toward a queer feminist rereading of Taylor Swift and maternity, Swift's own problematic feminist politics complicate this picture. In particular, she has been justifiably accused of performative allyship with the queer community and problematic white feminism. Given all this, what does it mean to call Swift "mother"?

"Mother"

The word "mother," as it is used to describe Taylor Swift and other pop stars, comes from queer, predominantly Black ballroom culture of the 1980s.[2] Ballroom "houses" (groups of drag performers forming a found family) competed as teams in balls, led by their house mothers. These were usually queens with more experience who could mentor their "children," many of whom had been exiled from their biological family and considered their houses to be their new families.[3] Like other Black and feminist re-imaginings of motherhood, this use of mother resists patriarchy and white supremacy and challenges the hegemony of a particular construction of motherhood as biological, pure, nurturing, and natural.[4] However, Swifties calling Taylor Swift "mother" have lost much of this original meaning of the mother as a queer figure of relational care.

Taylor Swift and Philosophy: Essays from the Tortured Philosophers Department, First Edition. Edited by Catherine M. Robb and Georgie Mills.

Queer and Black feminist theories of motherhood challenge the identification of motherhood with biological birth, making space for other conceptions of motherhood that extend from adoptive motherhood to non-traditional and non-patriarchal forms of family and social group. Drawing on these theories of motherhood, we argue that a political reading of Taylor Swift must account for both the dominant and marginalized concepts of the mother. The appropriation of the word "mother" from queer and Black culture has become a major motif of Swift's fans' social media without always embracing the goals of queer, Black feminism. At the same time, Swift's recent public statements, videos, and music have affirmed more inclusive models of feminism and hinted at a proximity with queerness. Though it did not originate with Swift, the non-traditional mother motif projects queerness and feminism and challenges dominant conceptions of motherhood.

In so doing, the motif of Swift as mother suggests alignment with such feminist concepts as Audre Lorde's Black feminism and Shelley Park's "mothering queerly." However, Swift's individualistic persona prevents a full embrace of the relational politics of care and reciprocity that emerges from feminist theories such as Joan Tronto's "caring democracy" and Adriana Cavarero's maternal inclination. Below, we outline Taylor Swift's engagement with feminism, her relationship to the concept of motherhood, and her association with queerness, before examining how these elements fit together to position Swift as a post-modern pop icon.

Taylor Swift and Feminism

Taylor Swift has always been entangled in gender politics, drawing on a multiplicity of meanings around femininity and feminism. Her early image leaned on a conventional brand of white femininity that one cultural commentator called "a cross between Shirley Temple, Doris Day and the Sunbeam bread mascot."[5] She continued to project this theme of innocence, niceness, and the girl next door throughout her first three album cycles ("eras" in Taylor-speak), using images like princesses, castles, and suburban rural white teenage romance—what feminist philosopher Simone de Beauvoir (1908–1986) calls the "exquisite flowers, rare lace"[6] of traditional femininity. These tropes of innocence are historically connected to stereotypes of femininity that white women in North America and Europe have *been confined within*, as white feminist philosophers like de Beauvoir argue. However, the innocence trope has also *benefitted* white women in a social hierarchy that sees Black women as sexually promiscuous and sexual property, as Black feminist theorists like Patricia Hill Collins have pointed out.[7]

Indeed, Swift's feminism could be characterized as second-wave feminism, which arose around the 1960s in white-dominated political movements and emphasizes equality for women. For example, Swift sings in "The Man," "I'm so sick of running as fast as I can / Wondering if I'd get there quicker / If I was a man." These ideas owe much to second-wave feminist philosophers like de Beauvoir, who pointed out that women were confined to activities around childrearing while men are given space for "transcendence," or seeking freedom and enlightenment.[8]

Although she "came out" as a Democrat and started posting about systemic racism in 2018, Swift has mostly focused on palatable themes of economic empowerment (especially around her rerecording of her back catalogue starting in 2021), agency,[9] and women supporting women,[10] sometimes through a simplistic lens that does not acknowledge structural injustices like racism.[11] As a result, her feminism has been called "marketplace feminism," or a consumer branding of feminism that is cool, fun, accessible, depoliticized, and often taken up by celebrities.[12] Also called "celebrity feminism," this public image often projects vague messages of empowerment without much explicitly political commentary.[13] However, the amount of criticism of her political engagement is perhaps disproportionate to her actual *faux pas*, "revealing a distrust of young female subjectivity difficult to separate from the distrust of Swift's political competence and intentions."[14]

Swift's most interesting engagement with feminism may be her playfulness with gender stereotypes in her ever-changing public image—sometimes performing them, sometimes pushing them to excess in parody, and sometimes inverting them. For example, her 2014 album *1989* includes a parody of herself as a crazy man-eater in "Blank Space (Taylor's Version)": "Got a long list of ex-lovers / They'll tell you I'm insane." She dresses in drag for "The Man" to comment on gender expectations in a masculinist industry; she challenges the archetype of hysterical femininity in "mad woman"; and she comments on gendered expectations for romantic relationships in "Mastermind": "the wisest women had to do it this way / 'Cause we were born to be the pawns in every lover's game."

This gender play allows fans to identify with *one* of her "eras" or identities or with the *idea* that she could contain multitudes, thereby giving fans permission to embrace their own multifaceted complexity. Postmodern philosophy rejects the dominance of one single meaning in favor of a multiplicity of meanings, identities, and interpretations.[15] Through Swift's constant reinvention—and her fans' diligent interpretations and reinterpretations of these reinventions—she has become a postmodern icon of multiplicity and free play.

Is it feminist for Swift to play with her image and gender roles? Though not radical or intersectional, Swift's self-referential, postmodern play with a multiplicity of selves resists the impulse to reduce her to a pop star for teenage girls crying over their breakups, a caricature that itself reflects cultural norms of infantilizing women without children.

Taylor Swift and Mothering

Swift's relationship with motherhood only entered public discourse in her more recent "eras." While she has mostly resisted responding to press inquiries about being unmarried and childless, the topic of motherhood surfaces in the song "peace," where she tells her muse (presumably Joe Alwyn) she would be willing to "give you a child."[16] In "Anti-Hero," she writes the dark side of imagined motherhood, enacting a hypothetical adult son and daughter-in law fighting over their inheritance after Swift's death. She also plays on the centuries-old trope of the undesirable, cat-owning spinster, saying: "Someone is going to think I'm undateable for a lot of reasons before they think I'm undateable because I have two cats."[17] She has continued to highlight her cats in her social media presence, her official website, the *Miss Americana* documentary, and even her lyrics: "Guess I'll just stumble on home to my cats / Alone, unless you want to come along" ("Gorgeous").

Playing with her public image as a childless woman frozen in adolescence against a backdrop of an ageist popular culture that refuses to see older and middle-aged female musicians as sexual,[18] Swift highlights her unconventional gender presentation. This playfulness echoes ideas developed by contemporary psychoanalytic feminist philosophers like Nancy Chodorow and Julia Kristeva. Chodorow critiques and extends Sigmund Freud's (1856–1939) theories to emphasize the socially constructed nature of the assumption that women would be mothers,[19] while Julia Kristeva draws on psychanalytic theory to highlight the tension between biological motherhood and the cultural meaning-making around motherhood.[20] Yet even theorists like Kristeva rely on an essentialist concept of motherhood that reduces motherhood to innate biological characteristics: contemporary queer and feminist theorist Judith Butler critiques Kristeva and argues that even feminist accounts of women and mothers can be essentialist. Butler argues instead for a "culturally constructed body" that will be "liberated, not to its 'natural' past nor to its original pleasures, but to an open future of cultural possibilities."[21] We can understand Swift's postmodern gender play as opening a future of cultural possibilities. Swift plays adeptly with stereotypes of women as mothers and the assumption that she should have children. Perhaps the figure of Taylor Swift as mother to her fans helps us move beyond purely biological understandings of motherhood.

Taylor Swift as Queer Mother?

Like so much mainstream slang, the Swifties' use of "mother" has its origins in Black culture, particularly the queer, primarily Black ballroom culture of the 1980s. Motherhood in this sense is not about childbearing, but about relational care and excellence. In the documentary film *Paris Is Burning* that profiled the ballroom culture of the 1980s, Carmen Xtravaganza likens her house mother to a "real" mother and highlights relational care in a found family—her house mother gives her birthday presents and takes her in when her biological mother kicks her out, and although they fight, they are bonded by love and care. In *Paris Is Burning*, house mother Willi Ninja defines motherhood as leadership and excellence: "You know, you have to have something to offer in order to lead. The mother usually becomes the mother because she's usually the best one out of the group. ... It's the mother that's the hardest worker and the mother gets the most respect."[22]

As drag and ballroom entered the mainstream, especially through the reality competition show *RuPaul's Drag Race*, it began to be appropriated by straight and white audiences, culminating in white pop singer Megan Trainor's 2022 song "Mother," a song utterly devoid of the original meanings of the term centering around relational care in found family. Enter "mother" into the mainstream lexicon, and by 2023 Taylor Swift fans on TikTok and Twitter were calling Swift "mother" and commenting "she's so mother for that" or "mother is mothering" when Swift released new music or performed a provocative dance on the Eras Tour. A cursory investigation into Taylor Swift-focused online spaces indicates that many Swifties did not know the queer Black origins of this use of "mother" when they adopted it.[23] And Swift suggested that she did not know these origins either, saying during the Eras Tour in May 2023 in Philadelphia: "What's that thing you guys have been saying online? You're always like 'Mother is Mothering,' which I think you mean in a totally different context than Mother's Day, but I just thought of it because it made me think of the word that you use when you're like turning it into a verb, like good for you, that's cool." Swift's ignorance of the term's resonance here highlights a lack of attention to marginalized voices within her fandom who had pointed out the term's origins.

And yet, despite the limitations of Swift's own engagement with queerness and Blackness and the heteronormativity and whiteness of the majority of her fanbase, there is a small but vocal and growing community of fans engaged in queering Swift's music. Self-proclaimed "Gaylors" are fans, many themselves queer, who pick up on lyrics and other signs that they argue hint that Swift is gay or pan/bisexual. These hints include Swift's frequent use of rainbow imagery and the colors of the lesbian and bisexual flags, lyrics like "You can want who you want / Boys and boys and girls and girls" ("Welcome to New York (Taylor's Version)"), the dedication of "Dress" to Loie Fuller, and a quote from *Miss Americana* in which Swift says "gay pride" is one of the "things that make me, me." Despite Swift calling the LGBTQ community "a community that I'm not a part of" in 2019,[24] Gaylors controversially believe that Swift will come out publicly as queer any time now. The "You Need to Calm Down" music video—which spotlit queer and drag celebrities, includes the lyric "step on his gown," and encourages viewers to donate to GLAAD—added fuel to the fire. Interpreting Taylor Swift through a queer lens is thus happening on two fronts: from the Gaylors and from the mainstream of her fanbase, who call her "mother," a term appropriated from queer Black and Latinx ballroom culture. Gaylors did not, to our knowledge, start the trend of calling Taylor Swift "mother" and calling her "mother" is not predicated on an explicitly queer reading of her music (in fact, many fans who call her "mother" are unaware or dismissive of Gaylor theories). Rather, calling Taylor Swift "mother" is an inadvertent appropriation of a queer term that runs parallel to Gaylors' separate project of queering Swift. At the same time, Gaylor fans do seem to have built a found family in digital spaces around queer reinterpretation and myth-making. Gaylors have thus carved out space for a queered conception of mothering *within* the heteronormative constraints of the Swiftdom.

This queering of the concept of the mother has an antecedent—albeit one that Taylor Swift does not reference and that is not a major topic of discussion among Swiftie online spaces—in feminist scholars who argue we ought to expand our conception of mothering beyond the straight, cisgender, nuclear family to include revolutionary forms of mothering such as queer and Black mothering. Many queer and women-of-color feminist theorists have argued for an expansion of mothering to account for a broader cultural conception of mothers, similar to the expanded definition of mothers from ballroom culture. For example, queer theorist Shelley Park argues that we ought to challenge the equation of motherhood with biological birth and instead acknowledge those who are "mothering queerly," from adoptive motherhood to non-traditional and non-patriarchal forms of family and social group. In expanding our conceptions of what real motherhood looks like, Park argues, we are "queering motherhood," or acknowledging the subversive potential of parenting.[25] In the context of a growing movement to interrogate the idealized figure of the mother and the inevitability of childrearing,[26] these queer theories of mothering address the postmodern fracturing of the figure of the mother in the twenty-first century.

In a similar vein, Black feminist scholars have pointed out how mothering while Black is itself a radical form of resistance to white supremacy and patriarchy. For example, Black feminist theorist Audre Lorde (1934–1992) challenged hegemonic conceptions of motherhood as biological, pure, nurturing, and natural. She laid bare the ways that Black women are forced to mother under conditions of hatred and to release their children into a world of anti-Black hatred.[27] Lorde and others have theorized Black motherhood as especially relational, building on communities beyond the nuclear family because of such social forces as the Great Migration and the mass incarceration of Black men.[28] This innovative rethinking, largely overlooked by the white mainstream, expands motherhood beyond childbirth to relationships of care, dovetailing with queer feminists' calls for a more expansive vision of mothering. By bringing together these cultural texts—on the one hand, the Swiftdom and its queering by Gaylors and fans who call Swift "mother," and on the other hand, feminist theories of mothering that argue for a more expansive conception of mothering as care and resistance—we can better understand what it might mean to consider Taylor Swift as a queered mother figure. Together, the Gaylor community and commentary by queer and Black philosophers of mothering point to the possibility of understanding Taylor Swift as a mother beyond biological mothering.

Taylor Swift, Postmodern Mother

If Taylor Swift is mother to her fans, she is the most postmodern of mothers. She is a savant of reinvention, multiple meanings, and speaking to multiple audiences simultaneously. She toggles her public image between "the girl-next-door/millionaire, the hopeless romantic/savvy businesswoman, and a silly teenager/serious adult singer-songwriter,"[29] inhabiting this multiplicity of images in the "Look What You Made Me Do" music video and a CapitalOne commercial. Indeed, she has become more self-aware of this multiplicity and even centered her personal brand *on* rebranding during the album rerecords and Eras Tour. But given the ambiguity of her public image and her evasive responses to interviewers who ask her the real meaning of her music, we may never know the full scope of Swift's conception of her mothering.

We could consider Swift a mother as defined by ballroom culture: a role model and mentor to a found family, modeling excellence and becoming a mother by being the best at what she does. But Swifties, a disproportionately white audience,[30] do not typically understand the 1980s Black and Latinx drag origins of "mother." Rather, Swift is a mother figure in the sense that she models excellence and postmodern reinvention. In this sense, Swift has become a queered postmodern mother figure.

As feminist and queer theorist Craig Jennex puts it, it is precisely "*because* of their malleable nature" that pop icons like Swift "can become objects of fantasy and identification" for audiences in this way.[31] Swift is the queen of reinvention and the postmodern free play of self-image and "pluralistic willingness to include multiple meanings or narratives"[32] of her work. So audiences ultimately get to choose which version of her they consume, and they interpret her work in multiple ways. As Walter Benjamin (1892–1940) argues, the reception and afterlife of a work is often more important than any search for its original meaning.[33]

A political reading of Taylor Swift must ultimately account for both dominant and marginalized concepts of the mother—namely, queer and Black feminist concepts of mothering and the queer online space that Gaylors have created. If Taylor Swift is "a woman ... defined as a human being in quest of values in a world of values," as Simone de Beauvoir argues for all women,[34] can we tease out some values from this human being, her work, and the remarkable world of meaning that has been created around her?

The solidarity and empowerment experienced by Swift's fans comes less from her explicit political activism than from her postmodern multiplicity. For many of her fans, her self-awareness as an artist who contains multitudes (and multiple ways of inhabiting femininity)—and her reclamation of all these past selves in the postmodern project of rerecording her old albums and revisiting the fashions and sentiments of past "eras"—add up to a sense of agency and self-determination. By modeling reinvention and newfound maturity about her old selves, Swift-as-mother helps her fans mature and deepen their own relationships with their past selves.

"All the ways you're so ashamed of the person you were right before this moment," says a college student to a reporter at the Eras Tour, "You could so easily be ashamed of singing Taylor Swift in your bedroom. You could leave it behind. But she doesn't let you. She says, 'Look, I'm getting older, too.' You grow with her. What if we weren't ashamed of our eras? What if we realized they were always with us, and you just didn't have to feel shame about who you were?"[35] By compassionately revisiting her previous selves in the "Eras era" (as Swift called the period of her Eras Tour in a March 2023 Instagram post), Swift is showing her fans how to mother their past selves.

This is a form of growth and individual self-care, and Swift's brand revolves around excelling in her craft. Ultimately, however, this is a politics of individualism,[36] reflecting drag mother Willi Ninja's definition of motherhood as *leadership and excellence*. For Swift to cultivate a more radical politics of motherhood, she would have to develop a more relational, intersectional model of motherhood, one more similar to drag queen Carmen Xtravaganza's definition of motherhood as *love and care*. Feminist theories of mothering can help us imagine such a relational conception of mothering.

The work of contemporary maternal feminist philosophers shows an alternative vision of mother/mothering based on relational care. These feminist thinkers theorize relational care in different ways. For example, Joan Tronto's concept of "caring democracy" proposes a political ethos of care in which democracy cultivates caring relationships, economies are structured around supporting caretakers, and the political system cares for citizens.[37] As another example, contemporary feminist philosopher Adriana Cavarero theorizes a politics of relationality through the metaphor of the mother inclined toward her child in contrast to the figure of a vertical, upright, rational individual.[38] An artist who fully took on board these relational politics of care imagined by thinkers like Tronto or Cavarero would center reciprocity, collectivity, and relationships of care.

However, the Swiftdom does not necessarily reflect such a relational feminism of care, instead centering on individualistic standards of excellence and individuality of identity. Although Swifties often find identity in a collective fanbase similar to the diva-worship communities of gay men around Judy Garland or Lady Gaga,[39] Swift's lyrics and self-presentation typically rely on an individualism and "marketplace feminism"[40] that resist the relationality of Cavarero's maternal inclination and Tronto's caring democracy. She sings, "All of my heroes die all alone" in *Lover*'s "The Archer" and "You're on your own, kid / You always have been" in *Midnights'* "You're On Your Own, Kid." Although feminist themes and awareness of queer and Black identity have become more prominent in her recent work, the individualistic parameters and political economy of Swift's celebrity delimit the scope of her engagement with a more relational feminism.

And yet the fans and reception of Swift's work are not the mere result of the artist's intentions, and at least some of her fans choose to interpret her work as progressive in spite of these limits, reading queerness into her lyrics and creating relational communities of alternative interpretations within the fandom. The distinction between artist and art goes back at least to Plato's *Apology*, where Socrates observes that poets do not seem capable of explaining their own work.[41] The meaning of a work is created by the people who read and consume it. What fans do with her art and image is as powerful as what Swift herself does: a mother only exists as a mother in relation to her children.

Notes

1. Sam Sanders, "A Portrait of the Artist as Taylor Swift," *Into It: A Vulture Podcast* with Sam Sanders, October 20, 2022, at https://www.vulture.com/article/taylor-swift-midnights-into-it.html.
2. *Paris Is Burning*, dir. Jennie Livingston (Off White Productions and Prestige Pictures, 1990).
3. Marlon M. Bailey, "Gender/Racial Realness: Theorizing the Gender System in Ballroom Culture," *Feminist Studies* 37 (2011), 365–387.
4. Audre Lorde, "Eye to Eye: Black Women, Hatred, and Anger," in her *Sister Outsider: Essays and Speeches* (New York: Crossing Press, 2007), 145–175; Loretta J. Ross, "Preface," in Alexis Pauline Gumbs, China Martens, and Mai'a Williams eds., *Revolutionary Mothering: Love on the Front Lines* (Binghamton, NY: PM Press, 2016), xiii–xix.
5. Dodai Stewart, "Don't Go Calling Taylor Swift a Feminist, Says Taylor Swift," Jezebel, October 22, 2012, https://jezebel.com/dont-go-calling-taylor-swift-a-feminist-says-taylor-sw-5953879.
6. Simone de Beauvoir, *The Second Sex*, ed. and trans. H.M. Parshley (New York: Random House, 1989), 729.
7. Patricia Hill Collins, *Black Feminist Thought*, 2nd ed. (New York: Routledge, 2000), chap. 6.
8. De Beauvoir, *The Second Sex*.
9. Myles McNutt, "From 'Mine' to 'Ours': Gendered Hierarchies of Authorship and the Limits of Taylor Swift's Paratextual Feminism," *Communication, Culture and Critique* 13 (2020), 73, https://doi.org/10.1093/ccc/tcz042.

10. Vanity Fair, "Cover Preview: Taylor Swift Fights Back About Her Love Life, the Hyannis Port House—and Has Words for Tina Fey and Amy Poehler," *Vanity Fair*, March 5, 2013, https://www.vanityfair.com/culture/2013/03/taylor-swift-fights-back-tina-fey-amy-poehler.

11. Judy L. Isaksen and Nahed Eltantawy, "What Happens When a Celebrity Feminist Slings Microaggressive Shade? Twitter and the Pushback against Neoliberal Feminism," *Celebrity Studies* 12 (2021), 549–564, https://doi.org/10.1080/19392397.2019.1678229.

12. Andi Zeisler, *We Were Feminists Once: From Riot Grrrl to CoverGirl®, the Buying and Selling of a Political Movement* (New York: PublicAffairs, 2016).

13. Sue Jackson, "'A Very Basic View of Feminism': Feminist Girls and Meanings of (Celebrity) Feminism," *Feminist Media Studies* 21 (2021), 1072–1090.

14. Eric Smialek, "Who Needs to Calm Down? Taylor Swift and Rainbow Capitalism," *Contemporary Music Review* 40 (2021), 99.

15. Jean-François Lyotard, *The Postmodern Condition: A Report on Knowledge*, trans. Geoffrey Bennington and Brian Massumi (Minneapolis: University of Minnesota Press, 1984).

16. Fan speculation that the *Midnights* song "Bigger Than the Whole Sky" is about Swift experiencing a miscarriage is an example of fans' obsession with Swift's reproductive status and possible future motherhood.

17. Josh Eells, "Cover Story: The Reinvention of Taylor Swift," *Rolling Stone* (blog), September 8, 2014, https://www.rollingstone.com/music/music-news/the-reinvention-of-taylor-swift-116925.

18. Murray Forman, "Resisting the Politics of Aging: Madonna and the Value of Female Labor in Popular Music," in Susan Fast and Craig Jennex eds., *Popular Music and the Politics of Hope: Queer and Feminist Interventions* (New York: Routledge, 2019), 267–281.

19. Nancy Chodorow, *The Reproduction of Mothering: Psychoanalysis and the Sociology of Gender* (Berkeley: University of California Press, 1978).

20. Julia Kristeva, *Desire in Language: A Semiotic Approach to Literature and Art* (New York: Columbia University Press, 1980).

21. Judith Butler, "The Body Politics of Julia Kristeva," *Hypatia* 3 (1989), 117.

22. *Paris Is Burning*.

23. While many fans appear not to understand the term's queer Black origins, others worked to highlight it. For example, one Reddit user posted, "In this context 'mother' is a direct reference to 'drag mothers'—the (usually) older queen who put you in drag for the first time, showed you the ropes, helped you get your beat down, and made you part of their chosen family and loved you like you were born to it. And in that sense, with knowing where it comes from, I would absolutely call Taylor 'Mother' ... I know other swifties [sic] who have found their chosen families through this fandom. Taylor is absolutely Mother," at https://www.reddit.com/r/TaylorSwift/comments/14t60u3/am_i_the_only_one_weirded_out_by_swifties_calling/?rdt=61026 (accessed September 5, 2023). Thanks to Jessie Meltsner for this reference and to her and Anna Britt for many helpful comments on this chapter.

24. Abby Aguirre, "Taylor Swift on Sexism, Scrutiny, and Standing Up for Herself," *Vogue*, August 8, 2019, https://www.vogue.com/article/taylor-swift-cover-september-2019.

25. Shelley M. Park, *Mothering Queerly, Queering Motherhood* (Albany: SUNY Press, 2013).

26. Orna Donath, *Regretting Motherhood: A Study* (Berkeley: North Atlantic Books, 2017).

27. Lorde, "Eye to Eye: Black Women, Hatred, and Anger"; Ross, "Preface."

28. Dani McClain, *We Live for the We* (New York: Bold Type Books, 2019).

29. Mary Fogarty and Gina Arnold, "Are You Ready for It? Re-Evaluating Taylor Swift," *Contemporary Music Review* 40 (2021), 2.

30. "A Demographic Deep Dive into the Taylor Swift Fandom," Morning Consult Pro, March 14, 2023, at https://pro.morningconsult.com/instant-intel/taylor-swift-fandom-demographic.

31. Craig Jennex, "Diva Worship and the Sonic Search for Queer Utopia," *Popular Music and Society* 36 (2013), 351.

32. Smialek, "Who Needs to Calm Down?, 102.

33. Walter Benjamin, "The Task of the Translator," in *Selected Writings*, vol. 1, ed. Marcus Bullock and Michael W. Jennings (Cambridge, MA: Harvard University Press, 1996), 254–255.

34. De Beauvoir, *The Second Sex*, 52.

35. Taffy Brodesser-Akner, "My Delirious Trip to the Heart of Swiftiedom," *The New York Times Magazine*, October 12, 2023, sec. Magazine, at https://www.nytimes.com/2023/10/12/magazine/taylor-swift-eras-tour.html.

36. McNutt, "From 'Mine' to 'Ours,'" 73.

37. Joan C. Tronto, *Caring Democracy: Markets, Equality, and Justice* (New York: NYU Press, 2013).

38. Adriana Cavarero, *Inclinations: A Critique of Rectitude* (Stanford, CA: Stanford University Press, 2016), 1–16.

39. Jennex, "Diva Worship," 351.

40. Zeisler, *We Were Feminists Once*, 1–14.

41. Plato, *Apology*, in *Euthyphro; Apology; Crito; Phaedo*, ed. C.J. Emlyn-Jones and William Preddy (Cambridge, MA: Harvard University Press, 2017), 125.

"LOOK WHAT YOU MADE ME DO": REPUTATION, FORGIVENESS, AND BLAME

6

Can I Forgive You for Breaking My Heart?

Sophia Pettigrove and Glen Pettigrove

Almost every philosopher writing on forgiveness in the last 40 years, including one of the authors of this chapter, has assumed that forgiveness presupposes wrongdoing.[1] For example, contemporary philosophers David McNaughton and Eve Garrard write that "if there is no wrongdoing there is nothing to forgive."[2] Another contemporary philosopher, Lucy Allais, describes forgiving as "releasing a wrongdoer from blame." Blame, on her account, is a feeling that assumes "someone [has] culpably done something wrong."[3] Consequently, before you can forgive someone, according to Allais, you must believe they did something they shouldn't have done, because forgiving involves "ceasing to have blame-feelings towards someone who has wronged you."[4]

Taking our cue from a number of Taylor Swift's songs, in this chapter we challenge the assumption that forgiveness presupposes wrongdoing. Swift's lyrics frequently take up the question, "can I forgive you for breaking my heart?" Sometimes, the answer is a resounding no, as in "Picture to Burn": "If you come around saying sorry to me / My daddy's gonna show ya how sorry you'll be." If this heartbreaker is hoping to be forgiven, he'll be sorely disappointed. But in other songs, like "invisible string," forgiving a heartbreaker is described as both possible and beautiful: "Cold was the steel of my axe to grind / For the boys who broke my heart / Now I send their babies presents." These hatchets have been buried and these friendships restored. Whether the answer ends up being yes or no, the question is one that commonly arises for those whose hearts have been broken. Can I forgive the person who has broken my heart?

Heartbreaking

Heartbreaking is not an activity philosophers have spent much time discussing, so it will be helpful to reflect for a moment on what it involves. Heartbreaking is an activity defined by its outcome, namely, a broken heart. In this respect, it is like "deceiving." If I haven't managed to get

Taylor Swift and Philosophy: Essays from the Tortured Philosophers Department, First Edition. Edited by Catherine M. Robb and Georgie Mills.

another person to form false beliefs, then no matter how often I have lied, I haven't deceived them. Similarly, if no one is heartbroken, then no matter how badly I've behaved, I haven't been breaking hearts. Deceiving implies there is an intention to mislead someone. Heartbreaking, by contrast, does not imply anything about the heartbreaker's intentions. This makes it possible for Swift to sing, in "Afterglow," that "I'm the one who burned us down / But it's not what I meant." Heartbreaking is wholly defined by its consequences, namely, heartbreak, regardless of the intention behind it.

Heartbreak, in its widest sense, is a profound sadness about the damage or loss of something about which one cares deeply. In a narrower sense, it is profound sadness about a damaged or broken relationship. If you don't "feel anything at all" then, as Swift writes in "The Way I Loved You (Taylor's Version)," your "heart's not breaking." Another defining feature of heartbreak is the time required to get over it. No matter how sad you feel today, if you bounce back tomorrow and never again feel sad about the loss, then you were not heartbroken. Heartbreak lasts a long time. This aspect of heartbreak is frequently reflected in Swift's lyrics, as in "cardigan" when she sings "I knew I'd curse you for the longest time." Swift also recognizes there is no guarantee you will get over your heartbreak. In "Cornelia Street," she writes about "the kind of heartbreak time could never mend." Time is necessary, but not always sufficient, for healing after heartbreak.

"Making You a Villain"

Often when we think about heartbreak, and almost always when Swift sings about it, we have in mind a relationship that has gone wrong. For example, we might think of an ex who was unfaithful. When discovered, the infidelity evokes a mix of anger and sadness, and the once intimate relationship is disrupted. In the song "Should've Said No," the cheater "beg[s] for forgiveness" and asks the wronged party for "one [more] chance." Providing the unfaithful partner with the kind of forgiveness they seek would involve both letting go of hard feelings and resuming their romantic relationship. However, not every case of forgiving involves kissing and making up. It is possible to forgive and, at the same time, to part ways.[5] Nevertheless, overcoming hard feelings often goes hand in hand with restoring a broken relationship, and when people ask or offer forgiveness, they often think of it as a package deal.

Dramatic break-ups characteristically display "culpable wrongdoing," which is when someone can be blamed for doing something wrong, as is the case with infidelity. Infidelity is the breaking of an explicit, or sometimes implicit, promise. Infidelity often entails sneaking around, adding deception to the list of grievances. Finally, infidelity routinely involves abandonment, such as Swift's teenage love triangle from *folklore*, where the unfaithful party runs off with a new lover. Even when the unfaithful partner doesn't leave the relationship, there can be subtler forms of abandonment, such as failing to give a partner the attention and appreciation they deserve. As Swift puts it in "Girl at Home (Taylor's Version)," "While she waits up / You chase down the newest thing and take for granted what you have." Because wrongdoing is involved, forgiveness after this type of break-up neatly fits the standard philosophical account.

Sometimes, then, when the question, "can I forgive you for breaking my heart?" is being asked, what you are really wondering is whether you can forgive the other person for breaking faith, betraying trust, or deceiving you. You might have thought your partner was "Mr. Perfect" but instead discover he was "Mr. Casually Cruel," as Swift puts it in "Mr. Perfectly Fine (Taylor's Version)." These cases are well suited to philosophical accounts that assume forgiveness presupposes "culpable wrongdoing."

However, not every heartbreak involves wrongdoing. It is possible to be heartbroken even when the other person hasn't wronged us, hasn't failed to meet an obligation, and has given us everything they were meant to. Such cases raise interesting philosophical questions, both about forgiveness and about heartbreaking, as we will explore in the next section.

"What to Do When a Good Man Hurts You"

Let's consider three different cases of heartbreaking that might be morally innocent and observe the difference this makes for our overarching question about being able to forgive. The first case is one that Swift describes in "Midnight Rain," where a couple breaks up because they have incompatible dreams. He wants a traditional marriage and a comfortable future in his hometown. She wants to pursue an uncertain career, "chasing that fame" wherever it might lead. To pursue her dream, she chooses to end their relationship. When she does, he is heartbroken, "'cause he was nice" and has been emotionally invested in their relationship.

The second case of morally innocent heartbreak is a relationship where one person stops having feelings for the other. This person breaks off the relationship to search for the romance it lacks. This is hard for the person left behind, and even harder when the heartbreaker begins dating someone new.[6] In Swift's "right where you left me" we get a picture of one such heartbroken woman. The song contains no blame nor resentment for the heartbreaker, just a cry for help because the heartbroken narrator has ended up stuck and unable to move on.

The final case we will consider is that of unrequited love. For example, the song "Teardrops on My Guitar" describes being heartbroken because the person you have feelings for doesn't feel the same way. It hurts to cherish someone who does not cherish you back. Although we might at times irresponsibly let our hopes run away with our feelings, not every victim of unrequited love is irresponsible in this way. It is possible to faultlessly misread the cues that are given by the other person, but that doesn't make the heartbreak any less painful.

Can one person forgive another for breaking their heart in such cases? Part of what makes these examples interesting is that, in each of them, both heartbreaker and heartbroken appear to be innocent. You are not obliged, especially in a young relationship, to limit your aspirations to ensure they harmonize with your partner's dreams. Nor are you obliged to continue a relationship when you discover your dreams are deeply incompatible. Breaking up in such a circumstance is reasonable and perhaps required, even when you know it will hurt one (or both) of you.[7] At least sometimes, feelings faultlessly come and go. You have to get to know another person fairly intimately before you are in a position to know how well suited you are to one another. Finally, the fact that someone else has fallen in love with you in no way obliges you to feel the same way about them. If we think it is possible to forgive someone for breaking our heart in situations like these, it follows that we don't think culpable wrongdoing is a necessary condition for forgiving. We can forgive someone even if they haven't done something wrong.

We will return to this idea shortly, but first, it will be helpful to address one objection to our suggestion here. You could reject the proposal that heartbreaking can be innocent, because while it sounds possible in theory, it might be that in practice someone is always at fault. When dealing with complicated emotions we are bound to make mistakes and cause more hurt than we realize. Swift offers a nice example in "Back to December (Taylor's Version)": "you gave me roses and I left them there to die." Maybe the heartbreaker in this scenario could have reduced the hurt they were causing by appreciating their partner's loving actions, even when that love wasn't reciprocated. Breaking someone's heart is often done clumsily, and we can make mistakes that cause pain for the other person, even when the heartbreaker has the best of intentions.

Even well-meaning heartbreakers often break up ineptly, and this has the potential to increase the other person's undeserved pain. Nevertheless, it is implausible to think someone is always to blame whenever a person's heart gets broken. Sometimes the heartbreaker can be entirely unaware they are breaking someone's heart. The narrator in "Teardrops on My Guitar" describes being heartbroken because the object of her affections (Drew) doesn't return her feelings. Drew, who is committed to someone else, seems completely innocent in this situation. Furthermore, the lyrics show that the heartbroken narrator actively tries to conceal her feelings from him: "I fake a smile so he won't see / That I want and I'm needing everything that we should be." The song doesn't suggest Drew has done something wrong. Even so, it is understandable for the singer to be upset with him for choosing someone else and to feel heartbroken as a result.

Even when we know our actions will hurt the other person, sometimes breaking someone's heart now will save both parties more hurt down the line. The relationship described in "Midnight Rain" is doomed to end either in a break-up or in one (or both) of the parties feeling unsatisfied because of how different their aspirations are. Looking back on the break-up, the narrator of the song decides it was ultimately for the best: "I guess sometimes we all get / Just what we wanted." This result was only possible because they parted ways, albeit with broken hearts.

If we accept that a person can innocently break another's heart, that puts another spin on the question, "can I forgive you for breaking my heart?" We might decide that in a case like "Midnight Rain" there is nothing to forgive, because the breakup was for the best. In such a case, hurting the other is morally permissible because it spares them greater, future pain. If that's the case, one might think it impossible for the boy in "Midnight Rain" to forgive the person who broke his heart, since the heartbreaker has done nothing wrong. Similarly, in "Teardrops on My Guitar," although Drew may be the cause, or at least *a* cause of the teardrops on Swift's guitar, he doesn't satisfy what many assume is a requirement for forgiveness, because he hasn't wronged her. However, we don't think this fact rules out the possibility of forgiving him. To see why requires us to think again about the nature of heartbreak and forgiveness.

"Death by a Thousand Cuts"

When we talk about letting go of negative feelings toward someone who broke our heart, we often describe this as forgiveness even when the heartbreaker did not act badly. This practice is also reflected in Swift's songs, and there are good reasons for speaking this way.

One of the reasons we speak of forgiving someone for breaking our heart, even when there is no culpable wrongdoing, becomes evident when we examine the various harms that come with heartbreak, which are often undeserved or viewed as such by the person who is heartbroken. The most obvious harm in relation to heartbreak is emotional hurt. Swift likens the pain of heartbreak to being unable to breathe and being "haunted" by the person or the heartbreak.[8] The pain of heartache is compounded by its obsessiveness. While any emotion can capture our attention, heartbreak does so more firmly than most. It drags our attention back to what we have lost, making it difficult, sometimes impossible, to focus on other things. This quality is nicely illustrated in "this is me trying": "it's hard to be at a party when I feel like an open wound / It's hard to be anywhere these days when all I want is you." Swift also observes in "A Perfectly Good Heart" that once your heart has been broken there is no going back: "it's not unbroken anymore." Even when the heartbreak heals, it leaves scars.

The pain of heartbreak is not just the pain of failing to get what we wanted or losing someone we loved. It is the pain of being rejected. The realization in the song "Cold as You" that "I'm not what you wanted," raises the fear that I'm not good enough. It is not surprising, then, that getting dumped tends to undermine self-esteem. If this person, whose opinion I am vulnerable to, says I'm not good enough, it is hard to ignore.

Having one's heart broken can also have an impact on future relationships. A past relationship that went badly can affect your self-image and set expectations for future relationships that are hard to shake. Swift highlights this fact in "Begin Again (Taylor's Version)": "I think it's strange that you think I'm funny, 'cause / He never did." In this case, the song leaves us hoping the new relationship can give birth to new expectations. But not everyone is so fortunate. Heartbreak can make it hard to trust people again, as when Swift sings in "Haunted (Taylor's Version)" that "I can't trust anything now." This is especially so if the heartbreak takes you by surprise, leaving you questioning whether you have enough to offer a future partner, as Swift seems to allude to in her song "peace."

In a long-term relationship, heartbreak is often accompanied by the loss of things that were shared and of key parts of your identity. If a break-up requires moving out, then you may lose your home, your community, your favorite routine, and other aspects of yourself that were defined by your social and psychological relation to particular spaces. You often lose the dreams you had built together and end up "taking down the pictures and the plans we made" ("Babe (Taylor's Version)"). As a result, you may be left unsure of where you fit in the world: "If I can't relate to you anymore / Then who am I related to?" ("coney island"). When long-term relationships end, the things you have shared over time are either lost or changed. As Swift puts it, "All the years I've given / Is [now] just shit we're dividing up" ("happiness").

But it's not only the present and future that are changed. A break-up also changes the past. One's most joyful memories suddenly become painful. Your ex's "winning smile / Begin[s] to look like a smirk" ("happiness"). The meaning of the past is altered by the present. Time well spent is transformed into a series of missed opportunities. There were other relationships you could have pursued that might have led to happier endings.

Reflecting on the harms of heartbreak explains why we are often ambivalent about whether a heartbreaker can, in fact, be innocent and why we might still feel aggrieved when dumped, even when it's done in the nicest possible way by someone who does everything in their power to minimize the hurt. It makes sense, then, that the various harms associated with heartbreak would lead to estrangement or resentment between former partners even if the heartbreaker is not guilty of having wronged you. Although the heartbreaker may not have been obligated to behave differently than they did, their actions may, nevertheless, have caused deep and irreversible harm. Indeed, the harm associated with heartbreak can exceed that of many uncontroversial wrongs and can be correspondingly harder to get over.

This brings us to the second reason we might speak of forgiving someone for breaking our heart, even if they were blameless for doing so. The emotional and relational dynamics are similar after having our heart broken and after being wronged. When we are heartbroken, we are hurt, angry, or both. We might resent the heartbreaker for hurting us. The break-up and our reactions often lead to estrangement, at least in the short term. Then, at some later point, we distance ourselves from these hard feelings—perhaps overcoming them altogether—and often take steps to end our estrangement. This process is nearly identical to what we go through when someone hurts us through moral failure or wrongdoing. It is this process that philosophers like Allais take to be definitive of forgiveness. Given the similarity of the emotions, commitments, and relational dynamics involved in the two cases, we have good reason to think of them in the same terms.

A third reason we might use the term forgiveness in relation to some cases of getting over heartbreak comes into view when we look at it from the perspective of the heartbreaker. Given how painful heartbreak can be, some heartbreakers may feel every bit as badly as a wrongdoer suffering the pangs of conscience. Is this guilt? Some philosophers, such as Gabriele Taylor, have argued we should reserve the term "guilt" for the unpleasant emotion we feel when we believe we have failed to meet an obligation.[9] If so, then the innocent heartbreaker doesn't feel guilt, because they did not fail to meet an obligation. However, it is extremely common to feel misplaced guilt when one's actions have hurt another, even when one is blameless. The emotions heartbreakers feel, such as regret or remorse, can feel like guilt. And when heartbreakers who feel this way reach out to ease their regret or the other person's pain, this often manifests as a request for "the green light of forgiveness," as Swift describes it in "happiness." These similarities between what it feels like to be a regretful heartbreaker and what it feels like to be a regretful wrongdoer recommend using the same concept to describe what sometimes happens after heartbreak, when the person whose heart you broke releases you from that regret.

The final reason to use the word "forgiveness" to describe what happens in some cases of overcoming heartbreak is that we don't have another term that captures this unique emotional and relational journey. "Forgiveness" is the most common label for letting go of hard feelings and ending a period of estrangement after one has suffered undeserved harm at the hand of another, even if this harm was caused by someone who is "morally innocent."

Thus, there are good reasons for thinking we *can*, in fact, forgive someone for breaking our heart, even if their heartbreaking did not involve culpable wrongdoing. First, the victim of heartbreak, like the victim of wrongdoing, has suffered undeserved harms that can be as serious as those caused by wrongdoing. Second, the emotional and relational journey a person takes after having their heart broken (however innocently) can be similar to the journey taken after being wronged. Third, the emotional journey that regretful heartbreakers take closely resembles the one taken by regretful wrongdoers. Finally, we lack a term that captures these moral, emotional, and relational dynamics as well as "forgiveness." Based on these reasons, we recommend revising the standard philosophical definition of forgiveness to include not just victims of wrongdoing but also victims of undeserved harms like heartbreak, even when the person who caused those harms has done nothing wrong.

"The Green Light of Forgiveness"

How might reflecting on heartbreak encourage us to think about forgiveness? We propose that forgiving involves no longer holding some fact about the past against someone in the present. There are a number of ways we might hold the past against a person. We might be angry at them. We might refuse to have anything to do with them. We might hold them at an emotional distance. We might bring the past up in conversation, giving voice to our hurt or blame. If we bite our tongue, we might still find that whenever we think of them, we think of the past—for example, referring to someone in an interview as "the boy who broke up with me over the phone in 27 seconds when I was 18."[10] Forgiving involves being able to relate to the other person without our past always getting in the way. This may not be all that forgiving involves, but it involves at least this much.[11]

Facts about the past that might reasonably be held against someone today include cases of wrongdoing. But other kinds of facts about the past can also haunt the present, and not all of these are candidates for forgiveness. For example, no longer holding their childhood enthusiasm for Shaun Cassidy against someone would not count as forgiving. The kinds of facts that matter for forgiving are facts that might reasonably cause hard feelings or lead to estrangement. And, importantly, this includes cases in which one person's actions hurt another, who didn't deserve to be hurt, even when the first person acted within their rights and did not fail to meet any of their obligations.

Why is thinking about heartbreak through the lens of Swift's songs philosophically interesting? Our answer is that thinking about heartbreak more carefully invites us to revise a key assumption in almost every philosophical account of forgiveness. But it is worth noting the wider significance of these reflections. When philosophers talk about ethics, they often "give considerations of right and wrong ... priority over our other concerns and over other values."[12] Philosophical work on forgiveness routinely reflects this priority. An enormous number of cases where forgiveness might come up are cases involving wrongdoing, and so it is unsurprising that common definitions of forgiveness start with wrongdoing. But right and wrong are not our only ethical concerns. Wrong actions are not the only kinds of actions that can reasonably provoke hard feelings, nor are they the only causes of estrangement. Swift's work takes us through the first-person perspective of what heartbreak feels like in many different circumstances, and through music she invites her audience to know the pain of heartbreak all too well. As Swift has shown us, the range of relationships we might need to repair is not limited to those that have been damaged by wrongdoing. The lyrics in Swift's songs demonstrate that paying attention to heartbreak can remind us to look beyond right and wrong to some of the other things that matter.

Notes

1. Glen Pettigrove, "The Forgiveness We Speak," *The Southern Journal of Philosophy* 42 (2004), 375–376.
2. David McNaughton and Eve Garrard, "Once More with Feeling: Defending the Goodwill Account of Forgiveness," in Kathryn Norlock ed., *The Moral Psychology of Forgiveness* (London: Rowman & Littlefield, 2017), 96.
3. Lucy Allais, "Feeling Blame and Feeling Forgiveness," in Glen Pettigrove and Robert Enright eds., *The Routledge Handbook of the Philosophy and Psychology of Forgiveness* (New York: Routledge, 2023), 215–216.
4. Allais, "Feeling Blame and Feeling Forgiveness," 215.
5. For further discussion, see Glen Pettigrove, *Forgiveness and Love* (Oxford: Oxford University Press, 2012).
6. Swift captures this experience in "right where you left me" when she sings, "I could feel the mascara run / You told me that you met someone."
7. Michael Brady, *Emotional Insight* (Oxford: Oxford University Press, 2013).
8. See, for example, Swift's songs "Breathe (Taylor's Version)," "Haunted (Taylor's Version)," "Death by a Thousand Cuts," "cardigan," "happiness," and "Beautiful Ghosts."
9. Gabriele Taylor, *Pride, Shame, and Guilt* (Oxford: Oxford University Press, 1985), 97–100.
10. *The Ellen Show*, "Memorable Moment: Taylor Swift on Joe Jonas," YouTube, November 11, 2008, at https://www.youtube.com/watch?v=amh859mNeKI.
11. For more on what forgiveness involves, see Pettigrove and Enright eds., *The Routledge Handbook of the Philosophy and Psychology of Forgiveness*.
12. T.M. Scanlon, *What We Owe to Each Other* (Cambridge, MA: Harvard University Press 1998), 1.

7

How to Forgive an Innocent
Taylor, Kanye, and the Ethics of Forgiveness

Sarah Köglsperger

Yo, Taylor, I'm really happy for you, I'mma let you finish, but Beyoncé had one of the best videos of all time! One of the best videos of all time!
—Kanye West, 2009 MTV Video Music Awards.

It's okay, life is a tough crowd / 32 and still growin' up now / Who you are is not what you did / You're still an innocent.
—Taylor Swift, "Innocent (Taylor's Version)"

The infamous incident at the 2009 MTV Video Music Awards is one of those iconic moments in pop culture history that people still remember vividly. The nineteen-year-old Taylor Swift had just won the award for Best Female Video, when her acceptance speech was suddenly interrupted by Kanye West, who jumped on stage, took the microphone from her, and declared that "Beyoncé had one of the best videos of all time!" What followed was widespread public outrage against Kanye. At the same award ceremony the following year, Taylor performed her previously unreleased song "Innocent" for the first time, which was widely interpreted as a response to the incident. In the song, the protagonist shows sympathy toward a wrongdoer and expresses the belief that he is "still an innocent." The song received mixed feedback. While some saw it as a moment of forgiveness and sympathy toward Kanye, others saw it as "slams disguised as forgiveness," as a "patronizing, condescending sermon," or as "petty."[1] Criticisms like these were especially provoked by the childhood imagery included in the lyrics.

Are the critics right to say that "Innocent" is not an instance of forgiveness, but rather a petty condescending slam? Or do these critics misunderstand Taylor's intention to forgive Kanye for stealing her VMA moment? When considering these questions, a puzzle arises. It doesn't make sense to forgive someone if we think they are innocent. If they are innocent, then there would be nothing to forgive. Forgiveness presupposes that there is

Taylor Swift and Philosophy: Essays from the Tortured Philosophers Department,
First Edition. Edited by Catherine M. Robb and Georgie Mills.
© 2025 John Wiley & Sons, Inc. Published 2025 by John Wiley & Sons, Inc.

someone to forgive for some wrongdoing. An innocent person who hasn't committed any wrong or who is not responsible for his actions is not blameworthy. Our anger or resentment toward someone would be misplaced if there is nobody or nothing to be angry at in the first place.

By focusing on the VMA incident and its direct aftermath, we will see how Taylor's song "Innocent" could be seen as an instance of forgiveness, even though innocence normally precludes the possibility of forgiveness.

Why Snatching Microphones Is Wrong

Forgiveness is a potential response to personally having been wronged, and being innocent means either having done nothing wrong or not being responsible for one's action. To determine whether "Innocent" is an expression of forgiveness, we need to first look at the action in question and ask whether Kanye in fact wronged Taylor, or whether he was, in this sense, innocent. Did Kanye wrong Taylor? Intuitively we might think that it's problematic for Kanye to take the microphone from Taylor in the middle of her speech, and pronounce that Beyoncé should have won the award instead. But maybe we are mistaken. We could also see Kanye's action not as aiming to demean Taylor, but as standing up for justice. Maybe he was truly convinced that Beyoncé should have won, and saw it as a great injustice that she did not receive the award. Not respecting Taylor's interests and feelings were then only a side-effect of the more important aim of putting things right.

Even if that were the case, Kanye's action could still be seen as wrong. It was presumptuous that he assumed he had the authority to jump on stage and interrupt Taylor, and it was presumptuous to think that Beyoncé needed to be defended by him. After all, Beyoncé did go on to win another award later that evening, for best Video of the Year—a more prestigious award than the one Taylor won. So, Beyoncé did not need Kanye's help to stand up for an injustice.

Additionally, it is difficult to say whether Beyoncé not receiving the award could have been an injustice, since art has a subjective aspect. If two artworks have a similar aesthetic value, we have some discretion in our attitudes toward the artworks.[2] Some people might prefer Beyoncé's video, others might prefer Taylor's, still others might find both equally good. Because the value and quality of art is partly a matter of subjective taste and discretion, it is not appropriate to consider someone as objectively wrong for having a different view about who should have won the award. We might disagree based on our taste, but this is not a reason to stop an award ceremony, as there could be no real injustice occurring when one person is given the award over the other. However, Kanye had the hubris to take his opinion as the authoritative one, thereby also disrespecting the decision of the judges, as well as the procedural norms of the event.

Regardless of how great one finds Beyoncé's video, it is plausible to see Taylor as being entitled to finish her speech without interruption. So, Kanye wronged Taylor by interrupting and disrupting her speech.

What exactly is the nature of Kanye's wrongdoing? The contemporary philosopher Jeffrie Murphy claims that intentional wrongdoings can be insulting because they involve a lack of respect for the victim's "equal moral worth." That is, the wrongdoer treats the victim as if they are less of a person, and worth less respect. The wrongdoer might convey a message like "I count, but you do not" or "I am here up high, and you are there down below."[3] Even though not every wrongdoing involves an attempted lowering of the victim's moral status, this one seems to. Kanye presumed to have the authority to interrupt Taylor and snatch the microphone from her. This act did seem insulting to Taylor, and treated her with less moral worth.

Innocence and Childhood

Taylor doesn't explicitly discuss the nature of the wrongdoing in "Innocent." Rather she addresses the wrongdoer. While she does not mention names and does not directly refer to the VMA incident, it is hard to doubt that she intended the song as a response to Kanye. Some lyrics clearly allude to the incident, referencing Kanye's age at the time ("32 and still growin' up now") and referring to the month the VMAs took place ("You'll have new Septembers"). That Taylor's first live performance of "Innocent" was at the same award show the year later, and started with a video clip in the background showing the incident, made it more obvious to whom the song is addressed.

The discussion so far has shown that Kanye's action was wrong, in that it treated Taylor with less respect and moral worth, and Taylor's song "Innocent" is a response to this wrongdoing. The next question is whether "Innocent" can be considered an instance of forgiveness. To answer that we need to consider whether the wrongdoer in the song is responsible. This is what some critics deny—they claim that the wrongdoer in the song is perceived as an innocent, and so does not need to be forgiven. Let's look more closely at why the critics might have a point here.

There are two possible ways that "Innocent" could *not* be an instance of forgiveness. The first possibility is that the protagonist does not regard the wrongdoer as responsible; the wrongdoer is as "an innocent," someone who is not an appropriate target for blame and forgiveness. This interpretation seems to work, since the lyrics of the song describe the wrongdoer as "still an innocent." It's clear that the wrongdoer in the song cannot be an innocent in the sense that he did nothing wrong, as the lyrics make it clear that there were some wrongs committed: "Left yourself in your warpath," and, "Did some things you can't speak of / But at night you live it all again." Nonetheless the song's imagery of childhood suggests that the wrongdoer is not mature enough to be responsible for his actions. For example, Taylor writes, "Wasn't it easier in your lunchbox days? / Always a bigger bed to crawl into," and "Wasn't it easier in your firefly-catchin' days? / And everything out of reach."

Taylor seems to compare Kanye to a child, telling him that he is still growing up, and so the critics seem justified in their concern that the song is condescending or patronizing. Regarding someone as a child means not regarding him as a (fully) responsible person. Children are not yet full members of the moral community. They cannot yet sufficiently control their behavior and they lack sufficient understanding of what morality demands and how others ought to be treated. Thus, comparing someone to a child is condescending and disrespectful when, in fact, the person is an adult with normal capacities for moral action.

As the philosopher Peter Strawson (1919–2006) has claimed, seeing someone as responsible means taking them seriously as a person capable of adhering to moral values, and reacting to their wrongdoings with blaming attitudes like resentment.[4] This would mean that in "Innocent" the protagonist does not see any reason for resentment, and so no need for forgiveness, since the wrongdoer's actions do not carry enough moral significance. If the wrongdoer does not understand the moral norms he violated, and the wrong cannot be demeaning, then there is no need for resentment. In this way, the protagonist of the song would dismiss the wrongdoing, just like you would dismiss the wrongdoings of a child. You would let it slide, because they were not responsible for what they did.

Is this really what Taylor means when telling the wrongdoer that he is "still an innocent"? Does she consider Kanye as childlike, as if he doesn't understand what he was doing, as if he is not a responsible person? If so, then Taylor would be unrealistic and unkind in her understanding of the situation. But if Taylor does not regard Kanye as a child, then perhaps she is deliberately condescending. This, however, does not seem to fit the character of who she was at the time. In the *Miss Americana* documentary, Taylor speaks of her desperate need to be liked, and says that her "entire moral code as a kid and now is a need to be thought of as good."[5] Even though we cannot fully exclude the possibility, it seems implausible that the same girl who claims she needs to be thought of as good would intentionally write a song with condescending lyrics. So, to be charitable, let's see if we can find other interpretations of what is going on in this song.

Moving on without Forgiveness

Here is another, more charitable way to interpret the song as not an instance of forgiveness: perhaps the protagonist acknowledges the wrongdoer's responsibility, but chooses not to forgive him, by distancing herself from the wrongdoer and his action. There are ways in which we might overcome resentment, or not feel resentment in the first place, without forgiving. Not every instance of overcoming resentment is also an instance of forgiveness. Your resentment might wither away over time, or you might forget what happened to you, without any decision involved. Or you might decide to let go of the resentment because it is just too exhausting to hold on to it. If the resentment is a risk to your mental health, you might relinquish it for your own benefit, while also fully accepting that you have not forgiven the other person, and that they were responsible for the wrongdoing.

Taylor seems to understand this pretty well, at least by now. In an interview in 2019—ten years after the VMA incident—when asked about her habit of addressing the haters in her songs, she said: "People go on and on about you have to forgive and forget to move past something. No, you don't... You just become indifferent and then you move on."[6] A paradigmatic example of this in her discography is "I Forgot That You Existed." There she describes that, after a wrongdoer was living "rent-free" in her mind for a long time, one magical night she just became indifferent toward him, moving on without forgiving.

Sometimes we can take on a detached perspective from which we don't experience resentment. In his essay "Freedom and Resentment," Peter Strawson describes different conditions that may lead us to modify or suspend our resentment and other reactive attitudes.[7] One condition might be that the wrongdoer is an innocent—a child or anyone else who does not yet understand fully the moral norms that govern our social world. In that case, we adopt an "objective attitude" toward the person—holding back our emotional involvement, and seeing them from a detached point of view.

Sometimes, though, we shift our attitude even in the case of mature adults. We have this "resource," as Strawson calls it, and sometimes use it as a refuge "from the strains of involvement."[8] As the contemporary philosopher Pamela Hieronymi explains in her analysis of Strawson's essay, sometimes the emotional effort of engaging with certain people is too much, or we are too exhausted to respond with resentment, so we disengage for our own self-protection.[9] Even though we notice that someone is a responsible adult, we might still take on an objective attitude for our own sake. This kind of attitude is reflected in "I Forgot That You Existed," when Taylor sings, "it was so nice / So peaceful and quiet / I forgot that you existed / It isn't love, it isn't hate, it's just indifference."

This is not, however, what seems to be going on in "Innocent." There is no sign of indifference or disengagement. And the two songs also couldn't be more different musically. While the indifference described in "I Forgot That You Existed" is accompanied by cheerful and fun sounds, "Innocent" is a gentle pop ballad, which Taylor delivers in a tender voice sounding full of sympathy. What's reflected in the music, as well as the lyrics, is not a detached attitude, but rather a protagonist who deeply cares about the wrongdoer, and wants to comfort him: "It's alright, just wait and see / Your string of lights is still bright to me / Oh, who you are is not where you've been / You're still an innocent."

From the analysis so far, then, the critical claim that "Innocent" merely contains "slams disguised as forgiveness" does not fit well with what is going on in the lyrics and music of the song. There is no sign of Taylor as detached and moving on without forgiveness. It also does not seem that Taylor intended to condescendingly compare Kanye to a child who cannot be held responsible. We cannot, of course, be sure about this. It is still possible that Taylor was condescending, even if maybe not intentionally. However, it's possible that "Innocent" can also be seen as a plausible instance of forgiveness.

"Today Is Never Too Late to Be Brand New"

If "Innocent" involves forgiveness, then we need to be clearer about what happens when someone forgives. What is the process the victim goes through? Forgiveness must happen without giving up the judgment that the action was wrong—nothing about forgiving should signal to the wrongdoer that his action was right or permissible after all. What must change, however, is the victim's view of the wrongdoer. The philosopher Jean Hampton (1954–1996) claimed that the forgiver must have a "change of heart" toward the wrongdoer.[10] According to Hampton, the forgiver changes her judgment about the person and stops seeing him as a "rotten" human being. This does not mean that she condones his action or his bad character traits. But, overall, she sees him as someone who is still capable of acting morally, with the wrong act not defining who he is. Through the decision to see the wrongdoer in a new, more favorable light, the victim rids herself of feelings like resentment, hatred, or indignation.[11]

This should sound familiar. It's almost as if the forgiver would tell the wrongdoer, as Taylor does, that "Your string of lights is still bright to me," or, "Who you are is not what you did," and, "Today is never too late to be brand new." Throughout "Innocent," the protagonist still sees the wrongdoer as a decent person, who is not defined by his past wrongs. Thus, when Taylor apparently tells Kanye that he is still growing up, or an innocent, we probably shouldn't understand it literally. Instead we should see it as her telling him that, despite what he did, she thinks that he is still sufficiently decent and his character is not determined by his past mistakes.

So, in order to forgive, we need to remove the wrong act as evidence of the person's character—we need to separate the person from his wrong action. How and why do we do this?

Repentance and Our Common Human Nature

The most obvious reason for separating our assessment of a person's character from the wrong act that they have performed is that the wrongdoer repents his action. When the wrongdoer distances himself from the action and condemns it too, he signals that he now respects the moral value that he violated, and we can reasonably let go of our resentment. By apologizing or making up for the wrong action, the wrongdoer lets us know that he also does not consider the action to be representative of who he is.

It's not clear if this applies to "Innocent" and the Kanye incident. At least the wrongdoer in "Innocent" seems to show some feelings of regret: "Did some things you can't speak of / But at night you live it all again." As outsiders to the situation, we cannot know if Kanye repented his action. He apologized publicly to Taylor on his blog, and on the *Tonight Show with Jay Leno* shortly after the incident. However, apologizing (the communicative act of admitting to having violated a norm) does not necessarily mean that the wrongdoer also repents. The apology could be insincere, and it's not clear if Kanye's apology was—Kanye took back his apology in 2013 saying that he "didn't have one regret," and apologized merely because he had "fallen to peer pressure."[12] Of course, Taylor couldn't foresee this at the time of writing "Innocent" and could have taken his apology as sincere (which maybe it was in 2009, who knows?)

What if we are not sure if the wrongdoer repents? Should we still forgive them? It's important to clarify something about the nature of forgiveness. The possibility or legitimacy of forgiveness does not depend on the wrongdoer but on the person who has been wronged. Forgiveness is possible and even admirable whether or not the wrongdoer repents. Forgiveness cannot be demanded, but is a deliberate choice made by the victim—something like a gift. In "Innocent" Taylor sings, "You'll have new Septembers / Every one of us has messed up too ... / I hope you remember / Today is never too late to be brand new." Here the protagonist empathizes with the wrongdoer by acknowledging that we all have made mistakes in the past. Contemporary philosophers Eve Garrard and David McNaughton explain the underlying thought that might be behind these lyrics. They argue that the reason for forgiving even an unrepentant wrongdoer is our common human nature, "and hence our shared human frailty and fallibility."[13] The recognition that we also have acted wrongly in the past, and will probably be wrongdoers in the future too who will be in need of forgiveness, gives us a reason of reciprocity to forgive others. Having this in mind, it is plausible to see "Innocent" as an instance of forgiveness.

However, we could still doubt how sincere forgiveness is when it is publicly announced by performing a song. Someone could suspect that "Innocent" was all about self-promotion and showcasing moral superiority, instead of genuine forgiveness. However, in the Taylor–Kanye case, public forgiveness makes sense. The wrongdoing happened publicly, Kanye was blamed by the public, and he publicly apologized. So, it was also important for Taylor to communicate the forgiveness publicly, so that not just the two parties but also the emotionally invested fans could move on. (And, given that

Taylor is known for channeling her personal experiences into her music, people expected her to do this through song.)

When we decide to forgive a wrongdoer, we don't change our judgment that he was responsible for the wrong, but we change our perception of the person, and this change of perception can be transformative. By ceasing to see the past as significant, we no longer see the person as someone who has wronged us, and we also no longer see ourselves as victims. This enables us as well as the wrongdoer (along with everyone else involved) to move forward and, as Taylor reminds us, to "be brand new."

Notes

1. See Leslie Gornstein, "Preach it! Taylor Swift Fools (Almost) Everyone," *Los Angeles Times*, September 13, 2010, at https://www.latimes.com/archives/blogs/ministry-of-gossip/story/2010-09-13/preach-it-taylor-swift-fools-almost-everyone; Jonathan Keefe, "Taylor Swift: Speak Now," *Slant Magazine*, October 25, 2010, at https://www.slantmagazine.com/music/taylor-swift-speak-now; Jon Caramanica, "At MTV Awards, Taylor vs. Kanye Part 2," *The New York Times*, September 13, 2010, at https://www.nytimes.com/2010/09/13/arts/music/13mtv.html.

2. On the challenge of combining subjectivity and objectivity in aesthetic theory, see Alex King, "Response-Dependence and Aesthetic Theory," in Christopher Howard and R.A. Rowland eds., *Fittingness* (Oxford: Oxford University Press 2022), 309–326.

3. Jeffrie Murphy and Jean Hampton, *Forgiveness and Mercy* (Cambridge: Cambridge University Press, 1988), 25.

4. Peter Strawson, "Freedom and Resentment," *Proceedings of the British Academy* 48 (1962), reprinted in Pamela Hieronymi, *Freedom, Resentment, and the Metaphysics of Morals* (Princeton, NJ: Princeton University Press, 2020), 107–133.

5. *Miss Americana*, dir. Lana Wilson (Tremolo Productions, 2020).

6. Taylor Swift, "Taylor Swift on 'Lover' and Haters," interview by Tracy Smith, *CBS News*, August 25, 2019, at https://www.cbsnews.com/video/taylor-swift-on-lover-and-haters.

7. Strawson, "Freedom and Resentment," 107–133.

8. Strawson, "Freedom and Resentment," 116.

9. Pamela Hieronymi, *Freedom, Resentment, and the Metaphysics of Morals* (Princeton, NJ: Princeton University Press, 2020), 11.

10. Murphy and Hampton, *Forgiveness and Mercy*, 83.

11. Murphy and Hampton, *Forgiveness and Mercy*, 83–87.

12. John Caramanica, "Behind Kanye's Mask," *The New York Times*, June 11, 2013, at https://www.nytimes.com/2013/06/16/arts/music/kanye-west-talks-about-his-career-and-album-yeezus.html?pagewanted=2&_r=0.

13. Eve Garrard and David McNaughton, "Conditional Unconditional Forgiveness," in Christel Fricke ed., *The Ethics of Forgiveness* (New York: Routledge, 2011), 103.

8

"This Is Why We Can't Have Nice Things"
Goodwill as a Finite Resource

Georgie Mills

In 2014 Taylor Swift was at the top of her game with her fifth album, *1989*. But alas her success and visibility led to increasing criticism, at times for incredibly trivial reasons. Headlines included comments about her weight, her friends, her "annoying" personality, her dating life, and her musical talent.[1] In 2016 it all culminated in an intense and gleeful online backlash after the release of an edited and illegally recorded phone call in which she seemed to approve of a Kanye West song that she had publicly complained about.[2] The hashtag #TaylorSwiftIsOverParty started trending on Twitter worldwide and haters rejoiced in having an excuse to bash the star.

Understandably, Taylor disappeared from public life until the release of *reputation* in 2017, an album that contains the track "This Is Why We Can't Have Nice Things." The song captures Taylor's disillusionment, reflecting on the trust, forgiveness, and social generosity that she had shown prior to her cancellation. Taylor had enjoyed throwing big parties, telling her guests that there were "no rules" in her house, and giving second chances to an unnamed addressee of the song. Taylor sings, "Why d'you have to rain on my parade?" before mourning the end of this period of hospitality and agreeableness, and characterizing it as something broken by those who "Stabbed me in the back while shaking my hand."

Ultimately, "This Is Why We Can't Have Nice Things" is an anthem about goodwill. Though the song's tone is bitter, its message is hopeful. Goodwill is fragile, and it is a limited resource. So when someone abuses your goodwill you need to withdraw it as an act of self-preservation and self-advocacy.

"It Was So Nice Throwing Big Parties"

So what is goodwill?[3] In business, goodwill is an intangible asset that adds value to a company based on that company's reputation and existing client base. For a celebrity, like Taylor Swift, the goodwill generated by one's

Taylor Swift and Philosophy: Essays from the Tortured Philosophers Department,
First Edition. Edited by Catherine M. Robb and Georgie Mills.
© 2025 John Wiley & Sons, Inc. Published 2025 by John Wiley & Sons, Inc.

reputation among fans and industry professionals might function something like goodwill in business. Profitability as an artist depends not only on artistry but on the fandom and their continued trust and interest in the work and the person. There is an intangible value that Taylor's career has that is above and beyond her musical prowess. Fans care about her as a person, and are heavily invested in their own participation in her success. This goodwill from the fandom is illustrated by the immense popularity of her Eras Tour, and the continued success of her rerecorded albums. Goodwill also plays a role in Taylor's collaborations with other singers, producers, and songwriters. Her excellent reputation as a colleague and collaborator results from her goodwill and it produces goodwill toward her.

Taylor's goodwill was at stake when her reputation was damaged by Kim Kardashian's release of a recorded phone call between Taylor and Kanye in 2016. Fans who invest time and passion in Taylor's career and music do so not just because of the quality of the music, but also because of their admiration and love for Taylor herself. Damage to Taylor's reputation could cause real damage to the goodwill of fans and collaborators.[4] This business-specific kind of goodwill may have been lost in her 2016 cancellation, but it is not the concept that best helps us to analyze "This Is Why We Can't Have Nice Things." What Taylor mourns in the song is not her reputation as such, but her lifestyle of throwing big parties, inviting people into her home, and being "friends again" with former antagonists, all of which could be seen as gestures of goodwill.

The goodwill Taylor is concerned with is a matter of mutual trust and honesty. When we show goodwill we bestow some benefit or convenience on the recipient with the understanding that this will be reciprocated. Goodwill, in this sense, is an extension of trust. To display goodwill is to show the recipient that you trust them to act honestly and fairly in your future dealings with one another. Goodwill is built over time; the more we know someone, the more likely we are to trust their intentions toward us. With this sense of goodwill, and in light of what happened to Taylor, we can understand "This Is Why We Can't Have Nice Things."

"Therein Lies the Issue, Friends Don't Try to Trick You"

Prior to the infamous 2016 phone call, Taylor had publicly forgiven Kanye West for interrupting her 2009 VMA acceptance speech. Taylor's song "Innocent," in which she sings "Your string of lights is still bright to me," was clearly a response to Kanye. Taylor extends empathy to the addressee, presumably Kanye, by reflecting on the difficulties of having made a mistake in public, and reassuring him that he is "still an innocent." Taylor was heavily criticized for this song at the time, with critics arguing that it was condescending and "A savvy insult masquerading as the high road."[5]

With this criticism there was a lack of goodwill on the part of the media. Taylor was only twenty-one years old at the time, and she may have miscalculated how the song would be received. So let's extend a little goodwill to Taylor ourselves and take the song at face value.

We can see "Innocent" as a display of Taylor's goodwill toward Kanye, predicated on an assumption of Kanye's own goodwill. The song paints a picture of an individual who, with all good intentions, made a bad mistake and hurt Taylor but also damaged his own reputation in the process. Taylor is extending goodwill to Kanye by not only expressing her continued esteem for him, but also by not attributing malicious intention to him, regardless of how much his actions hurt her at the time. Goodwill involves not only meaning well, but also expecting that those to whom you extend your goodwill will respond in kind. Charitably attributing good intentions to others is an act of goodwill.

This feature of goodwill, mutually charitable interpretations of each other's actions, can help us to understand the breakdown of goodwill that occurred between Taylor and Kanye. In the extended clip of a phone call between them in 2016, we hear Kanye asking Taylor to release his new song, "Famous," on her Twitter page. During the phone call, Kanye mentions that she features in the lyrics of the song. Taylor tentatively asks "Is it gonna be mean?" Kanye describes the lyrics as saying "Me and Taylor might still have sex" and "I made her famous."[6] In this exchange, Taylor's goodwill is not reciprocated. She hears Kanye out on his controversial lyric, and she trusts him to be honest about the content. She asks to hear the song when it is finished, and thanks Kanye profusely for taking the time to call her. However, Kanye never sends her the song, and the finished version contains the lyric "I made that bitch famous."

Taylor reacted with displeasure to the song's release, leading Kim Kardashian to release a short clip of the phone call in which Taylor thanks Kanye for the call and approves a song lyric, giving the impression that Taylor had already approved of the song in the form that was later released. Then came the huge media backlash against Taylor, the extensive hateful comments directed at her accompanying the #TaylorSwiftIsOverParty hashtag, and her disappearance from public life for a while before the release of *reputation*, an album that responds to her cancellation.

This series of events was a repeated failure of goodwill. At any point, some honesty and the assumption of good intention could have avoided the situation. If Kanye had told Taylor the real full lyric, if Kim had released the full unedited phone call, if Taylor had not taken the term "that bitch" so personally, this might have been a non-event. However, Kanye did not tell her the full lyric, and their call was illegally recorded and edited to have Taylor cheerfully approving lyrics. The public also failed to extend goodwill to Taylor. Her own public statement pointed out that there is no recording of her approving the lyric calling her "that bitch." But many members of the public chose to assume that she was lying, rather than consider that their information might be incomplete.

"I'm Shaking My Head, and Locking the Gates"

The message of "This Is Why We Can't Have Nice Things" is that goodwill runs out when it is abused or not reciprocated. Taylor had extended trust and friendship to Kanye, creating a "mended fence" between them after the 2009 VMA incident. With goodwill to Kanye, she assumed he had no intention to hurt or humiliate her when he interrupted, even if that was the outcome. Despite this mended fence, Taylor was recorded without her knowledge approving an incomplete song lyric, and had this recording distributed when she reacted to the real lyric.

In "This Is Why We Can't Have Nice Things," Taylor describes herself taking "an axe to a mended fence" and says she is "shaking my head and locking the gates." Clearly, the "nice thing" that we can't have is her goodwill. The first verse of the song describes the lavish parties that Taylor threw for her friends before she was cancelled. She describes herself as "feeling so Gatsby." This joyful participation in social generosity was certainly a display of goodwill. However, this generosity is hard to maintain when the friends you throw parties for might turn on you at any time. Later in the song, Taylor mourns "It was so nice being friends again / Here I was giving you a second chance / But you stabbed me in the back while shaking my hand." Her goodwill, in the sense of an expectation of trust and honesty, is destroyed. The "nice thing" that is broken is her ability to extend her friendship and attribute good intentions to actions. After all the abuse that Taylor suffered after Kim released a clip of her phone conversation with Kanye, it would be simply foolish for Taylor to continue her goodwill toward them.

"Forgiveness Is a Nice Thing to Do"

A central feature of goodwill is the expectation that it goes both ways. A gesture of goodwill is a display of trust that puts forth the hope and expectation that the trust placed in the recipient will turn out to be warranted, that the person who receives this trust will behave in the way that you are trusting them to behave. We hear this element of goodwill in "This Is Why We Can't Have Nice Things" when Taylor considers the possibility of forgiving the addressee of the song because "forgiveness is a nice thing to do." In the song, Taylor laughs off this possibility. She has already forgiven once, when it was plausible to imagine that the hurt was not done to her intentionally. To forgive a second time, when good intentions are implausible and snake emojis are rampant, is now impossible. Her goodwill is limited, and it has run out.

Though philosophical accounts of goodwill are scarce, philosophical support for not forgiving someone can be found. P.F. Strawson argues that to be angry with someone is to take them seriously as a member of the moral community.[7] It might satisfy Strawson to forego anger when we can reasonably extend some goodwill and trust that a transgression was done accidentally, but in the case of deliberate, calculated reputational damage, for Taylor to keep her goodwill going would be for her to fail to take Kim and Kanye seriously as members of the moral community. Perhaps they did not foresee how extreme and potentially damaging the backlash against Taylor would be, but they nonetheless knew that they had only told the most convenient part of the story. For Taylor to forgive this would not be the show of trust that goodwill represents. Rather, it would display a lack of trust in Kim and Kanye's ability to behave better than they did. The "nice" thing that we can't have on this occasion is forgiveness, as the ability for goodwill to provide it has reached its limit.

"Here's to My Real Friends"

One thing that is striking about "This Is Why We Can't Have Nice Things" is the contrast between the lyrics and the other musical elements. The lyrics tell of the bitterness of wanting to be nice and having to stop for your own protection. It's a song about losing friends and giving up on relationships, but the music sounds happy and upbeat. It feels raucous and gleeful in its delivery. Toward the end of the song, Taylor lists some forces in her life that haven't let her down such as her "real friends," her "baby," and her "mama," and she expresses her gratitude for their continued presence in her life in spite of "all this drama." She had a bad time after trusting the wrong people, but there are still people in her life who she can trust. In spite of the bitterness of the lyrics, it is a hopeful song in which she rejoices over her refusal to tolerate false friends any longer.

Taylor's relationships with close friends and family go beyond goodwill. As she expresses in the song, her gratitude to her mother is not based on her mother's receipt of cheerful benevolence or trust. Quite the opposite, Taylor expresses that her mother has "had to listen to all this drama" which does not sound cheery at all. While I'm sure that cheerful benevolence might be a part of Taylor's close relationships, solidarity and comfort in hard times is equally a part of closeness. Her close friends not caring "bout the 'he said, she said'" is not an act of goodwill, but an act of true friendship. This song shows us that the regard of Taylor's "real" friends is not so easily shaken. There is no need for goodwill because there is no need for extending trust and expectation of honesty; trust is already present thanks to the shared experience of friendship. Taylor's relationship with her mother is likewise not the result of goodwill, but of years of support and consistent familial love.

This contrast between the "real" friends and the "friends" who the song is addressed to tells us something else about goodwill. It's not only limited, but fragile. If someone extends goodwill to you but their goodwill is not reciprocated, then it will break. If it is reciprocated, then perhaps in time it may become unnecessary as the stability of the relationship outgrows the need for displays of trust. Goodwill is given in the hope that a more stable sentiment will follow. In that sense, it is a fragile and limited resource.

Given this fragility, we can read "This Is Why We Can't Have Nice Things" as a declaration of the limits of goodwill. Through her lyrics Taylor Swift has given a philosophical account of goodwill, telling us that goodwill is indeed a nice thing, but if you break it, I have to take it away.

Notes

1. A collection of such headlines appear in Swift's documentary, *Miss Americana*, dir. Lana Wilson (Tremolo Productions, 2020).
2. Chris Willman "Taylor Swift and Kanye West's 2016 Phone Call Leaks: Read the Full Transcript," *Variety*, March 23, 2020, at https://variety.com/2020/music/news/taylor-swift-kanye-west-phone-call-leaks-read-full-transcript-1203541363.
3. Immanuel Kant's (1724–1804) concept of "the good will" was developed as part of his broader ethical theory. According to Kant's view, the good will is the only source of unconditional goodness, because exercise of the good will is always good, regardless of circumstances. Though one's actions can have unpredictable consequences, Kant argues, if one's will is good then this represents something that is good for its own sake, rather than for the sake of some outcome. Philosophers differentiate this from the folk concept of goodwill. Kant's good will can be very loosely understood as the exercise of the will toward what is good under Kant's ethical framework. Kant's good will refers to the autonomous decision of the agent to act with purpose in accordance with duty, whereas goodwill refers to a less ethically charged kind of charitability or benevolence. It is the latter that Taylor seems to describe running out of in "This Is Why We Can't Have Nice Things." Since Kant's concept of the good will is not the concept of goodwill that helps us to understand Taylor's *reputation*-era goodwill drought, we will not go too far into detail here about Kantian good will. Suffice to say that, since most philosophy of goodwill appears in discussion of Kant, we may need to build our own philosophical account of goodwill in order to understand Taylor when she explains why we can't have nice things.
4. See chapter 9 in this volume, by Catherine M. Robb and Roos Slegers, for a fuller discussion of the nature of reputation.
5. Jon Caramanica, "At MTV Awards, Taylor vs. Kanye Part 2," *The New York Times*, September 13, 2010, at https://www.nytimes.com/2010/09/13/arts/music/13mtv.html.
6. Willman, "Taylor Swift and Kanye West's 2016 Phone Call Leaks."
7. P.F. Strawson "Freedom and Resentment," *Proceedings of the British Academy* 48 (1962), 187–211.

9

Taylor Swift's Philosophy of Reputation

Catherine M. Robb and Roos Slegers

Before the release of the album *reputation* in November 2017, Taylor had been publicly shamed by Kanye West at the 2009 MTV Video Music Awards, and publicly accused of lying by Kim Kardashian. These events were so scandalous that they became mainstream news, with the then US president Barack Obama calling West a "jackass," and Donald Trump calling for West to be boycotted.[1] Even though the public seemed firmly in favor of Taylor during these incidents, they initiated a sharp decline in her popularity. Critics accused Swift's female friendship group of being elitist "white feminists," suspected her relationship with actor Tom Hiddleston to be an inauthentic PR stunt, criticized her political neutrality, labeled her as "vacuous and self-absorbed," and claimed that we have all been "manipulated" into loving her.[2] Taylor suffered potent backlash on social media as the subject of the number one trending hashtag "#TaylorSwiftIsOverParty" to indicate that fans had stopped supporting her, and her social media feeds were inundated with snake emojis condemning her as a "snake."[3]

In the aftermath of this public criticism Swift announced in 2015, "I think people might need a break from me."[4] She took a long pause in her career, removed herself from the public eye, and stopped posting on social media, eventually clearing all the images from her accounts as if erasing her entire public past. In the 2023 *TIME* magazine interview to celebrate her being awarded Person of the Year, Taylor reflects on this period of her life as one in which she "had all the hyenas climb on and take their shots," and saying she was "cancelled within an inch of my life and sanity." These events had a profound impact on her well-being—she moved to a different country, was unable to leave her house, and lost trust in nearly everyone in her life. From this place of retraction, recluse, and distrust, the album *reputation* was born, written, and recorded in secret.

Taylor Swift and Philosophy: Essays from the Tortured Philosophers Department, First Edition. Edited by Catherine M. Robb and Georgie Mills.

Rage and Goth-Punk

Swift has spoken openly about *reputation* as a response to the public and social backlash that she had experienced in the previous years. She describes it as one of the most "cathartic" albums she has ever written, a "complete defence mechanism," and a moment of "rage."[5] The lyrics of many songs on the album reflect and explore the nature of Taylor's public image, the way others see her, and the way she sees herself. The lyrics also embrace a move away from her public image as a young and innocent country music or pop star, with more reference to alcohol, drugs, sex, and anger than on any of her previous albums.[6] The heavier music of *reputation* transforms Taylor from a teenage star or a pop princess into a "goth-punk" on a mission to reclaim her own reputation.[7] For the album she repurposes the image of the snake as her symbol of empowerment (not to mention that, being born in 1989, the snake is her Chinese zodiac animal).

Looking back, what does the controversial *reputation* era tell us about what reputation is and why it matters? What is it about having a bad reputation that was so devastating that it made Taylor doubt herself, hide away, and try to fight back? Why does reputation have this power?

"They Told You I'm Crazy"

Reputation is defined as a shared public opinion about the character and value of a person or group. As the contemporary philosopher and cognitive scientist Dan Sperber and his co-author evolutionary biologist Nicolas Baumard explain, your reputation is not formed because a few people have opinions about you, but because these opinions are "shared in a group," as part of public consensus or "common ground."[8] This helps explain why we describe someone's reputation using an abstract "they"— for example, "*they* say that Taylor has a reputation for not being able to hold down a man."

Who are "they"? When it comes to reputation, "they" does not point to any one specific person, but the public as a collective entity, an abstract and general group who develop a shared opinion about who someone is, their character and worth. Many people in this abstract group may not have had direct contact with the person about whom they are forming their shared opinion. This is especially true for Taylor—the public have a shared opinion about who she is, and very few of us have even met her.

In the lyrics on *reputation*, Taylor also recognizes that her own reputation and the reputations of those around her are a shared consensus of an abstract collective "they." References to "they" are scattered throughout different songs: "*they* told you I'm crazy" ("End Game"); "*they* got no idea about me and you" ("Dress"); "*they* say I did something bad" ("I Did Something Bad"); "*they* say, 'she's gone too far this time'" ("Don't Blame Me"); and, "*they* took the crown" ("Call It What You Want"). Even though Taylor also sings about the personal opinions she has of others, and that others have of her, when she sings about reputation it is clearly the shared judgments of the public "they" that she is evoking.

Reputation Is Fake

Given that reputation is formed by public consensus, it is for the most part "external" to us—dependent on what other people think about us, and up for others to decide.[9] As the contemporary philosopher Gloria Origgi claims, no matter how many good things we do, or however much we try to behave in ways that the public will interpret favorably, the control we have over our reputation is "limited and precarious."[10] This is because what you do, how other people interpret it, and then how it is formed into a reputation, does not follow a straightforward path. What you do and say is often distorted by public conversation, gossip, and hearsay, as the information travels from one person to another. Reputations are not true representations of our character but instead, according to Origgi, they are "the *refraction* of our image that is warped, amplified, redacted, and multiplied in the eyes of others."[11] Taylor Swift's reputation does not accurately describe who she really is. Rather, her reputation is a distorted and warped representation of her true character and value.

Swift clearly agrees—she does not consider her reputation to be part of who she really is. Instead, reputation is fake. Describing the rationale behind "Delicate," Taylor asks, "Could something fake like your reputation affect something real, like someone getting to know you?"[12] The idea of reputation being fake is further supported by Taylor's comments introducing "Delicate" during the *reputation* concert tour.[13] Addressing the audience directly, Taylor says she believes we all have something in common: the desire to find "something real," whether that be real friendship, real love, or just "someone who gets you." Similarly, we fear things that can get in the way of finding something real, like "having a bad reputation." Taylor elaborates: "preconceived notions," "gossip," or "rumors" can "threaten our chances of finding something real."

According to Taylor, then, a reputation can be an obstacle to getting the things you want most in life, which is even more frustrating because that reputation is fake, undeserved, and outside our control. The first lines of "Delicate" exemplify this: "My reputation's never been worse, so / You must like me for me." We must like Taylor for who she is—that is, despite her reputation, despite the gossip, the rumors, and the warped image of who "they" think she is. The "you" that is referred to in the song does appear to see Taylor for who she *really* is, or so she hopes—she knows "it's delicate."

The separation between who you really are and your reputation is a lyrical theme throughout *reputation*. For example, in "End Game," Taylor describes a number of things that others believe about her—that she's a player, that she's crazy—which she then rejects as not being true: "here's the truth from my red lips." In "I Did Something Bad," other people have accused her of doing something bad, but by contrast, according to her own interpretation of the situation, it felt good: "They say I did something bad / Then why's it feel so good?" In "Dress," the public don't know about the true nature of her relationship: "Everyone thinks that they know us / But they know nothing about / All of this silence and patience." And in "Call It What You Want," Taylor makes it clear that those who have shaped her reputation are liars—"All the liars are calling me one"—and do not really know her at all—"'cause he really knows me / (Which is more than they can say)." Taylor is clearly in agreement with the philosophical accounts of the nature of reputation: it is a fake public opinion about who you really are.

Feeling Seen

Even though our reputations are fake, it's clear that they still matter to us. The bad reputation that forced Taylor into hiding wasn't so easy to shake off. It was something she couldn't ignore, and it resulted in the creation and release of an album dedicated to reclaiming her public image. What could explain why we care so much about something that is a warped and distorted lie?

The Scottish philosopher and economist Adam Smith (1723–1790) gives us an answer, highlighting the relationship between reputation and wanting to be seen for who we really are. In his *Theory of Moral Sentiments*, Smith writes about our deepest desire: "not only to be loved, but to be lovely."[14] What we want more than anything in life is not just to receive love, but to feel like we are deserving of that love—because we are truly seen as being "lovely." Smith used the word "love" to mean any kind of positive regard, but he also uses the word "sympathy," which includes the affection and esteem that we feel with our friends, acquaintances, or even strangers. Smith claims that we want people to feel sympathy and love for us because they see who we really are, and because of this, we care what other people think of us. If people don't love us, we think that we are unlovable, but if people do love us, it's because there is something truly in us that is worth loving.

We see our behavior reflected in the eyes of others, and it is difficult, Smith points out, to think well of ourselves when people around us give us indications that we are not worthy, not beautiful, or not smart. Being aware of what counts as "attractive" or "cool" is central to the way that we think about ourselves and shapes how we act. From a young age we are taught to use the public as a mirror, reading the reactions of those around us to gain information about what is deemed "praiseworthy" and what is "blameworthy."[15] This is why we are so often tempted to do and say things that we believe will make others think well of us and produce a good reputation. In *Miss Americana*, Taylor tells us that she has also experienced this desire: "the main thing that I always tried to be was ... a good girl.... I'd been trained to be happy when you get a lot of praise ... I became the person who everyone wanted me to be."[16] This also might explain why Taylor felt compelled to reconnect with Kanye, going for dinner with him, taking his calls, and listening to his requests. Taylor claims that "all I ever wanted my whole career after that thing happened in 2009 was for him [Kanye] to respect me ... I just wanted his approval."[17]

The desire for others to think well of us also explains why we might tend to keep the less polished sides of ourselves hidden—because they make us feel self-conscious and vulnerable. Taylor shows us an example of this in the music video for "Delicate." The opening scenes show Taylor burdened by her status as a celebrity, with everyone looking at her, wanting to talk to her and touch her, which is why she is accompanied by four bodyguards who closely track her every move. She finds respite in a bathroom, where she makes funny faces in the mirror, and then becomes invisible with the help of a magical note. Feeling liberated, Taylor dances out of the bathroom, through the hotel lobby and into the streets, striking silly poses. She can dance like nobody is watching, and finally be herself without the worry of what others think of her. Watching the video, we get to see the "real Taylor," without her reputation getting in the way.

Taylor recognizes the desire to be seen not just for herself, but also for her fans. During the *reputation* concert tour, all the concertgoers wore friendship bracelets that lit up in the dark (a trend that carried on to the Eras Tour). The bracelets make the fans visible, and Taylor tells us that the bracelets enable her to "see every one of you"—even the people at the back who, given the massive size of the stadium may feel invisible.[18] Taylor knows that her fans have come to see her, but that they also wish to be seen by her in a meaningful way. Taylor gives us the feeling that she sees us for who we really are—because of our friendship bracelets, because of the songs that speak directly to our own desires and vulnerabilities. And we see Taylor despite her reputation—because she confides in us and shows herself "the way she really is."

"I'd Do It Over and Over and Over Again If I Could"

From the way that Taylor Swift sings, writes, and talks about reputation, we could reach the conclusion that reputation is completely beyond our control, separate from who we really are, just a fake portrayal shaped by people who don't know us. But philosophers like to complicate things.

The contemporary philosopher Yotam Benziman claims that there is an interesting paradox at the heart of what reputation is. Reputation depends on public consensus and is outside our control, but it is also "internal" to us, belongs to us, and is shaped by our actions. Your reputation is both external and internal to you, it belongs to others and also to you, as a description of who you are based on how you present yourself in public.[19]

This means that reputation is not entirely fake after all, and gives us important information about each other as part of "collective wisdom." Origgi writes that reputation is "the informational trace of our actions," and categorizes the credibility we earn "through repeated interactions."[20] So, we do have more control over our reputations than we may have originally thought, and reputation can provide useful knowledge about how people act and who they are.

Although Swift is adamant that reputation is fake, there are a few lyrics on *reputation* that hint at her being aware that reputations are shaped by our own actions and behaviors that can be representative of who we are. For example, in "I Did Something Bad," Taylor claims the actions that caused her reputation were the "Most fun I ever had," and that she'd do the same thing "over and over and over again if I could." Similarly, in "End Game," the reputation that precedes one of the song's protagonists is a result of their own "mistakes" and "choices." In the same song, Swift writes about things people know because of their "big reputations": "you heard about me, ooh / I got some big enemies (yeah) / … And I heard about you, ooh (yeah) / You like the bad ones too." The knowledge that is gained from their reputations is not negated, but instead affirmed with a "yeah." In "… Ready for It?" Swift claims that she "knew he was a killer" even though she had never met him before, and that he "knew [she] was robber" even though he had never met her before. In this case, their reputations gave them knowledge about each other, and this knowledge is not rejected or proven to be false at any other point in the song. Taylor thus depicts reputation as accurately representing a part of her and others' characters, and something that we have agency over.

The Tilted Stage

While some of Swift's lyrics show that she is aware of the causal relationship between her actions and her reputation, she is much more outspoken about the way her reputation has been imposed on her and used against her. Why does Swift emphasize reputation as being fake, harmful, and out of our control?

Not all reputations are made equal. The public shapes our reputations based on a whole host of assumptions and stereotypes, such as our gender, race, and sexuality. Although having a reputation is something everyone experiences, the concern with how others perceive us will play out very differently depending on our identity and place in society. For example, from a very young age, the signs we receive about what counts as beautiful and good are gendered. Girls are more readily praised for the way they dress than boys, and boisterous behavior will be condoned (or even encouraged) in boys more than in girls.

Furthermore, a reputation puts more burdens on women because the standards for their behavior have traditionally been more restrictive than those for men. For example, going on "too many dates" but not being able to "make them stay" (as Swift describes in "Shake It Off") is a charge more readily leveled against women than against men, a point that Swift also makes clear in "The Man": "They'd say I played the field before I found someone to commit to / And that would be ok / For me to do." A woman behaving in the same way as a man gets a negative reputation for being unable to "keep a man," while the man's reputation as a "player" is positive and makes them "more of a boss." Similarly, while a man showing his anger contributes to his power status, a woman's anger gets her a reputation for being "hysterical" or "shrill," or even a "bitch." As Swift tells us, "no one likes a mad woman" ("mad woman").

Taylor recognizes that there are double standards when it comes to how men and women are judged by the public, and how their reputations are formed. A woman's reputation is less likely to match who she really is, and will cast her behaviors and actions in a negative light. Taylor tells us that "there's a different vocabulary for men and women.... A man does something, it's strategic. A woman does the same thing, it's calculated. A man is allowed to react. A woman can only overreact."[21] Taylor explains how she too has experienced this: "If I did something good, it was for the wrong reasons. If I did something brave, I didn't do it correctly. If I stood up for myself, I was throwing a tantrum."[22] In response to the criticism of her "girl squad" being elitist, Taylor tells us, "I thought it [the public narrative] was going to be we can still stick together, just like men are allowed to do. The patriarchy allows men to have bro packs. If you're a male artist, there's an understanding that you have respect for your counterparts."[23] And in relation to the difference between men and women in business: "I'm sick of women not being able to say that they have strategic business minds—because male artists are allowed to."[24]

In her *reputation* era, Taylor not only offers an interesting illustration of the philosophical accounts of reputation, but also meaningfully contributes to these theories. While reputation is paradoxically both external to us and something that might represent who we really are, through the use of her lyrics and performances Taylor demonstrates that where the emphasis of this paradox lies depends on whose reputation we are talking about. If you are a woman, then, as Taylor writes in "Look What You Made Me Do," the public stage on which your reputation is formed is "tilted." This tilted stage is not only written about abstractly in her lyrics, but is performed as part of the *reputation* concert tour, where the stage on which she performed was literally tilted, expressing the uneasy ground on which Taylor has to walk in order to maintain and deal with her reputation. The "different vocabulary" involved in reputation is played out in front of us, and is more than just a philosophical theory.

It's not for nothing that the only lyric on *reputation* that explicitly mentions a reputation *not* preceding someone, not affecting the way that they see themselves, is sung by a man—"I got a reputation, girl, that don't precede me" ("End Game"). As a woman and as a celebrity whose public image makes global headline news, Taylor's reputation is more likely to be "fake," out of her control, and get in the way of her forming "real" connections. This makes the success of Taylor's *reputation* era even more of a victory. Taylor managed to get back at the ones who wanted to taint her reputation, and at the same time, communicated clearly to her fans that she sees them, and that she knows that they see her for who she really is.

Notes

1. Constance Grady, "How the Taylor Swift–Kanye West VMAs Scandal Became a Perfect American Morality Tale," Vox, August 26, 2019, at https://www.vox.com/culture/2019/8/26/20828559/taylor-swift-kanye-west-2009-mtv-vmas-explained.
2. Alice Vincent, "Taylor Swift: The Rise, Fall and Re-Invention of America's Sweetheart," *The Telegraph*, January 25, 2020, at https://www.telegraph.co.uk/music/artists/taylor-swift-rise-fall-re-invention-americas-sweetheart; Nate Jones, "When Did the Media Turn against Taylor Swift?," Vulture, July 21, 2016, at https://www.vulture.com/2016/07/when-did-the-media-turn-against-taylor-swift.html.
3. Jason Lipshutz, "Taylor Swift's 'Reputation,' Intact: Expect the Script to Once Again Get Flipped," *Billboard*, August 24, 2017, at https://www.billboard.com/music/pop/taylor-swift-reputation-intact-script-flipped-7941807.
4. David Renshaw, "Taylor Swift: 'I Think I Should Take Some Time Off. I Think People Might Need a Break from Me," *NME*, October 8, 2015, at https://www.nme.com/news/music/taylor-swift-84-1213866.
5. Randy Lewis, "Even at the Rose Bowl, Taylor Swift Forges an Intimate Bond with Fans," *LA Times*, May 19, 2018, at https://www.latimes.com/entertainment/music/la-et-ms-taylor-swift-reputation-tour-rose-bowl-20180519-story.html; Laura Snapes, "Taylor Swift: 'I Was Literally About to Break,'" *The Guardian*, August 24, 2019, at https://www.theguardian.com/music/2019/aug/24/taylor-swift-pop-music-hunger-games-gladiators; Sam Lansky, "2023 Person of the Year: Taylor Swift," TIME, December 6, 2023, at https://time.com/6342806/person-of-the-year-2023-taylor-swift.
6. Jon Caramanica, "Taylor Swift Is a 2017 Pop Machine on 'Reputation,' But at What Cost?," *The New York Times*, November 9, 2017, at https://www.nytimes.com/2017/11/09/arts/music/taylor-swift-reputation-review.html.
7. Lansky, "2023 Person of the Year: Taylor Swift."
8. Dan Sperber and Nicolas Baumard, "Moral Reputation: An Evolutionary and Cognitive Perspective," *Mind & Language* 27 (2012), 509–510.

9. Yotam Benziman, "Reputation and Morality," *Human Affairs* 30 (2020), 109–110.

10. Gloria Origgi, *Reputation: What It Is and Why It Matters*, trans. Stephen Holmes and Noga Arikha (Princeton, NJ: Princeton University Press, 2018), 171.

11. Origgi, *Reputation*, 4.

12. Nicole Mastrogiannis, "Taylor Swift's iHeartRadio reputation Release Party: Everything We Learned," *iHeartRadio*, November 11, 2017, at https://961kiss. iheart.com/content/2017-11-10-taylor-swifts-iheartradio-reputation-release-party-everything-we-learned.

13. *Taylor Swift: Reputation Stadium Tour*, dir. Paul Dugdale (Netflix, 2018).

14. Adam Smith, *The Theory of Moral Sentiments*, vol. 1 of the *Glasgow Edition of the Works and Correspondence of Adam Smith*, ed. David Daiches Raphael and Alec Lawrence (Indianapolis: Liberty Fund, 1982), 151.

15. Smith, *The Theory of Moral Sentiments*, 161.

16. *Miss Americana*, dir. Lana Wilson (Tremolo Productions, 2020).

17. Brian Hiatt, "Taylor Swift: The Rolling Stone Interview," *Rolling Stone*, September 18, 2019, at https://www.rollingstone.com/music/music-features/taylor-swift-rolling-stone-interview-880794.

18. *Taylor Swift: Reputation Stadium Tour*.

19. Benziman, "Reputation and Morality," 110–111.

20. Gloria Origgi, "Reputation in Moral Philosophy and Epistemology," in Francesca Giardini and Rafael Witteck eds., *The Oxford Handbook of Gossip and Reputation* (Oxford: Oxford University Press, 2019), 70.

21. David Morgan, "Taylor Swift: 'There's a Different Vocabulary for Men and Women in the Music Industry,'" *CBS News*, August 25, 2019, at https://www.cbsnews.com/news/taylor-swift-preview-sexist-labels-in-the-music-industry/?ftag=CNM-00-10aab6i&linkId=72505330&fbclid=IwAR0Tu6eR1hHvOgN7gbB10UfIAfOJHfucfWpI5BF7ZVpzcsb-khuCOIe_L9A.

22. Hiatt, "Taylor Swift: The Rolling Stone Interview."

23. Hiatt, "Taylor Swift: The Rolling Stone Interview."

24. Hiatt, "Taylor Swift: The Rolling Stone Interview."

10

"It's Me, Hi! I'm the Problem It's Me"

Taylor Swift and Self-Blame

Agnès Baehni

The most popular song on Taylor Swift's 2022 album *Midnights* is the track "Anti-Hero." Speaking about the song, Taylor says: "This song is a real guided tour throughout all the things I tend to hate about myself. We all hate things about ourselves."[1] What Taylor expresses in this song captures a recurring theme in both music and everyday life: the tendency to blame oneself without thinking twice about it. When referring to the importance of self-blame in Taylor's work, I am not implying that she always blames *herself* in her songs like she does in "Anti-Hero." Rather, my point is that her music reflects something that many of us do on a daily basis. In addition, not only does self-blame play an important role in Taylor Swift's musical repertoire, but as the documentary *Miss Americana* (2020) reveals, blame and self-blame have also been central aspects of her life since her rise to fame in 2008. Insisting that her "entire moral code as a kid and now is a need to be thought of as good," Taylor confessed that she often struggled with the need to maintain the image of a "good girl."[2]

In light of this, we face the following question: Should we blame ourselves more than others, like Taylor seems to suggest in songs such as "High Infidelity," "Would've, Could've, Should've," "Afterglow," and "Anti-Hero"? Taylor is often presented as a model for younger generations and as a feminist icon. But could it be that she is also exemplifying and fueling a tendency to over-blame oneself? If so, this could be particularly problematic for her audience, which is largely constituted of girls and young women, a demographic that often experiences disproportionate levels of blame, both from oneself and from others.[3]

To settle this question, we'll consider an asymmetry in our intuitions about the ethics of self-blame and other-blame. The asymmetry is this: for a given wrongdoing, let's say arriving late to a concert, it often seems morally appropriate for someone to blame *herself* more than it would be morally appropriate for others to blame her.[4] This is "The Blame Asymmetry Claim." Is this true? And if so, why is it true?

Taylor Swift and Philosophy: Essays from the Tortured Philosophers Department, First Edition. Edited by Catherine M. Robb and Georgie Mills.

Don't Blame Me (But Let Me Blame Myself?)

Contemporary philosopher Dana Nelkin provides an interesting explanation of the above-mentioned asymmetry. In her view, it can be explained in light of the following philosophical principle: "All other things equal, it is harder to justify risking harm to others than to ourselves."[5] We find echoes of this principle in many of our everyday actions. As an illustration, consider Taylor's actions during her Eras Tour in 2023. During this tour, she sometimes performed in extreme conditions, for instance in Rio de Janeiro where temperatures exceeded 40 degrees Celsius (104°F) and where videos showing her gasping for air caused concern among her fans.[6] Contrast this with her decision to postpone a show in Buenos Aires because of bad weather conditions saying, "I love a rain show but I'm never going to endanger my fans or my fellow performers and crew."[7] What Taylor expresses in this quote is that certain risks she is willing to accept for herself cannot be tolerated when it comes to other people's health.

Let's come back to self-blame. Both self-blame and other-blame are painful when we are subjected to them, and so, according to Nelkin, when blaming ourselves or others we risk inflicting undue harm if we blame more than is warranted. Since one is justified in risking more harm to oneself than to others, and since blame involves a risk of harm, one is justified in blaming oneself more than others for a similar offense. So, on Nelkin's view, there is nothing wrong with self-blame being a recurring theme in Taylor's music, because it reflects a general fact about the ethics of our blaming practices. That is, we are justified in blaming ourselves more than others because we are justified in taking more risk when it comes to ourselves than to others.

I Knew You Were (in) Trouble

Nelkin's proposal is appealing but it raises some questions. A first question is whether *risk* is the right concept when thinking about the ethics of self-blame. Indeed, the intuition underlying the claim that Taylor is justified in risking her health more than her fans' health, or that one is justified in blaming oneself more than others, is not merely that we are justified in *risking* more suffering to ourselves. It is rather that we are justified in inflicting more suffering on ourselves than on others. For instance, Taylor would be more justified in ruining her own career than someone else's. This is because what is at stake in these cases is not merely the potential risk, but suffering itself.[8] Blame usually involves a form of suffering—it is never pleasant to be blamed or to blame oneself, even when it is deserved. Thus, the more pressing question with regards to the ethics of self-blame is whether we are justified in inflicting more suffering on ourselves than on others for the same wrongdoing.

My suggestion is that the relevant concept when thinking about the ethics of self-blame should not be *risk*, but rather suffering or harm. If we accept an asymmetric principle about self-blame, it needs to be: "All other things being equal, it is harder to justify inflicting suffering on others than on oneself." For now, I have not given a definitive answer to the question of whether we should blame ourselves more than others. I have simply argued that if we are seeking to explain this asymmetry in light of a general moral principle, we need to abandon the notion of risk and concentrate instead on the idea of suffering. For now, it remains unclear whether Taylor's work might be fueling an unjustified tendency to over-blame oneself, or whether it reflects a justified moral asymmetry.

A second point of concern is that Nelkin's analysis of what matters in blame might be misguided. She suggests that what matters is that we blame *enough*, but I think that what matters is that we don't blame *too much*.[9] Nelkin's proposal overlooks a fundamental insight into what morality is about: morality is more about avoiding suffering and increasing well-being than it is about ensuring that wrongdoers get their due. Although there are many dissimilarities between the legal and moral realms, it is worth noting that this is what the presumption of innocence is based on: it is often more of a problem to punish or blame someone too much than to blame or punish someone insufficiently.

The two problems mentioned so far are related. Since Nelkin assumes that what matters is that we blame enough, it makes sense that she focuses on risk. If we care about blaming enough, we will probably often blame a lot to ensure that wrongdoers get what they deserve, and then we risk wronging them if we over-blame. Instead of risk, I suggest that we focus on suffering, and that we keep in mind that what matters in blame is that we don't blame someone too much. However, just focusing on suffering is not enough. We also need to point to the precise feature of the relationship we have with ourselves that explains the asymmetry between the justification of inflicting suffering on ourselves and others. In the next section, I suggest we can blame ourselves more than others because we *know* ourselves better. This is in line with one of the major lessons Taylor draws in her documentary *Miss Americana* (2020)—the need to be self-aware and to know oneself.

Self-Blame and Self-Knowledge

One promising way to make sense of the asymmetry between the ethics of self-blame and other-blame is to consider the role of knowledge and self-knowledge in the justification of our blaming practices: perhaps it is appropriate for Taylor to blame herself more than it would be for others to blame her because she has *self-knowledge*.[10] She knows why she did a particular action and she knows the kind of person she is, as she sings in

"ME!" for example, "I know that I'm a handful, baby, uh / I know I never think before I jump." The idea is that, by knowing herself, she might have access to aggravating conditions that would justify her in blaming herself more than others.

Nevertheless, according to Nelkin, this explanation might not work for three reasons.[11] First, it is possible that the asymmetry having to do with knowledge doesn't always hold, whereas our intuitions about the moral asymmetry remain. This means that even when we don't know our minds better than the minds of other people, the intuition according to which it is morally appropriate to blame oneself more than others remains. I disagree. Let's imagine that Taylor has complete amnesia for what she did yesterday because a crazy scientist erased her memory. In this case, she cannot access her past thoughts just like she cannot access other people's thoughts. Since she has no idea about her motives or intentions, it is reasonable that she should be as cautious in blaming herself as she would be in blaming another, even though she remains, in some sense of the term, *herself*. Now imagine a reverse situation: Taylor has access to a machine that allows her to read other peoples' minds and to know their intentions and motives in the same way as she knows her own. In this case, she would be justified in blaming them as much as she would blame herself for the same wrongdoing. So, it looks like our ethical intuitions vary according to variations in the "knowledge" parameter.

Second, Nelkin insists that we might not be able to know ourselves better than others.[12] It is indeed hard to generalize the claim that we are more accurate about ourselves than about others. I want to defend a much more modest claim: we are not *always* more accurate, but we *often* are. If I see Taylor on the stage, I have no way of knowing what her thoughts are. Maybe she is enjoying the show, or maybe she is anxiously waiting for it to end. Contrary to this, I have some sort of access to my mental states (what goes on in my head). For instance, I know why I am now getting closer to the stage, because I am enjoying the concert very much and I want to snap a good picture before it ends.

Finally, even if we are radical self-knowledge skeptics, that is, if we think we can never know ourselves better than others, we can still point to a relevant difference having to do with knowledge. Let's imagine again that Taylor arrives late to a meeting—maybe she is justified in blaming herself more than others would be, because she knows there was no traffic jam, that she woke up late, and so on. She has access to relevant facts about herself that don't have anything to do with her mental life.

As Nelkin remarks, if we have special access to our own mental states, this might not explain that we should blame ourselves more, but rather that on certain occasions we should blame ourselves less, since "we might also sometimes have better access to excusing conditions."[13] In line with this reasoning, consider the following lyrics from Taylor's song "Don't Blame Me": "don't blame me, love made me crazy." Here she seems to point to an excusing condition for her actions. The fact that self-knowledge provides excusing conditions is not a problem. On the contrary, it captures something central about the degree to which we should blame ourselves— sometimes we should blame ourselves more, and sometimes less than others, depending on whether we have access to aggravating or excusing conditions. This reflects the general treatment of self-blame in Taylor's work. Although there is much self-blame in her lyrics, there is also compassion for herself (and in particular for her younger self being blamed by others), for example, "When you can't blame it on my youth / And roll your eyes with affection" ("Nothing New").

And so, we don't have any *systematic* reason to blame ourselves more than others. We can blame ourselves more than others only because we often know ourselves better than we can know others, and in knowing ourselves better we can be aware of aggravating conditions.[14] If we could know others as well as we know ourselves, then it would be permissible to blame them to the same degree as we blame ourselves.

Private Blame and Overt Blame

In *Miss Americana* Taylor claims that "When you are living from the approval of strangers, one bad thing can cause everything to crumble."[15] This makes it clear that Taylor, like many of us, is concerned with the approval of others. We care about what people think of us, but, luckily, we are often ignorant of whether they are blaming us. Indeed, there are roughly two ways of blaming people: we can do it privately or we can express it overtly.[16]

In overt blame the person who is blamed is aware of being blamed. This is what happens when someone tells you, "Hey, you really should not have done this!" Taylor does this in some of the songs directed at her ex-boyfriends, such as "Picture to Burn" and "All Too Well." Usually, when we blame ourselves, we are directly aware that we blame ourselves, whereas we can blame others privately.[17] The fact that we are aware of our self-blame makes it overt. Taylor refers to this conscious aspect of self-blame in "I Knew You Were Trouble" when she sings, "He's long gone / When he's next to me / And I realize / The blame is on me."

These two different forms of blame, private and overt, come with different moral implications: while some situations may not warrant overt blame, it is possible that they would still make private blame appropriate. If your spouse accidentally breaks your favorite piece of Taylor Swift merchandise after a very difficult day at work, it might be appropriate to blame them privately, but inappropriate to express your blame to them overtly.

In assessing whether blame is morally appropriate we can use the norm of "proportionality," which tells us that in order for blame to be morally appropriate, the harm it does to the wrongdoer must be proportionate to the gravity of the offense. This norm explains why we would blame someone who stole our ticket to a Taylor Swift concert more than someone who forgot our birthday—because stealing a ticket is worse than forgetting a birthday. Since private blame involves less harm to the individual being blamed than overt blame, it can be appropriate in cases when overt blame is not. Think of cases in which it is unclear how bad the offense is, or cases such as those mentioned above in which the person is justified in blaming the culprit silently, but where the culprit, for some reason, deserves to be cut some slack.

"... Ready for It?"

Recall the following points: We saw that the proportionate harm norm can warrant private blame while forbidding overt blame. We also saw that all self-blame is overt because we are directly aware of it. If we combine these two points, we see that the proportionate harm norm sometimes warrants other-blame (given that it can be private) while forbidding self-blame (since it is always overt). This is because overt blame inflicts greater harm than private blame on the recipient. Thus, it appears that we should sometimes blame ourselves *less* than others should blame us.[18] The explanation for this is very simple: it is possible to ignore that one is subjected to other-blame, while it is impossible to ignore that one blames oneself.

And so, in the end, is it true that we should blame ourselves more than others, like Taylor's work suggests? My answer is that it depends on two parameters. On the one hand, whether we can know ourselves better than others, and, on the other hand, whether we are focused only on overt blame:

1. We should blame ourselves *less* than we blame others for the same wrongdoing if by blame we mean "all kinds of blame considered" (private and overt), and if there is no difference between how we know ourselves and how we know others.
2. We should blame ourselves and others *the same* if we know ourselves and others the same, and if by blame we only mean overt blame.
3. We should blame ourselves *more* than others if we only focus on overt blame (both self- and other-) and if we accept that there is a difference in how we know ourselves and others.

Since it is likely that there *is* a difference between how we know ourselves and how we know others, and since we often care about how much people blame us to our face, not merely how much they blame us privately, the third solution is the one that is the most promising. Such an instance of self-blame, featuring self-knowledge, is exemplified in the song "Dear John" when Taylor sings, "Well maybe it's me / And my blind optimism to blame."

Here she seems to be aware of her tendency to be overly optimistic, and this justifies her blaming herself. Nevertheless, if we are justified in blaming ourselves more than others, this is not because of a fundamental asymmetry between the self and others but because of a contingent feature of the self-relationship: the fact that we usually know ourselves better than others.

We can conclude that there's nothing wrong with the recurring theme of self-blame in Taylor's work. Her lyrics are in alignment with justified intuitions about our moral practices: we are often justified in blaming ourselves more than others. Swift's work should be seen as an invitation for self-reflection. It's necessary to be aware of one's own faults in order to improve, and self-blame can be a useful tool to achieve moral progress.

Despite this positive aspect of Taylor's work, one might still wonder about the extent to which the self-blame that she describes in "Anti-Hero," for instance, stems from external sources ("… at teatime, everybody agrees"). Does her self-blame come from the blame others put upon her in a problematic way? Hopefully, the answer is no. It's important to consider self-blame in Taylor's lyrics in the more general context of her work and public presence, which generally advocates self-esteem and autonomy from the opinions of others. So, the good news is that we can probably continue listening to Taylor's songs without blaming ourselves.

Notes

1. Taylor Swift (@taylorswift), Instagram, October 3, 2022.
2. *Miss Americana*, dir. Lana Wilson (Tremolo Productions, 2020).
3. See for instance Itziar Etxebarria, M. José Ortiz, Susana Conejero, and Aitziber Pascual, "Intensity of Habitual Guilt in Men and Women: Differences in Interpersonal Sensitivity and the Tendency towards Anxious-Aggressive Guilt," *The Spanish Journal of Psychology* 12 (2009), 540–554.
4. Dana K. Nelkin, "How Much to Blame? An Asymmetry between the Norms of Self-Blame and Other-Blame," in Andreas Brekke Carlsson ed., *Self-Blame and Moral Responsibility* (Cambridge: Cambridge University Press, 2022), 98.
5. Nelkin, "How Much to Blame?, 111.
6. Let us nevertheless remember that one of Taylor's fans, Ana Clara Benevides Machado, died of heat exhaustion at one of her shows in Brazil.
7. Maanya Sachdeva, "Taylor Swift Cancels Buenos Aires Show Due to 'Unsafe' Conditions," *Independent*, November 10, 2023, at https://www.independent. co.uk/arts-entertainment/music/news/taylor-swift-buenos-aires-argentina-eras-tour-b2445507.html.
8. One might resist the idea that there could be a form of justified harm, since injustice or unfairness might be built in the concept of harm. In order to avoid this worry, I suggest using instead the notion of "suffering," which is more neutral. For a discussion on whether the notion of harm should be moralized, see Nils Holtug, "The Harm Principle," *Ethical Theory and Moral Practice* 5 (2002), 357–389.

9. Nelkin, "How Much to Blame?, 112.
10. Nelkin, "How Much to Blame?, 106.
11. Nelkin, "How Much to Blame?, 107.
12. Nelkin, "How Much to Blame?, 107.
13. Nelkin, "How Much to Blame?, 108.
14. Another way of explaining the asymmetry in our intuitions about blaming ourselves and others is to say that we hold ourselves to different standards from others. It seems to me that this explanation can be traced back to the fact that we generally know ourselves better than others. We hold ourselves to higher standards often because we know that we have the capacity to do better.
15. *Miss Americana.*
16. See, for instance, Mona Simion, "Blame as Performance," *Synthese* 199 (2021), 7595–7614.
17. I won't be assuming the stronger claim that we always know it when we blame ourselves, since it is possible that we are sometimes blaming ourselves unconsciously by entertaining recurring thoughts, or having certain self-regarding emotions without identifying them as self-blame.
18. When discussing her account, Nelkin herself observes that "A different hypothesis might seem to jump out at this point: self-blame is essentially harmful or painful where other-blame isn't, or, at least, self-blame is more directly connected to something essentially painful than is other-blame"; Nelkin, "How Much to Blame?, 110. For a discussion of the fact that self-blame is essentially painful, see Andreas Carlsson, "Blameworthiness as Deserved Guilt," *The Journal of Ethics* 21 (2017), 89–115.

"THE GIRL IN THE DRESS WROTE YOU A SONG"

11

Begin Again (Taylor's Version)
On Taylor Swift's Repetition and Difference

King-Ho Leung

In "You Belong with Me (Taylor's Version)," the 2021 rerecording of her now-classic 2008 pop ballad, Taylor Swift makes one subtle change in the lyrics. While the second verse in the original version goes "I'm in *the* room, it's a typical Tuesday night," in the rerecorded version she now sings "I'm in *my* room, it's a typical Tuesday night." *The* room becomes *my* room—Taylor's room—and the song truly becomes *Taylor's* version. On the surface level, Taylor's rerecording of her early career albums is simply a reactive response to ownership disputes with her record company, as it has been largely interpreted and reported in the media. But at the philosophical level, Taylor's act of rerecording is an active affirmation of her own music through the act of repetition.

Repetition is common in contemporary pop music. So, in what sense is Taylor unique in her approach to repetition as singer-songwriter? In this chapter we'll explore the different ways in which repetition is at work in Taylor's songwriting and album production. In particular, we'll draw on Søren Kierkegaard (1812–1855) and Gilles Deleuze (1925–1995), to see Taylor Swift not simply as a musician of repetition but also as a philosopher of repetition.

Repetition versus Recollection

Taylor's songwriting frequently features the repetitive literary device known as *inclusio*, where the opening and closing sentences of a piece are similar, if not identical. A clear example of this is found in Taylor's debut single "Tim McGraw," in which the opening line is repeated at the end of the song: "He said the way my blue eyes shined / Put those Georgia stars to shame that night / I said 'that's a lie.'" Other examples of the opening lyrics being repeated in the closing of the song include: "Teardrops on My

Taylor Swift and Philosophy: Essays from the Tortured Philosophers Department, First Edition. Edited by Catherine M. Robb and Georgie Mills.
© 2025 John Wiley & Sons, Inc. Published 2025 by John Wiley & Sons, Inc.

Guitar" ("Drew looks at me / I fake a smile so he won't see"), "Love Story (Taylor's Version)" ("We were both young when I first saw you"), "Haunted (Taylor's Version)" ("You and I walk a fragile line / I have known it all this time / But I never thought I'd live to see it break"), and "Cornelia Street" ("'I rent a place on Cornelia Street' / I say casually in the car"), among many others.

However, there are also songs where the opening line is repeated as the closing line, with a difference. Such songs include "Mary's Song (Oh My My My)," which opens with, "She said, I was seven and you were nine / I looked at you like the stars that shine / In the sky," and finishes 80 years later with "I'll be eighty-seven; you'll be eighty-nine / I'll still look at you like the stars that shine / In the sky." A similar change can be found in "Red (Taylor's Version)," which begins with "Loving him is like / Driving a new Maserati down a dead-end street," but ends with "His love was like / Driving a new Maserati down a dead-end street." This signifies a temporal transition with a shift from the present continuous tense ("Loving him *is* like ...") to past tense ("His love *was* like ..."). This indicates that the narrator of the song is finally moving on from "loving him" and discovering how she has changed, encountering herself anew as a different person. In these songs, repetition comes with a difference. One might even say that repetition makes the difference.

Taylor's repetition with a difference is not simply used to represent changes in time, but also changes in emotions, or even changes in our sense of self. For instance, in "I Almost Do (Taylor's Version)," the entire opening verse is repeated to close the song, but with one slight difference, so that the repetition is not identical. In the opening verse Taylor sings, "I bet / This time of night you're still up ... And I *bet* / Sometimes you wonder about me," and the phrase "I bet" is repeated four times. But the lyrics in the closing verse are changed slightly to "I bet / This time of night, you're still up ... And I *hope* / Sometimes you wonder about me." In this final non-identical repetition, the "I bet" that is repeated no less than ten times throughout the whole song changes to "I hope." This conveys a difference in the emotion and disposition of the narrator, as well as a sense of hope for a future relationship with her love.

We often think of repetition as backward-looking: we repeat something from the past, as though we are trying to recall some past event or relive the "good old days." But the notion of repetition sometimes has a different meaning in philosophy. For instance, in his 1843 book *Repetition*, the Danish philosopher Søren Kierkegaard draws the following distinction between "repetition" and "recollection":

> Repetition and recollection are the same movement, except in opposite directions, for what is recollected has been, is repeated backward, whereas genuine repetition is recollected forward. Repetition, therefore, if it is possible, makes a person happy, whereas recollection makes him unhappy.[1]

According to Kierkegaard, it is recollection that is backward-looking. We recall things as though we were looking back at them in a rear-view mirror (as Taylor memorably sings in "White Horse (Taylor's Version)"). By contrast, repetition is a forward movement. When we repeat something we are always creating something new. Kierkegaard observes that, unlike recollection, we only repeat things because we enjoy them and want to affirm them, which is presumably why so many people listen to Taylor's music on repeat. In this sense, repetition is a way of moving forward in life. We choose to repeat things and activities that we like, songs that we enjoy, while we get on with our lives and move forward in time. We do not repeat things we don't like or activities that make us unhappy. Instead we abandon them like those things left behind in "White Horse," in the "rear-view mirror disappearing now."

But aren't many of Taylor's most well-known songs, especially from her early "country" period, about recollection? Recalling and reliving painful memories of hurt and heartbreak? Let's consider "Back to December (Taylor's Version)." At first, this song may sound like a tragic ballad about the singer-narrator constantly revisiting and reliving the past, going "back to December all the time," to recall a former love whom she's wronged, misses, and wishes to reunite with. But despite going "back to December all the time," this song is not simply about backwards-looking recollection, fixating on a past event that one cannot change, reliving the same past event over and over again. Rather, at its heart the song is a forward-looking kind of repetition. Listening, we find out that the singer-narrator does not simply go back to December all the time to recall the past, but to rewrite it: "I go back to December, *turn around and change my own mind* ... I go back to December *and make it alright*." We do not go back to December to recall and relive the past that we cannot change, but to turn things around and make them alright, to repeat it with a difference and create something new.

Repetition in Recording

We tend to think of repetition in terms of sameness and identity. For example, when we listen to Taylor's "All Too Well (Taylor's Version)" on repeat, we are listening to the *same* song on repeat. However, according to the French philosopher Gilles Deleuze, in his book *Difference and Repetition*, this conception of repetition overlooks the way in which repetition presupposes and creates a difference and something new.[2] Every time we play and listen to "All Too Well (Taylor's Version)" is a new experience. Even if we listened to the song on repeat for an hour, our experience of listening at 2:10 a.m. would be different from our experience of the song at 2:00 a.m.—it could be a difference in terms of emotions, sleepiness, physical location, or simply because it is at a different time. Listening to the song in a car getting lost upstate in autumn is a different experience from listening to it while dancing around the kitchen in the refrigerator light, which is also different from listening to the song when going through heartbreak. The act of repetition, such as the act of listening to the same song on repeat, is always connected to the experience and expression of difference. According to Deleuze, to repeat is to generate something new and different, and not just recall or recollect something from the past.

This way of understanding repetition in terms of the creation of newness and difference is represented in a number of Taylor's songs, perhaps most notably in "Love Story (Taylor's Version)." In this song, the narrating character Juliet addresses the lyrics to Romeo, and is clearly based on Shakespeare's classic tragic love story *Romeo and Juliet*. In addition to repeating the opening lyrics as the closing line ("We were both young when I first saw you"), Taylor's retelling and repetition of Shakespeare's famous story ends not with a tragic ending as in the original. Instead, the characters are given a different ending: Romeo "knelt to the ground and pulled out a ring" and asks Juliet to marry him. This is a new and happy ending markedly different from Shakespeare's original. By retelling this famous love story with repetition and difference, Taylor is at once repeating Shakespeare's original story but also, at the same time, creating a new ending in her own unique way.

So far we've mostly considered Taylor's earlier work, from what we might call her "country" days. However, the use of repetition as the re-creation and production of something new and different becomes even clearer as Taylor gradually moves to more mainstream pop music. Consider her 2012 album *Red* (now rerecorded as *Red (Taylor's Version)*), which many see as her first transition to pop. At the outset of "State of Grace (Taylor's Version)," the opening track, we hear a repetition in the song's arrangement, with the heavy drumbeat and delay-pedal electric guitar riff. We also hear repetition in the vocalization in the background of the chorus, where a repeated "never" is added as a secondary track to echo the "I never …" sung by Taylor in the primary track. "I never (never) saw you coming … I'll never (never) be the same." The new sweeping "pop" sound of this opening track from *Red* announces a different sound for Taylor that is signaled by the use of repetition. In the chorus, for example, Taylor sings that she is experiencing difference, as something she did not expect ("I never saw you coming") and is herself becoming someone different ("I'll never be the same"). What comes from the repeated "never" is not similarity or being identical to something else, but difference: never being the same, and experiencing new things that one could never see coming.

The song that comes after "The State of Grace (Taylor's Version)" on *Red (Taylor's Version)* is the title track. In its chorus, we hear delayed and repeated electronically manipulated vocal sequences of the lyric "red, -ed, -ed, -ed," inserted as a secondary audio track following Taylor's own pronouncement of "loving him was red" in the main vocals. The "red, -ed, -ed, -ed" sequences are first played in the note of E and then repeated in the note of F#. Later on, in the penultimate track of the album, "Starlight (Taylor's Version)," we hear the notes E and F# again, repeated as a sequence throughout its chorus, where "starlight, starlight" is sung several times in F# and E ("star" in F#, and "light" in E). In this way, "Red (Taylor's Version)" is non-identically repeated as "Starlight (Taylor's Version)": another repetition with a difference. The album is mirrored by two songs, the second track and the second-to-last track, where their titles ("Red" and "Starlight") are repeated multiple times in the choruses in the notes of E and F#. The repetition of difference no longer simply appears internally within individual tracks, but now spans across different songs throughout *Red* as a whole, an album which notably ends with a song title that is all about repetition: "Begin Again."

Repetition as Rebirth

As Taylor ventures further into pop with *1989* and subsequent albums, her use of repetition and difference continues.[3] Taylor described *1989*, the 2014 album following *Red*, as her "very first, documented, official pop album." Indeed, in the album's first single, "Shake It Off" (now Taylor's Version) we hear an evident departure from (a "shaking off") Taylor's previous style and a conscious attempt at pop songwriting with repetition at its core. Throughout the song, we hear repetitions of different word-sequences such as "hate, hate, hate," "shake, shake, shake," "break, break, break," "fake, fake, fake." The song title "Shake It Off" is repeated thirty-six times, and is often preceded by a repetitive lyric, "I, I, I … I shake it off."

The conscious and explicit repetition of the song's title phrase in the recordings is found not only in "Shake It Off," but also in many other tracks on *1989*: from the opening track "Welcome to New York" (repeated 29 times) to other hit singles, such as "Out of the Woods" (repeated 34 times) and "Bad Blood" (repeated 15 times), to other tracks like "I Wish You Would" (repeated 19 times), "Wonderland" (repeated 21 times), and "All You Had to Do Was Stay" (repeated 22 times)—a song which also references and seems to repeat with a difference Taylor's earlier track "Stay Stay Stay" from *Red*. For this reason, Taylor was given the title "the Queen of Repetition" by journalist Emily Thompson Ward, who further observes that there are a variety of words and themes, such as red lips (mentioned 8 times), dancing to the beat (14 times), and burning flames (8 times), that are repeated in different contexts and manners across the songs in *1989*.[4]

This extravagant deployment of repetition in *1989* conveys not simply an "official" shift from country to pop as a different genre, but more importantly the birth of a new and different Taylor. As Taylor herself explains, the album is entitled *1989*, after her birth year, because it represents a "rebirth" for her.[5] As our philosophical analysis of the songs has shown, this rebirth is brought about through the use of repetition that produces newness and difference. Taylor's rebirth was not a one-off event but a repeated phenomenon. Indeed, sometime after the release of *1989*, Taylor blanked out all her social media accounts on August 18, 2017, and soon after uploaded graphics and videos of CGI snakes, culminating a week later in the release of the lyric video of "Look What You Made Me Do," which notably proclaims that "the old Taylor can't come to the phone right now … 'cause she's dead." What we have is no longer "the old Taylor," but Taylor the "snake" instead.

The imagery of the snake, as widely reported and interpreted by the media, is often seen as a reference and response to Taylor's feuds with other celebrities.[6] It is also relevant that her birth year, 1989, is the year of the snake in the Chinese zodiac. But what is particularly interesting about the snake imagery is how it appears in the lyric video for "Look What You Made Me Do," in the form of an "ouroboros." The ouroboros is an ancient symbol of a snake or dragon eating is own tail, which represents the unending cycle of life, death, and rebirth. It is striking that this ancient symbol for eternal cyclic renewal is the central image that appears for the choruses in the lyric video. This song not only declares the death of old Taylor, but also reports her rebirth: "Honey, I rose up from the dead, I do it all the time." Much like she goes "back to December all the time," Taylor's rebirth or indeed resurrection in her *reputation* era happens not just once but "all the time."

While "Look What You Made Me Do" and the other hits from *reputation* (2017) are largely dark and grey, Taylor's next album, *Lover* (2019), is considerably lighter and brighter, with colorful butterflies replacing the snake as the album's main imagery. In fact, in the opening of the music video for "ME!" a snake bursts and turns into a swarm of butterflies. Despite the dissimilarity in tone and the differences between snakes and butterflies, like *reputation*'s snake, the butterfly imagery of *Lover* conveys another rebirth. A new Taylor breaks free from her old self like a butterfly emerging out of its cocoon. She also does so in a way that explicitly references her self-titled debut album *Taylor Swift* (2006), which features patterns of butterflies on its cover. *Lover* is in this way a new debut, indeed a new *Taylor Swift*: it is another rebirth, a rebirth repeated with a difference.

Repetition and Rerecording

This chapter began by discussing Taylor's rerecording of her early albums, and it seems fitting to conclude by revisiting or indeed repeating this issue, but with a difference. As mentioned before, the rerecording of the "Taylor's Versions" emerged out of a dispute over the ownership of the master recordings of Taylor's first six albums. So Taylor's rerecording raises questions about ownership, authenticity, and originality.[7] Are Taylor's Versions the authentic or indeed original versions of Taylor's songs? Can a rerecording, which is something new, also be something original?

Deleuze writes that "repetition differs in kind from representation," because repetition always generates something new and different, whereas representation always refers back to some original.[8] For example, a poster of Taylor is a representation of Taylor the person who lives and breathes. As a representation, the Taylor we see on the poster has less reality than the original Taylor in real life. In this way, representations have a lesser reality than the originals they represent, and their value is derived from the value of the original. The poster of Taylor only has value because it represents the "original" living and breathing Taylor, and only derives its value from the fact that we value the original Taylor. So, by calling the rerecordings "Taylor's Versions," Taylor is insisting that they are not subordinate "representations" of the original master studio recordings, but rather repetitions which, as Deleuze would say, are not the subordinate idea found in a representation.[9] The "Taylor's Versions" are not mere copies of some original better thing, and are no less original or authentic versions of the songs penned by Taylor herself.[10]

Taylor's rerecording of the "Taylor's Versions" calls into question the originality of the previous studio recordings, and the very idea of what counts as an "original" Taylor. As the background voice in "22 (Taylor's Version)" asks: "Who's Taylor Swift anyway?" Perhaps this is a question that Taylor is seeking to answer through her ongoing repetition of difference, the recurring "rebirth" of different selves in her music. As she writes upon the release of the "Taylor's Version" of *1989*: "I was born in 1989, reinvented for the first time in 2014, and a part of me was reclaimed in 2023 with this album I love so dearly.... This moment is a reflection of the woods we've wandered through and all this love between us still glowing in the darkest dark."[11] As Taylor recognizes here and in many of her memorable songs that we listen to, on repeat, part of our experience of existing in the world or "wandering through the woods" is the quest to figure out who we are and what we want. By repeatedly questioning her own identity and reinventing herself, perhaps Taylor is, like each and every one of us, as she sings in the fourth song on her very first album, "trying to find a place in this world."

Notes

1. Søren Kierkegaard, *Fear and Trembling: Repetition*, ed. and trans. Howard V. Hong and Edna H. Hong (Princeton, NJ: Princeton University Press, 1983), especially 131.
2. Gilles Deleuze, *Difference and Repetition*, trans. Paul Patton (New York: Columbia University Press, 1994).

3. See Deleuze, *Difference and Repetition*, 76: "Difference inhabits repetition ... difference allows us to pass from one order of repetition to another."

4. Emily Thompson Ward, "Taylor Swift: Queen of Repetition," The Odyssey, November 10, 2014, at https://www.theodysseyonline.com/taylor-swift-queen-repetition.

5. David Renshaw, "Taylor Swift to Release 'Very First Official Pop Album' in October," *NME*, August 19, 2014, at https://www.nme.com/news/music/taylor-swift-199-1241766.

6. Lisa Respers France, "Taylor Swift and Snakes: The Backstory," *CNN*, August 23, 2017, at https://edition.cnn.com/2017/08/22/entertainment/taylor-swift-snakes/index.html.

7. Taylor's rerecording her "own" (*eigen*) versions of her music is also an expression of Martin Heidegger's (1889–1976) conception of "repetition" as a way of affirming one's authentic (*eigentlich*) mode of existence.

8. Deleuze, *Difference and Repetition*, 18.

9. Deleuze, *Difference and Repetition*, 57.

10. In this way, Taylor's rerecording non-identically repeats Deleuze's ambition of "overcoming Platonism" with his philosophy of repetition by "denying the primacy of original over copy"; Deleuze, *Difference and Repetition*, 66.

11. Taylor Swift, "My name is Taylor and I was born in 1989," X [Twitter], October 27, 2023, at https://twitter.com/taylorswift13/status/17177535933 88790096/photo/4.

12

Is Taylor Swift's Music Timeless?

A Metaphysical Proof

Patrick Dawson

Time is a very important theme for Taylor Swift. She sings of the seasons, the days of the week, and the times of the clock. She invests meaning in age: at fifteen "you're gonna believe them" ("Fifteen (Taylor's Version)"), at seventeen you "don't know anything" ("betty"), but at twenty-two "everything will be alright" ("22 (Taylor's Version)"). Given all these references to time, it might seem strange to say that there is no time in Taylor Swift's world. But in this chapter, I hope to prove just that. Swift has risen above time. Perhaps, by listening to her music, you could too. While some commentators have already called Swift's music "timeless," I will attempt to prove it, by comparing Swift's timelessness to the theories of several contemporary and famous philosophers, including Immanuel Kant (1724–1804), Martin Luther (1483–1546), and J.M.E. McTaggart (1866–1925).

What Is Timelessness?

What does it take for a musician to be timeless? It depends who you ask. In everyday life, we might call a musician timeless if their songs speak to people of any age or era. These artists remain household names even decades or centuries after they stop producing music. Think of Mozart, The Beatles, and Aretha Franklin. Is Taylor Swift among such names? This is a hard question to answer, since Swift remains a contemporary artist. We can't know for sure, today, if she will still be popular in 20, 50, or 250 years. But this is hardly satisfying for today's Swift fans, who might not live to see these times. "Surely," we cry out, "Taylor must be timeless?" We need answers. Perhaps a different approach can produce them.

Outside of everyday life, in the philosophical field of metaphysics, "timeless" has a different meaning. Timelessness is a serious and much-discussed theory. Simply put, it is the view that time is fundamentally

Taylor Swift and Philosophy: Essays from the Tortured Philosophers Department, First Edition. Edited by Catherine M. Robb and Georgie Mills.

unreal. The word "fundamentally" is important here. We can all agree that there *seems* to be time, in at least some sense. But what about when we examine reality on the most precise scale? What if we break down each object into its individual atoms, and break down the atoms into each of the states they move through? Perhaps time doesn't exist at this scale. If so, then that might cast a very different light on our everyday experiences of time. Could those experiences be nothing more than an illusion? Are we merely being tricked into believing in time, due to some quirk in our perceptions or minds? Like any good piece of philosophy, answering these questions just leads to more questions. If time is an illusion, could we peer through the veil, and break free of that illusion? Could listening to Taylor Swift's music help us to do this?

One complicating factor here is that philosophers disagree about what it would even mean for time to be "unreal."[1] We've never quite agreed about what time is, or what it would be if it existed. So we can't agree on what timelessness is, either. To grapple with this, we'll discuss three different conditions that famous philosophers across history have taken to be hallmarks of timelessness. In all three cases, we'll see that the themes contained in Taylor Swift's lyrics meet these conditions. Swifties can therefore declare with confidence that she is a timeless artist, in the most rigorous metaphysical sense of the word.

Is Taylor Swift Located in Time?

Let's begin by thinking of time as a series of *locations*. Any event, such as the birth of Taylor Swift, has occurred or will occur at some particular time, like 5:17 a.m., December 13, 1989. The physicist Isaac Newton (1642–1727), for example, believed that every event occurs at an objective location in time, just like an objective location in space. Some events have earlier locations, while others have later locations, but everything fits nicely into a single, well-ordered timeline. Modern physicists like Albert Einstein (1879–1955) took this idea even further, claiming that time is entirely unified with space, into one single structure of "space-time." The exact differences between these views don't matter here. The important point is, according to these views, every event has a precisely defined location, and is therefore related to every other event by proper temporal distances.[2] The release of *Speak Now* and its rerecording, for example, are separated by 4638 days: no more, no less.

But what if, deep down, the world doesn't contain such an orderly temporal structure? What if each event is neither located at any objective time, nor separated from other events by any objective duration?[3] In such a world, each event would be cut off from the others, without existing together in any unified temporal structure. By analogy, consider the various locations that pop up in the music video for "ME!" The first half takes place among houses on a single street. The houses themselves might be quirky, but they still sit in orderly rows, one after the other. Some houses have a higher street number, while others have a lower. They all fit into a single, linear structure. But in the second half of the video, we flicker through all sorts of places: we zoom into Brendon Urie's heart, we dance on-stage at a concert, we march and jump around a town square, and then we perch on mysterious neon platforms. Here, there is no order or structure. Instead of being connected by well-defined distances, or street numbers, these various places are totally disconnected from each other. Similarly, in a timeless world, there is just a bunch of disconnected events. None of these events are higher or lower, or earlier or later. Instead, each event just exists, without existing at any particular, ordered time.

The philosopher Immanuel Kant (1724–1804) believed in a view like this. He claimed that while time-ordering is part of our experience, it does not exist externally from us. Time is merely something we project onto the world, as a result of how our minds and experiences function. Kant thought the external world was deeply mysterious: we can never properly know about things as they are "in themselves." But he believed that time, specifically, was not something that was out there, among those external things. More recently, another version of this type of timelessness has been defended by contemporary philosopher Julian Barbour.[4] In his view, reality consists in a set of disconnected moments. Each event is connected to the others in the same moment, but each entire moment is cut off from the others. Any perception we have of moments being ordered into a single series of time is merely an illusion.

I suggest that Taylor Swift is living in this kind of world. While she does talk of days, months, and seasons, she uses these labels as a way of capturing feelings, sensations, or experiences, rather than denoting objective locations along a single, linear timeline. An event at midnight is not objectively at midnight. Rather, we just label it that way based on whatever suits the mood. Regardless of the positions of the Sun or the Earth, we might label midnight differently, if we happened to experience it differently. Midnights might become our afternoons ("Anti-Hero"). If it's one of those nights, we might have breakfast at midnight ("22 (Taylor's Version)"). Swift uses other time-labels in the same, flexible way. You want to leave the Christmas lights up until January ("Lover")? You feel like going "Back to December"? Go for it: there's nothing objective about the months and how you use them. Each event or moment just contains whatever feelings and experiences it contains, without needing to stand at some absolute temporal location. Like Immanuel Kant, Swift thinks of time as a feature of our experiences, rather than as something fixed, linear, or external.

The song "august" captures this well. Swift sings of a pseudo-relationship, plans made and abandoned, sexual awakenings, the salt air and the sun. The focus is not really on the duration or timing. Which year's August was it? How old were they? Was this affair confined to the dates August 1st to

31st, or was it a bit longer? These questions miss the point. August is not really a time, here, but more of a *vibe*, one of fleeting romance and the dying summer. Rather than committing Swift to the reality of August, as a time, this song only emphasizes time's fluidity and unreality. The same goes for "Christmas Tree Farm." The farm lives in Swift's heart. Christmas is more of a mood, and less of a specific day. Time is an illusion, and that means you're allowed to listen to "Christmas Tree Farm" on any day of the year.

Before we move on, there's something else worth noting about this theory of timelessness. There is a debate amongst Swifties about how we should chronologically order Swift's albums. Many of them have been rerecorded, and often in a different order to their original releases. But arguing over this could be missing the point. Taylor Swift's albums are not chronologically ordered at all, because *nothing* is chronologically ordered at all. Each album just exists, capturing whatever sensations it captures. These albums don't exist in a manner that is confined to specific times, because Taylor Swift's music is timeless.

So far, we've looked at one way in which Swift's world might be timeless. Namely, she might not be confined to a single, linear ordering of times. But this isn't the only way philosophers have understood timelessness. In the view of some philosophers, a mere ordering isn't sufficient for time anyway. After all, a row of houses on the street is ordered, but not in the specific sense of being *time*-ordered. So, perhaps there's some other special ingredient that characterizes time. If the universe lacks this ingredient, then it lacks time, regardless of whether there is an ordering or not. For the rest of this chapter, we'll consider some suggestions philosophers have made for what this special ingredient could be. In each case, we'll see that Taylor Swift remains timeless, even across the multiple senses in which philosophers have defined it.

Is Taylor Swift Fixed and Eternal?

One special ingredient we might associate with time is *change*. If there's no change, there's no time. On the face of it, change does seem to exist. Once, Taylor Swift had no Grammys, but now she has many. We might think differently of this so-called change if it turned out that Swift was *fated* to win those Grammys from the beginning. If the future is already fixed, if everything that will ever happen is already decided upon, then we might not see the variations from time to time as constituting true change. As contemporary philosopher Nicholas Gisin puts it, if "everything was set and determined at the big-bang ... [with] nothing more to add because there is no possibility to add anything ... [then] time would merely be an enormous illusion."[5]

Over the years, philosophers have developed many different variations on this idea of a fixed future. To summarize a few of them: "determinism" is the view that everything that will ever happen in the future can, in theory, be worked out from how things are now; "fatalism" is the view that the world is being guided toward some fate, and our actions are powerless to change it; "eternalism" is the view that everything in the future already exists, just as the present does, in a single, particular state.[6] The differences between these views are subtle, and those who believe in one might also believe in some of the others. I'll loosely refer to these ideas together, when referring to the future as fixed, settled, or closed. By contrast, if the future were unfixed, unsettled, or open, then there would be genuine change in what exists, or what is true or false, as time passes by. With every passing moment, new decisions would be made about what occurs next. According to some philosophers, this is what characterizes genuine change, and so is required in order for time to be real.

The view of time we are discussing here should not be confused with another view, "necessitarianism," which claims that there is no possibility or chance at all. Even in a fixed world, there are other possible ways that things could have been. But according to these views, it is already settled as to which of the possible worlds we live in. While there are different possibilities and a chance that things could be different, we are already living in the possibility that has been set. To say that the future could turn out different is exactly like saying the past could have been different. It's true, but it's a bit hopeless, because the future (like the past) has already been decided upon.

So what about Taylor Swift's world? Is the future already fixed and settled? It seems so. Fate, determinism, and the certainty of heartbreak is the bread-and-butter of Swift's philosophy. While she does talk of possibility in songs like "the 1," it comes with exactly that hopeless air of possibilities already decided. You could have been the one—but you're not. In fact, the very idea of "the one" exposes Swift's belief in a fixed, fated future. Similar concepts abound in her music, such as the "wrong" person for you ("Speak Now (Taylor's Version)") or the person you "belong" with ("You Belong with Me (Taylor's Version)"). Swift even dedicates a whole song to the concept of "karma"—the inevitable coming-around in the future, that follows from the actions of today ("Karma").

Confident in this fixed future, Swift often sets herself to play the role of the oracle. She knew that she and Jake Gyllenhaal were never, ever, ever getting back together ("We Are Never Getting Back Together (Taylor's Version)"). Likewise, in "Blank Space (Taylor's Version)," Swift plots the entire trajectory of a relationship that is yet to even begin. Similar foretellings of relationships and their endings can be found in songs like "Love Story (Taylor's Version)," "The Last Time (Taylor's Version)," and "New Year's Day." In fact, Swift often seems to have a clearer grasp of the future than she does of the past. She forgot that you existed ("I Forgot That You Existed"). She doesn't start it, but she can tell you how it ends ("Vigilante Shit").

So, while Swift's music is, itself, fresh and creative, the world it depicts has a fundamentally changeless feeling to it. In those rerecorded bangers that we put on repeat, Swift affirms again and again that she is still feeling twenty-two ("22 (Taylor's Version)"). In "New Romantics (Taylor's Version)," she tells us in chorus after chorus that every day is like a battle, and just as repeatedly, every night with us is like a dream. In many ways, this changelessness is part of Swift's appeal: we can listen to these songs over and again, and they still feel present to us, still speak to the same feelings, even for a new generation of listeners.

Swift's prophesying reaches its peak in "Mastermind," as she tells the story of a romance in which she has orchestrated every detail. None of it was accidental—it was all by design. The picture that Swift paints is a very traditional one for philosophers. Throughout the history of philosophy, numerous thinkers have argued that we cannot control our fortunes, and that the entire course of history has already been determined by some higher power. Our fates are predestined, even if only the chosen few can perceive them: the saints, the oracles, the multi-platinum singer-songwriters. By adopting this view, Swift is throwing her lot in with philosophers like the ancient Greek stoics, Martin Luther (1483–1546), Baruch Spinoza (1632–1677), and a host of others. So even if we can't know whether Swift will remain a household name for eternity, she has clearly *glimpsed* eternity, and has been inspired by it in her songwriting. That makes her timeless in a much deeper sense of the word.

Is Taylor Swift Passing through Time?

So far we've looked at change as the first special ingredient that might be needed for time. Now let's look at a second ingredient, which comes from one of the most famous time skeptics in Western philosophy, the English–Scottish philosopher J.M.E. McTaggart (1866–1925). He argued that there is no *passage* of time.[7] According to McTaggart, the reality of time requires more than locations, like Monday, Tuesday, and Wednesday. There also needs to be a transition or flow from one time to the next. First, Monday is present, then Tuesday, then Wednesday. It's not enough for there to merely *be* times—we must be *moving* in time, toward the future and away from the past. If we aren't moving in time, through the passage of time, then "true" time does not exist, at least according to McTaggart.

This argument has been developed and refined by more recent philosophers. McTaggart takes the passage of time to consist in a change in the *objective* present. However, contemporary philosopher Lisa Leininger argues that the passage of time just requires a march from each moment into the next, regardless of whether any one of those moments is objectively present or not.[8] Time is like a river: each point or moment along the river doesn't just exist, but also *flows* into the next one. Flow can be thought of in a positive way: it supposedly gives the universe a dynamism that would not be found in a mere series of times. But temporal flow is also constraining: we are forced to march forward at one second per second,[9] toward the inescapable future, and forever screened off from the inaccessible past.

In Taylor Swift's music, we don't find ourselves constrained in this way. Instead, Swift has released several songs that explicitly rail against the notion of time's steady flow. To the young, she says "Never Grow Up," and to her lovers, she says "Stay Stay Stay" and "Forever and Always." Swift rejects and cries out against the march from the past toward the future. In "All Too Well (10 Minute Version) (Taylor's Version) (From The Vault)" she puts it clearly: "Time won't fly, it's like I'm paralyzed by it."

At first glance this seems pretty negative, which is in line with McTaggart's view. No flow means no time, and that's that. But Swift's lyrics also bring out a liberating side to this form of timelessness. Rather than being trapped in a slow, steady march, Swift is free to jump in and out of whichever moments she likes, in whichever order she likes. The sagas depicted in tracks like "All Too Well (Taylor's Version)" and "The Story of Us (Taylor's Version)" are flickering whirlwinds of episodes, which Swift freely dips in and out of, jumping across space and time however she sees fit. Similar journeys are taken by Swift in the many flashbacks and daydreams that are scattered throughout her work. Swift breaks the structure of time as easily as closing her eyes in "Love Story (Taylor's Version)," or waking up in "Death by a Thousand Cuts." Swift is clearly not stuck at a specific present time, screened off from the past, and slipping toward the future. Instead, like in "The Very First Night (Taylor's Version) (From The Vault)," her music can fly, pick us up, and go back in time. Many Swifties probably listen to these songs as a way of transporting themselves out of the place and time they inhabit. This is another, very clear sense in which Swift has achieved timelessness.

The picture of reality we get from Swift's music doesn't contain an orderly passage or flow, onward into the future, which is what McTaggart took to be necessary for time. But it also isn't static. Even while being timeless, the world is dynamic. We might say that there is a "Swiftness" to the world, despite time being unreal. There aren't very many metaphysical views that fit into this category of "dynamic timelessness," though it isn't entirely unheard of.[10] Regardless, it's fair to say that this view is very specific to Taylor Swift. And in her classic style, we find an Easter egg tipping us off to her unique brand of metaphysics, right at the end of the rerecording of *Speak Now (Taylor's Version)*. The world is: "Timeless (Taylor's Version) (From The Vault)."[11]

Notes

1. A range of views are discussed in chapters 1 and 2 of Sam Baron, Kristie Miller, and Jonathan Tallant, *Out of Time: A Philosophical Study of Timelessness* (Oxford: Oxford University Press, 2022).
2. Technically, in Einstein's relativity theory, different observers can disagree about events' separations in time. But there is another, similar notion, called "proper time," which is objective and observer-independent.
3. In some frontier theories of physics, there are no temporal relations, but causal relations provide an alternative structure. See Sumati Surya, "The Causal Set Approach to Quantum Gravity," *Living Reviews in Relativity* 22 (2019), 5.
4. Julian Barbour, *The End of Time: The Next Revolution in Physics* (London: Weidenfeld & Nicholson, 1999).
5. Nicolas Gisin, "Time Really Passes, Science Can't Deny That," in Renato Renner and Sandra Stupar eds., *Time in Physics* (New York: Springer International, 2017), 2.
6. For details about the differences, see Elizabeth Barnes and Ross Cameron, "The Open Future: Bivalence, Determinism and Ontology," *Philosophical Studies* 146 (2008), 291–309.
7. J. Ellis McTaggart, "The Unreality of Time," *Mind* 17 (1908), 457–474.
8. Lisa Leininger, "Temporal B-Coming: Passage without Presentness," *Australasian Journal of Philosophy* 99 (2021), 130–147.
9. If you find "one second per second" confusing, you're not alone. Some have argued that this idea is incoherent, and so with it the entire notion of temporal flow. For a response and discussion see Ned Markosian, "How Fast Does Time Pass?" *Philosophy and Phenomenological Research* 53 (1993), 829–844.
10. For an example see again Surya, "The Causal Set Approach," particularly section 6 on dynamical forms of timeless causal set theory.
11. The author would like to thank the Tortured Poets Department's finest, Olivia Hall, for feedback on this chapter.

13

"I Remember It All Too Well"
Memory, Nostalgia, and the Archival Art of Songwriting

Rebecca Keddie

"I use songs almost like photographs so that I can go back and remember a time and remember exactly what it was like to experience it."[1] It's September 2019, and Taylor Swift is introducing "Cornelia Street" the eighth song of City of Lover, a one-off show in Paris celebrating the release of her seventh studio album. It's a song about the connection between memory and place, how we infuse places with emotion because they remind us of certain people and moments in our lives. By comparing the song to a photograph, in the quote above, Taylor describes how music too can become a touchstone for memory—the song "Cornelia Street" reproducing the emotional effect of the street itself. From the very first line, "We were in the backseat / Drunk on something stronger than the drinks in the bar," we are situated immediately in a moment in time and place. As the song unfolds it weaves together specific memories, from a drunken car ride to walking barefoot through the kitchen, to show how the story of the relationship has become so deeply entangled with place that, were it to end, it would become simply too painful to "walk Cornelia Street again."

The capacity for music to act as a touchstone of memory has been deeply woven into Taylor Swift's work from the very beginning of her career. On June 19, 2006, Taylor's first single, "Tim McGraw," was released. At its core, it is a song about the evocative power of music, and its capacity to provide a way back to the memories of a relationship: "when you think Tim McGraw / I hope you think of me." This first single acts as a thematic cornerstone for Taylor's subsequent career, where a central part of listening to Taylor's music is the feeling that it is akin to leafing through the pages of her diary, providing insight into her life and emotions. Considering songs as photographs and diaries evokes the image of a personal "archive"—a collection of things that form a memory of who we are. Philosophically this connects with the work of Michel Foucault (1926–1984) and Jacques Derrida (1930–2004), who employed the concept of the "archive" to think

Taylor Swift and Philosophy: Essays from the Tortured Philosophers Department, First Edition. Edited by Catherine M. Robb and Georgie Mills.
© 2025 John Wiley & Sons, Inc. Published 2025 by John Wiley & Sons, Inc.

about human memory on an individual and collective scale. These philosophical understandings of the "archive" provide a useful framework for thinking about the role of memory in Taylor Swift's songwriting and persona, and the way that we, both individually and collectively, project our own meanings onto her music.

"Say You'll Remember Me"

In *Archive Fever*, Derrida argued that we possess a compulsive desire to "collect, organize, and conserve," to protect against "forgetfulness, amnesia, the annihilation of memory."[2] This archive fever, a desire to act against erasure, or being forgotten, can be seen across Taylor Swift's songwriting as a way of asserting and capturing her memories of relationships: "I see your face in my mind as I drive away" ("Breathe (Taylor's Version)"); "I still see it all in my head / In burning red" ("Red (Taylor's Version)"), "I'm right where you left me" ("right where you left me"). Taylor also urges others to remember: "capture it, remember it" ("Fearless (Taylor's Version)"); "please picture me in the weeds" ("seven"); "say you'll remember me" ("Wildest Dreams (Taylor's Version)"). In "august," a track from her eighth album, *folklore*, Taylor writes of a relationship where its brevity and fragility leaves it vulnerable to slipping away "into a moment in time," lost in a summer haze that can't be recaptured when September arrives. However, the song acts as a defense against this erasure, as a record of the relationship otherwise forgotten, as she urges the subject: "But do you remember?"

Another way we can think about the relationship between song-writing and memory is with reference to what philosopher Paul Ricoeur (1913–2005) calls the "archival trace," which is the idea that something of the past is preserved in the archive.[3] For Ricoeur the archival trace embodies a paradox, suggesting both visibility and invisibility. The "trace" is something we can perceive in the here and now, because it is captured in the archive, but at the same time, the "trace" is evidence that the person or activity that left the trace is no longer visible and is in the past.[4] This notion of the archival trace can be a useful lens for viewing the reflective activity of songwriting, and perhaps no song in Taylor's discography better embodies this archival trace than "marjorie" on *evermore*.

The track sees Taylor grieving her grandmother Marjorie, who died when Taylor was thirteen years old. However, the absence caused by her death finds its counterpoint in Marjorie's ongoing presence in Taylor's mind and in her dreams: "What died didn't stay dead / You're alive, you're alive in my head." In the bridge, Taylor's grief extends to the lack of material records of her grandmother, and a desire for an archival trace, as she laments, "Should've kept every grocery store receipt / 'Cause every scrap of you would be taken from me." Given the lack of material records of Marjorie, the song works to take the place of a personal archive, with memories and life lessons archived in the form of lyrics and sound. Taylor even goes as far as to include a literal archival trace of her grandmother. Scour the song credits for "marjorie" and you'll see Marjorie Finlay's voice captured and immortalized in the backing vocals.

"Speak Now"

"Hold on to the memories / They will hold on to you," Taylor repeats in "New Year's Day," suggesting that memories are produced through repeated acts of remembrance. To think about memory in this way is central to what Derrida sees as the paradox of the archive. Archiving is driven by the desire to capture and stabilize memory, but the richness and complexity of memory can never truly be captured as something fixed. By determining what is remembered and what is forgotten, we create memory and knowledge, rather than merely capturing it. We can never return exactly to the moment as it was, so our act of remembrance is a re-creation of it.[5] Foucault also found a connection between memory and knowledge, and the power that it gives us. He claims that knowledge and power are fundamentally connected: power operates through knowledge, and knowledge is a form of power.[6] To control our archive is to exercise power over the stories we tell ourselves. To acknowledge that there is an "archival art" to Taylor's songwriting is to acknowledge the way that she uses memory, asserting and reclaiming power and knowledge through songwriting.

Taylor's third studio album, *Speak Now (Taylor's Version)*, exemplifies this. It's an album that charts the emotional turbulence of moving from her teenage years into adulthood, as well as the transition to a life lived in the spotlight. The album is about reclaiming power through "speaking now" and asserting the validity of one's memories. Using the imagery of the archive, in the original album prologue Taylor frames the tracks as a "series of open letters ... made up of words I didn't say when the moment was right in front of me."[7] As such, the songs take the place of other physical traces or archival records, capturing thoughts and feelings that otherwise would have gone unrecorded, asserting a power through speech that counters the powerlessness that Taylor experienced within the relationships she's writing about. For example, in "Mean (Taylor's Version)," she turns a critic's weapon back against him, wielding "words like knives and swords" to reclaim a sense of power lost through a harsh review. In "Better Than Revenge (Taylor's Version)," revenge is enacted in the form of a song, and in "Innocent (Taylor's Version)," Taylor steps up to speak into a microphone that was previously taken from her.

The clearest and most potent example of this use of memory as power is in "Dear John (Taylor's Version)," where Taylor's naivete in the relationship she describes is contrasted with the clarity that comes with hindsight. She sings of a relationship with a manipulative older partner: "And I lived in your chess game / But you changed the rules every day." Upon reflection she is able to see the relationship for what it is—"I see it all now that you're gone"— and the lyrics make explicit the mistreatment that wasn't clear to her at the time. Through songwriting, Taylor reclaims her power, singing in the outro: "The girl in the dress wrote you a song / You should've known." The power of the archival record to define the narratives we tell about ourselves and others is so potent that twelve and half years later, on the eve of the release of the rerecorded *Speak Now (Taylor's Version)*, during the Minneapolis stop of the Eras Tour, Taylor urged fans not to "defend me on the internet against someone you think I might have written a song about 14 billion years ago."

Taylor's project to rerecord her first six albums has made the role of memory in her songwriting more relevant than ever. The rerecording process has allowed her to revisit and reinterpret her past work, advancing subtle narrative shifts as she returns to albums and eras from earlier in her career. At first glance, this act of rerecording may seem contrary to the spirit of the archive, a discarding of the old in favor of the new Taylor's Versions. But actually archiving does not simply capture memory but continually creates it.

The archive is never static or fixed, but is always being made. For the philosopher Stuart Hall (1932–2014), the archive should be understood as a "living archive ... whose construction must be seen as an on-going, never-completed project."[8] This is because memory is not truly about the past, but the way that the past is actively reinterpreted and brought to bear on the present. This is true of all of Taylor's music, which is open to continual reinterpretation, but the idea of an active archive becomes explicit with the rerecordings. For example, in "All Too Well (10 Minute Version) (Taylor's Version) (From The Vault)," the memories of the relationship depicted in the song are rearranged and reconfigured. In the original, the narrator mourns the loss of a relationship, collating and arranging the memory traces of the relationship into an archive. The material ephemera of an old scarf, plaid shirt, and autumn leaves, are rendered into song lyrics. But in the rerecorded ten-minute version, the memories take on new meaning and significance: a keychain tossed on the ground becomes a symbol of an ongoing disregard that was not at first visible, an unequal power dynamic made explicit. In this return to the archive, memories are reformed and power is reclaimed.

"Passed Down Like Folk Songs"

"One day we will be remembered," Taylor sings in "Long Live (Taylor's Version)," a track where she uses the theatrical imagery of history-book heroes and slain dragons to sing of a hope that the music she creates, and the experience of playing that music live, will not be lost, as she tells the listener, "When they point to the pictures, please tell them my name." This hope is central to Derrida's understanding of the archive. To have "archive fever" is not just to be concerned with personal remembrance, but to be concerned with legacy and a desire to create something that will speak of us when we are gone.[9] It is only in the act of making memories public ("externalizing" our memories), that the archive is created.

The relationship between music and legacy is explored throughout Taylor's discography, including in her two 2020 albums, *folklore* and *evermore*, where the central framework for her songwriting shifts from being more straightforwardly diaristic, toward a focus on storytelling. Indeed, folklore involves the knowledge, customs, and stories that are passed down in a culture from one generation to the next. By adopting the language and imagery of folklore, Taylor is playing with how songwriting acts as archive, how it establishes legacy, and how our emotions and memories can be "passed down like folksongs" ("seven"), as she asks, "isn't it romantic how all my elegies, eulogize me?" ("the lakes").

As implied by the concept of folklore, these stories are never straightforward renditions of the past. Instead, central to the album are questions about how knowledge is constructed, how we know what we know, and what it means for something to be true. As Taylor writes in the prologue: "the lines between fantasy and reality blur and the boundaries between truth and fiction become almost indiscernible. Speculation, over time, becomes fact."[10] The tracks on *folklore* and *evermore* entangle Taylor's own stories with those of historical figures and fictional characters: the romantic poets, Emily Dickinson, socialite Rebekah Harkness, teenagers (August, Betty, and James), her grandparents, and even an embittered ghost surveying her own funeral. Muse merges with surrogate, with the fictitious, and with herself, as she asks: What stories do we tell of ourselves and others, and what stories will others tell of us when we are gone?

As Foucault and Derrida understand it, the archive does not contain knowledge as much as it produces it. The form and the structure of the archive determines what knowledge the archive produces. The act of archiving gathers and preserves the traces of one memory at the expense of another; remembering is not possible without also forgetting. Much of Taylor's songwriting operates like an archive in this manner, sitting at the intersection between concealing and revealing, remembering and forgetting, public and private. "Dear Reader," the closing track of the 3 a.m. edition of *Midnights* addresses this head on. The title evokes the opening line of a diary entry and frames the track as confessional, drawing the reader in and inviting them to listen to the innermost thoughts and feelings that Taylor is "spilling out to you for free." Simultaneously the track works to undermine this sense of disclosure, as there is a call to "burn all your past files," and a warning that the listener should not take her word for it—"the greatest of luxuries is your secrets."

On *reputation*, an album created in a moment of public backlash, Taylor engages with the idea of truth and knowledge as fundamentally constructed. In the album prologue she writes, "we think we know someone, but the truth is that we only know the version of them they have chosen to show us," and, "this is the first generation that will be able to look back on their entire life story documented in pictures on the internet." At the same time, she points to the failure of the incessant documentation to produce truth, noting how there will be "slideshows of photos backing up each incorrect theory," about who or what is the subject of each album track.

This theme is explored further in the music video for "Look What You Made Me Do," where Taylor satirizes some of her more infamous and controversial public moments, from the girl squad of the *1989* era, to her much-ridiculed desire to be "excluded from the narrative." However, the music video is not only a performance of self-awareness, but also an act of meta-commentary, as she nods to her role in constructing these various iterations of her own public image. In one scene she stands at the center of the shot, her dancers in at V formation behind her all clad in "I heart TS" T-shirts, a reference to a T-shirt worn by a rumored ex. In doing so she blurs the line between reality and performance, suggesting an element of choreography to aspects of her public presentation.

"I'll Show You Every Version of Yourself Tonight"

"These songs maybe started out being about something that happened to me, or in my life ... but my dream is that when they go into your world they become about your life."[11] It's the Eras Tour in Tampa, Florida, and Taylor speaks these words to the crowd of 70,000 gathered in the Raymond James stadium, as well as to the many thousands more tracking the tour's every move on social media. It's an acknowledgment of the way that songs archive not only Taylor's experiences, but our own, as we superimpose our memories and emotions onto the lyrics and sounds. "Fifteen (Taylor's Version)" becomes about our own teenage years, "Mean (Taylor's Version)" about our own detractors, "Clean (Taylor's Version)" recounts a time we overcame something in our lives, and "right where you left me" is about a time where we couldn't.

"mirrorball" engages with these ideas directly. In the song, Taylor imagines herself as a mirrorball, a shimmering, decorative object made up of lots of small mirrors, suspended above a dance floor, a constant source of entertainment. This entertainment comes from the light produced by the mirrorball's own "shattered edges," but simultaneously from the way it reflects ourselves back at us: "I'll show you every version of yourself tonight." On the opening night of the Eras Tour in Glendale, Arizona, Taylor chose to play "mirrorball" as one of the first two surprise songs of the tour, pairing it with her first single "Tim McGraw." Just as

Tim McGraw's songs became sites upon which she constructed memories of her own life all those years ago, "mirrorball" acknowledges how the positions have been reversed. As we seek to find ourselves in Taylor, we feel she is shining, even in a crowd of thousands, just for us.

The way that archives act as sites of collective memory construction is central to Derrida's understanding of the archive, and in fact he argues that it is in the passage from private to public that records are made into archives.[12] This points to how archives are not just spaces where we see ourselves as individuals, but where communities and societies construct collective memory and identity. As the philosopher Maurice Halbwachs (1877–1945) argued, individual and collective memory is fundamentally connected, because the presence of the group is essential for prompting and validating personal memory.[13] All music can become sites of collective cultural memory, but this is especially the case for Taylor Swift's music, with its ubiquity and sustained cultural relevance. Few artists in the twenty-first century can boast so many lyrics that have become part of our shared lexicon. We "shake it off" ("Shake it Off (Taylor's Version)"), bemoan that "I'm the problem it's me" ("Anti-Hero"), announce we're in our *reputation* era, and hardly a twenty-second birthday passes without a quipped "I don't know about you, but I'm feeling 22" ("22 (Taylor's Version)").[14]

Beyond an abundance of ubiquitous phrases, Taylor's music is so powerful in its ability to collectively construct memory, because her work chronicles, with a sharpness and expressive rawness, the volatility and emotional turbulence of being a young adult. Her albums provide a shared cultural touchstone through which our individual experiences are given collective meaning, and upon which we construct new memories. When we listen to "You Belong with Me (Taylor's Version)," we may recall our own experience of unrequited teenage crushes and embarrassing adolescent awkwardness, but we are just as likely to recall our experience of listening to the song, singing along with a friend at the back of a bus, or in the crowd at a concert, hands raised in the shape of a heart.

Nostalgia and the archive have also become a big part of Taylor Swift's public persona. From the album *reputation* onward, we see Taylor lean into a sense of "self-mythology." In the music video for "Look What You Made Me Do" she marshals into action her past personas, her current self (or at least one iteration) poised atop a teeming mass of easily recognizable past selves. In doing so these past personas are rendered more relevant than ever, as she stands literally on their shoulders. However, there is an inherent tension here; self-mythology goes hand in hand with self-destruction. In the next shot, this tower crumbles, and Taylor announces through the phone that her old self is dead. This reflects a philosophical understanding of memory, not as something belonging to the past, but as cyclical, continually working to produce the present. In the words of contemporary philosopher Marya Schechtman: "memories smooth over the boundaries between the different moments in our lives, interpreting and reinterpreting individual events and experiences in the context of the whole" so that we can produce a coherent narrative of the self.[15] The old Taylor(s) are simultaneously dead, and at the same time, more alive than ever.

This engagement with her past and the role of memories in the construction of the self is becoming an increasing part of Taylor's work. The Eras Tour looks back through her musical catalogue, revisiting the sound and aesthetic of each album, and *Midnights*, her tenth studio album, is both thematically and sonically retrospective. Billed as "the stories of 13 sleepless nights scattered throughout my life," the album considers the mental time-traveling we do as we lie awake, journeying through the archives of our mind, and how we hope this retrospection will lead to self-discovery: "that just maybe, when the clock strikes twelve ... we will meet ourselves."[16]

Similarly, Taylor's project of reclaiming her master recordings was not simply about reclaiming artistic output, but also about reclaiming past versions of herself and her memories: "He's got my past frozen behind glass / But I've got me" ("it's time to go"). In the music video for "I Can See You (Taylor's Version) (From The Vault)," a vault track from the *Speak Now* rerecording, Taylor uses the metaphor of a heist to depict the rerecording process, andromorphically depicting the *Speak Now* album as Taylor herself, complete with the era's signature curls and writing up her arms. Furthermore, by turning the rerecording releases into big events, with "Easter eggs" hinting at the next album, live on-stage announcements, and accompanying vault tracks, fans' own nostalgia for the albums is mobilized, as we feel we are revisiting and reclaiming the accompanying eras in our lives as well.

Memory is a central theme across Taylor Swift's discography, and increasingly the memory work of her songwriting has found its counterpart in aspects of her public presentation. The philosophical notion of the archive, especially as it appears in the work of Derrida, is grounded on a tension between remembering and forgetting, a desire to destroy and also a desire to preserve. Approaching Taylor Swift's work through the lens of the archive illuminates the way her songwriting is built on the opposing poles of remembering and forgetting, private and public, fiction and fact, self-destruction and self-mythologizing. This allows her to capture the inherent tension in doing intimate memory work on a public stage, for the world to see and reinterpret. The archive, as much as it is concerned with our personal memories, will always be public, a site of collective memory construction. As much as Taylor Swift's songwriting is about her life, it is about all our lives as well.

Notes

1. Robert Anderson "Taylor Swift City of Lover Concert," You Tube, April 10, 2021, at https://www.youtube.com/watch?v=vjLb5u5y3Aw.
2. Jacques Derrida, *Archive Fever: A Freudian Impression*, trans. Eric Prenowitz (Chicago: University of Chicago Press, 1996), 11.
3. Paul Ricoeur, *Time and Narrative*, vol. 3, trans. Kathleen Blamey and David Pellauer (Chicago: University of Chicago Press, 1988), 119.
4. Ricoeur, *Time and Narrative*, 19.
5. Derrida, *Archive Fever*, 17.
6. Michel Foucault, *Discipline & Punish: The Birth of the Prison*, trans. Alan Sheridan (London: Viking, 1977), 27.
7. Taylor Swift, liner notes to Speak Now (Big Machine Records, 2010).
8. Stuart Hall, "Constituting an Archive," *Third Text* 15 (2001), 92.
9. Derrida, *Archive Fever*, 12.
10. Taylor Swift, liner notes to folklore (Republic Records, 2020).
11. See You Leda, "Taylor Swift's Eras Tour Introduction Speech," You Tube, April 17, 2023, at https://www.youtube.com/watch?v=iQHOxLqtAEg.
12. Derrida, *Archive Fever*, 2–3.
13. Maurice Halbwachs, *On Collective Memory*, trans. Lewis A. Coser (Chicago: University of Chicago Press, 1992), 69.
14. For more on this see Cynthia Gordon, "The Linguistic Phenomenon behind Taylor Swift's Superstardom," Georgetown University, Ask a Philosopher, July 7, 2023, at https://www.georgetown.edu/news/the-linguistic-phenomenon-behind-taylor-swifts-superstardom.
15. Marya Schechtman, "The Truth About Memory," *Philosophical Psychology* 7 (1994), 13.
16. Taylor Swift, liner notes to *Midnights* (Republic Records, 2022).

14

Taylor's Version
Rerecording, Narrative, and Self-Interpretation

Jana Alvara Carstens

Lately there's been a new shift that has affected me personally and that I feel is a potentially harmful force in our industry, and as your resident loud person, I feel the need to bring it up. And that is the unregulated world of private equity coming in and buying up our music as if it is real estate. As if it's an app or a shoe line. This just happened to me without my approval, consultation, or consent.

—Taylor Swift, acceptance speech at *Billboard*'s Women in Music, 2019[1]

When news first got out in 2019 that Taylor Swift intended to rerecord her first six albums, reactions in the media were skeptical, if not downright mean.[2] Conventional wisdom said she would end up looking foolish, wasting her time, money, and effort. She herself was doubtful if people would care.[3] Rerecordings were, after all, nothing new. If the likes of Prince and Def Leppard couldn't pull it off to acclaim or achieve commercial success, then why would Taylor be the exception?

A few years later, we know just how much of an exception Swift is. With each rerelease, she topped the charts, broke records, and gained the admiration of the media and fans alike. Why was she the lucky one, while so many before her fell short?

There are many possible reasons why her rerecording project turned out to be so successful, with the loyalty of her fans being one of the reasons the works have sold well (remember the time Taylor's account on iTunes accidentally released seven seconds of static, and the static track topped the charts in Canada).[4] Another reason could be that everyone loves watching a combination of justice and revenge play out in real life. Through her rerecordings, Swift reclaimed her work from the owner of Big Machine Records, Scooter Braun, while also outing him as a "manipulative bully."[5] The secondhand satisfaction of watching a "mad woman" carrying out her "vigilante shit" with "karma" on her side, is better than fiction.

Taylor Swift and Philosophy: Essays from the Tortured Philosophers Department, First Edition. Edited by Catherine M. Robb and Georgie Mills.
© 2025 John Wiley & Sons, Inc. Published 2025 by John Wiley & Sons, Inc.

However, to get to the root of what makes her rerecording project special, one must ask why she has such widespread support. In this chapter, I want to suggest that it is Swift's mastery of "narrative" that makes both fans and the public root for her, and makes this rerecording project such a success. Narrative holds a special fascination for philosophers because narrative can be used to shed light on what it means to be a person and how we carry out our actions. Some philosophers maintain that storytelling is intrinsic to our nature. They argue that our capacity to act is intimately tied to our ability to tell stories. Building on this idea, philosophers ranging from Aristotle (384–322 BCE) to the contemporary Charles Taylor have argued that living well necessitates crafting overarching narratives about our lives. On a more everyday practical level, narrative allows us to make sense of our lives, gives them coherence, and helps us with emotional resolution. By looking at instances of how Swift illustrates different philosophers' theories of narrative, we can appreciate her storytelling genius even more, and learn how narratives can help us understand ourselves better.

The Old Taylor Is Resurrected

In the music video for "Look What You Made Me Do," we see, at one point, a *reputation*-era Taylor standing atop a mountain of old Taylors— each of them clearly recognizable from their iconic outfits. *reputation* Taylor kicks them away from the top. You might think she is trying to erase her past stories and selves. But, by deliberately portraying the old Taylors, Swift is in fact saying that she acknowledges their existence and is including them in her story. The message is clear: *reputation* Taylor is taking charge of the narrative (at that time), but she also doesn't mind showing her old selves and poking fun at them and their gaffes. She is after all the queen of accepting "cringe."[6] There are many different Taylors, but they are all still one and the same person: Taylor Swift. And she seems to be saying she can live with that.

In fact, what Swift is illustrating is a long-standing philosophical debate about personal identity or selfhood. Selfhood, broadly speaking, is the conscious awareness or idea that you have of yourself as being, well, you. You're not the bed or the chair you're sitting on, you're not a suburban legend or a blank space, you're you. When trying to define what a self is, two opposite viewpoints in philosophy tend to arise: the self as something ever-evolving, ever-changing, and different from moment to moment (otherness), and the self as stable and unchanging (sameness).

Consider it for a moment. On the one hand, your physical body, your understanding of yourself, and your thoughts, emotions, and sensations are constantly changing. As you go through life, no two moments are the same. Honestly, it's more chaotic than getting tickets to the Eras Tour. If we look at a person from this viewpoint, it seems like there's no consistency or predictability. You're constantly shifting to something else, hence the idea of otherness or being "other-than-self."

On the other hand, you know you are the same person. You don't wake up each morning surprised to find that you exist. You know you are the same being that existed yesterday, five years ago, on so on. When you meet up with your friends, they don't introduce themselves to you again. When you do something strange, people say, "wow, that's so out of character." There's something about you that endures, and hence is the same.

What is up with that? It seems like we are walking contradictions: with each passing second, we change and turn into something else, but somehow also remain the same person. Philosopher Paul Ricoeur (1913–2005) embraces this weird contradiction. He describes being human as having an inherent tension within oneself, and says that we shouldn't try to argue away or downplay contradictory aspects of ourselves. To do so would leave us with only part of the picture. To get a full picture of ourselves, and account for these sides, Ricoeur suggests that narrative is particularly helpful.

Narratives seem to echo human identity because stories are also made up of disparate elements (plot twists) while maintaining an overarching consistency (they are part of the same story). This gives us a hint about how we can understand these aspects of ourselves as being together. Ricoeur argues that we have narrative identities. We can think of ourselves as characters in our life stories. When we "emplot" ourselves in this way (put ourself as the character of the story), we are both able to account for how certain character traits have been formed in ourselves (in the past through change), and make sense of ourselves as being the same, as having a certain kind of character by which we and others can recognize us.[7]

Swift is especially adept at walking this tightrope: she keeps both her otherness (changes) and that quintessential "Swiftness" in balance. The outfits change and the eras change, but the red lips persist. We see this dynamic in the video of "Look What You Made Me Do," but it is particularly striking during her rerecording projects.

Nothing New (Taylor's Version)

When an artist reiterates their old work, as in the case of a rerecording, they revive their old selves, and the tension between who they were in the past and the image they have built up of themselves in the meantime is placed in the spotlight. It's a tricky spot to be in because the artist might need to revisit feelings they no longer feel, or reiterate beliefs they no longer hold. Both the artist and their fans might find it a bit awkward, stale, or cringe. But for Swift, this does not seem to pose a problem.

She is a true "plotter": a mastermind who takes random elements or discontinuous events and ties them together in a continuous coherent story. Throughout her career, there have been plenty of times to practice: she has changed genres, gone through eras and phases, and has killed (and resurrected) old Taylors. One could say that by the time the rerecordings rolled around, she was ready for it.

Swift's ability to not only acknowledge her different selves (whether from the past or the present), but also to connect them with that image of her that persists (her sameness), is arguably one of the reasons why she nailed her rerecordings. Even though some of her old songs and selves might have been a bit embarrassing or childish for the current Swift to rerecord and re-embody, she did not try to edit the younger Taylor. Instead, she reproduces almost exact copies of her original songs—with the exception of "Better Than Revenge (Taylor's Version)," but we'll get to that. Swift doesn't feel the need to gloss over the changes or the differences that she has embodied. Instead, she seems to intuitively grasp that, to tell a good story, one has to be comfortable with showing the tension between change and sameness, between plot twists and the whole story. She stands by her story, as she stands by her previous selves at the end of the "Look What You Made Me Do" music video.

Our Song

Besides showing us that stories capture the complexity of being a person, Swift's choice to create near-identical rerecordings of her originals also illustrates that she is well aware of the reciprocal and shared nature of stories. Contemporary philosopher Allen Speight points out that we tend to forget that there is also a passive element in storytelling.[8] When we think of narrative, the emphasis is often on the active narrator, reflecting on themselves and telling *their* story. What we neglect is that narrators also absorb or take in the narratives around them: when telling their stories, they tap into larger narratives. In other words, the narrator is not only a provider or giver of stories, but also someone who takes or receives stories from the social sphere.

This passive or receiving side of narrative points to the fact that in addition to the tension between otherness and sameness within ourselves, we also have to account for other people. Storytelling isn't something that happens in a bubble: the stories we tell are told in collaboration with others, because of others, and for others. We can only arrive at a more comprehensive understanding of ourselves (tell the full story), when we acknowledge how other people help us to sustain our stories and actions.

Taylor seems to be aware of this passive and communal aspect of stories. She is mindful of both herself and her listeners as receivers, and that her story is in fact not just her story: it's ours. She explicitly acknowledges this about her songwriting process: "I go through this process where I feel things, I write a song about that thing, I show it to you and I go, 'Do you like it? Did you ever feel this way too?' And so when you guys are at a show, if you even nod your head or make eye contact with me or sing the words to a song during a show, that to me validates that emotion and makes me feel like I wasn't alone in feeling it."[9] Not only does she tap into other people's stories and retell them, but she also shares her stories and gives them to us, hoping that we too will draw on them and make them our own. This is probably why she refrains from saying who a song is about, so that we can interpret the stories as part of our narratives (although, when she was younger and more of a novice storyteller, she gave more hints).

Because Swift is aware of the shared nature of stories, she avoids the temptation of trying to control the narrative through tactics such as editing, retakes, or censoring. One would, for example, almost have understood it if she had decided not to rerecord "Innocent" (a song that was presumably penned about a certain someone who interrupted her at the VMAs and then subsequently betrayed her and stabbed her in back). But she knows that "Innocent (Taylor's Version)," like all the other songs from her rerecorded albums, is no longer just her story. This song might have helped—and will help—others to work through a similar situation in their lives, and they would miss it if it were gone.

Swift further acknowledges the shared nature of stories when she responds to fans' requests (within reason). She released a longer version of "All Too Well" because the fans wanted it (while also rerecording the shorter original version for those of us who might miss it). Another, somewhat hilarious example (and not part of the scope of her original rerecording project, but too good not to mention), was when fans complained that there wasn't enough Lana Del Rey on the original version of "Snow On The Beach (feat. Lana Del Rey)." Apparently Swift was listening, and a few months later rereleased "Snow On The Beach (feat. More Lana Del Rey)."

Begin Again

Swift's rerecording project also serves as an example of the dynamic nature of narrative and the narrative self. Contemporary philosopher Adriana Cavarero deliberately speaks of the "narratable" self, and not of the "narrated" self.[10] Cavarero argues that to deem a person's story as fully told, and therefore complete, is to diminish their complexity to a mere "what," an object with a fixed essence that we think we can grasp and fully understand. Cavarero emphasizes that the uniqueness of an individual's life is never fully exhausted; it is perpetually open to retellings, embellishments, and new chapters. This perspective aligns seamlessly with Swift's artistic journey, as she breathes new life into her existing body of work, underscoring the perpetual evolution of narrative and self-understanding.

We also see this sensibility when we look at the words Swift used when she first announced that she would also be releasing previously unreleased songs that didn't make the final cut on the original albums, in addition to the rerecorded tracks: "I want you to have the whole story, see the entire vivid picture ..."[11] These previously unheard tracks, "from the vault," provide us with new perspectives or more information about what originally happened in that Era (in that part of Taylor's story and narrative). They are like messages in a bottle, coming to us from a different time, and once we open them, we learn a little bit more about the original moment in which they were penned.

By adding these previously unreleased songs to her body of work, Swift not only expands the existing narrative but also reframes the existing tracks (stories) on each album. When we listen to "Castles Crumbling (Taylor's Version) (From The Vault)" on *Speak Now (Taylor's Version)*, we learn, for example, that the younger Swift wasn't only contending with growing up and navigating the pitfalls of love (with the exception of "Long Live (Taylor's Version)"), but she was also scared of disappointing fans and having her fame implode.

When we listen to "I Bet You Think About Me (Taylor's Version) (From The Vault)," we learn even more about the snooty ways of the person that Taylor possibly refers to in "We Are Never Ever Getting Back Together (Taylor's Version)." And the addition of "I Can See You (Taylor's Version) (From The Vault)" changes not only how we interpret the *Speak Now* album and how we perceive the *Speak Now* Swift, but also affects how we interpret her work as a whole. Originally, we didn't see this side of her until much later. But now, the timeline has changed, and we know that this side of Taylor existed in conjunction with her more chaste princess-like self. It also alerts us to the fact that she perhaps wasn't quite ready to share that side of her story, perhaps fearing how it would change how we saw her at the time.

The songs that Swift adds through her rerecording project show us that she is well aware of the open-ended nature of stories and the rich complexity of a person's life. When she tells a story, she doesn't close the door on it. We see her revisit narratives and narrative themes: going back and sometimes completely changing the narrative. She shows us that we can change our perspective or provide more explanations of what happened through the stories we tell and that there is always more to say. We can always begin again.

Better Than Revenge

Earlier, I wrote that Swift sticks to her story, so what does it mean when we discover changes in her rerecordings? We first have to distinguish between accidental changes and deliberate changes. Some accidental changes can be attributed to the inevitable: for example, her voice has matured, and the music production of each track is hard to imitate perfectly. But accidental changes also include those subtle changes that perhaps only avid listeners of the original recordings would pick up on:[12] things as seemingly insignificant as the missing breath in "Last Kiss (Taylor's Version)."[13] Originally, when she sang the lines "And I hope the sun shines and it's a beautiful day / And something reminds you, you wish you had stayed," she took a shaky inhale, almost sounding like she was holding back a sob. In the rerecorded version, the sharp inhale is gone.

This accidental change reveals that narrative isn't just a cognitive exercise. Contemporary philosopher J. David Velleman argues that narratives are often felt, rather than rationally or consciously thought through.[14] To understand ourselves and the narrative, we cannot leave out the role of emotions. When Swift set out to rerecord this song, she probably didn't mean to change a thing. But the older and wiser Swift cannot help but *feel* the story differently, and this changed how she delivered this song.

Deliberate changes to Swift's rerecordings are another story. For months leading up to the release of *Speak Now (Taylor's Version)*, there were heated arguments over "Better Than Revenge" and whether she should leave out the controversial lyric, "But she's better known for the things that she does / On the mattress." One side of the debate said that it would be disingenuous of her to rewrite history and that she should trust her listeners to take into consideration that the track came from a different time. The other side said that the lyrics needed to be retired and that it couldn't be reiterated, because Swift knew better.

When the rerecorded album finally came out, she had ultimately chosen to replace these lyrics with the more innocuous, "He was a moth to the flame / She was holding the matches." This time, during the retelling of this story, Swift deliberately and consciously chose not to reiterate her past words (while probably also *feeling* that it was wrong). This does not erase the fact that a more controversial version of the song still exists, nor is Swift trying to erase her past or what she said. Instead, her unwillingness to repeat these words shows growth or narrative progression: she knows better now.

The Story of Us (Your Version)

Telling and retelling stories isn't just something we happen to do. Interpreting and reinterpreting the world around us—or, put differently, telling and retelling stories—is the way in which we understand ourselves. Ricoeur writes that, for a person to carry out their actions and interact with others, they need to make sense of the world around them. Stories are guides to help us become more of ourselves, since understanding, or making sense of something, is to understand our relation to that thing, and hence to better understand ourselves.[15] Interpretation is self-interpretation. For example, when I interpret cats as cute and intelligent, I come to understand myself as someone who likes cats. In other words, the story I tell about cats tells me something about myself. On a more complex level, if you try to analyze why you like listening to Taylor Swift, this not only tells us something about Taylor, but also about you, and reveals a part of what you are like and who you are.

Most of us who listen to Swift are already aware of this principle (of coming to understand oneself through understanding something else, or someone else). As one journalist describes their experience of the Eras Tour: "It's a journey through her past, starring all the different Taylors she's ever been, which means all the Taylors that *you've* ever been."[16] When she shares her story through her music, we take a journey through her story, and come out on the other side, still ourselves, but somehow changed, our own narratives and self-understanding expanded. When listening to her music, we might exclaim "She describes exactly how I feel!," acknowledging that when we interpret her music, we interpret ourselves too.

While we can come to understand ourselves through others' stories, we also shape our understanding of ourselves through the stories we tell about ourselves. Philosopher Charles Taylor (who should be every Swiftie's favorite philosopher for the very logical reason that he shares a name with her) refers to humans as self-interpreting animals.[17] The self, or who you are, is not some static thing, but a continuous storytelling action. Stories are a way of *doing* things, and not just a way of *representing* the world.[18] In other words, stories are not things that are completely independent of us once we tell them: we interact with them and they change us, even as we author them.

Swift's example of nuanced and continuous storytelling not only offers an explanation of why we find her rerecordings compelling, but also serves as a kind of instruction or guide on how we can use narrative to make sense of ourselves and our actions, and even help us to orient our future actions. As Ricoeur writes, awareness of our narrative identity allows us to link ourselves more clearly as agents with our own actions and aims, thus resulting in the fact that we are "better readers and authors of our own lives."[19] Swift's storytelling and re-storytelling through the rerecordings is a practical demonstration of this principle. Taylor illustrates how embracing our narrative can lead to a profound self-understanding and open up avenues of action.

Notes

1. Rebecca Schiller, "Taylor Swift Accepts Woman of the Decade Award at *Billboard*'s Women in Music: Read Her Full Speech," *Billboard*, December 13, 2019, at https://www.billboard.com/music/awards/taylor-swift-woman-of-the-decade-speech-billboard-women-in-music-8546156.

2. See, for example, Michael Hann, "Taylor Swift's Great Re-Recording Plot: Icy Revenge or a Pointless Setback?," *The Guardian*, August 22, 2019, at https://www.theguardian.com/music/2019/aug/22/taylor-swift-six-albums-scooter-braun; Bill Werde, "What's the End Game? Why Taylor Swift's Plan to Re-Record Her Old Albums Is So Perplexing (Guest Column)," *Billboard*, August 26, 2019, at https://www.billboard.com/music/music-news/whats-the-end-game-why-taylor-swift-plan-re-record-old-albums-perplexing-8528342.

3. Miranda Siwak, "Taylor Swift Confesses 'Nobody Knew If Rerecorded Albums Would Be 'a Success' amid Maren Morris Duet," *US Weekly*, June 2, 2023, at https://www.usmagazine.com/entertainment/news/taylor-swift-unsure-if-rereleases-would-succeed-amid-maren-duet.

4. Jason Hughes, "Taylor Swift Realizes She Tries Too Hard after Her 'Static' Single Hits Number One in Canada (Video)," The Wrap, October 24, 2014, at https://www.thewrap.com/taylor-swift-realizes-she-tries-too-hard-after-her-static-single-hits-number-one-in-canada-video.

5. Taylor Swift, "For years I asked, pleaded for a chance ..." Tumblr, June 30, 2019, archived from the original on Internet Archive, at https://web.archive.org/web/20210212230900/https://taylorswift.tumblr.com/post/185958366550/for-years-i-asked-pleaded-for-a-chance-to-own-my.

6. Hannah Dailey, "Taylor Swift's NYU Commencement Speech: Read the Full Transcript," *Billboard*, May 18, 2022, at https://www.billboard.com/music/music-news/taylor-swift-nyu-commencement-speech-full-transcript-1235072824.

7. Paul Ricoeur, *Oneself as Another*, trans. Kathleen Blamey (Chicago and London: University of Chicago Press, 1992), 118–119, 124, 140–141.

8. Allen Speight, "The Narrative Shape of Agency: Three Contemporary Philosophical Perspectives," in Allen Speight ed., *Narrative, Philosophy and Life* (Dordrecht: Springer, 2015), 49–60.

9. Chris Willman, "Taylor Swift Brings Her Epic Empath Energy to SoFi Stadium for a Grand Six-Night Stand: Concert Review," *Variety*, August 4, 2023, at https://variety.com/2023/music/concert-reviews/taylor-swift-sofi-stadium-concert-review-tour-haim-1235688111.

10. Adriana Cavarero, *Relating Narratives: Storytelling and Selfhood*, trans. Paul A. Kottman (London: Routledge, 2000).

11. Taylor Swift, "I'm thrilled to tell you that my new version of Fearless (Taylor's Version) is done and will be with you soon ..." X [Twitter], February 11, 2021, at https://twitter.com/taylorswift13/status/1359854050544615425/photo/2.

12. Katie Goh, "'I Made My Peace': Fans Divided over Taylor Swift's Re-Recording Project," *The Guardian*, April 15, 2021, at https://www.theguardian.com/music/2021/apr/15/i-made-my-peace-fans-divided-over-taylor-swifts-re-recording-project.

13. Dylan Kickham, "Swifties Are Mourning 1 Major Change Taylor Made to Her Version of 'Last Kiss,'" Elite Daily, July 8, 2023, at https://www.elitedaily.com/entertainment/taylor-swift-shaky-breath-removed-last-kiss-memes.

14. J. David Velleman, "Narrative Explanation," *The Philosophical Review* 112 (2003), 1–25.

15. Ricoeur, *Oneself as Another*, 18.

16. Rob Sheffield, "'This Is Extraordinary': Why the Eras Tour Is Taylor Swift's Greatest Live Triumph Yet," *Rolling Stone*, May 29, 2023, at https://www.rollingstone.com/music/music-features/taylor-swift-eras-tour-1234743135.

17. Charles Taylor, *Human Agency and Language: Philosophical Papers 1* (Cambridge: Cambridge University Press, 1985), 45–76.

18. Giuseppe Zaccaria, "Trends in Contemporary Hermeneutics and Analytical Philosophy," *Ratio Juris* 12 (1999), 274.

19. Ricoeur, *Oneself as Another*, 159.

"WITH MY CALAMITOUS LOVE AND INSURMOUNTABLE GRIEF"

15

Taylor Swift on the Values and Vulnerability of Love

Macy Salzberger

Stripped down with delicate vocals, piano accompaniment, and the occasional string instrument, "hoax" by Taylor Swift feels painfully intimate. The ballad recounts the heartbreak of a relationship with someone who knows you too well to not have your best interests at heart. With a melancholic yet somehow hopeful whisper, Swift sings: "Stood on the cliffside / Screaming, 'Give me a reason' / Your faithless love's the only hoax / I believe in / Don't want no other shade of blue / But you / No other sadness in the world would do." On first listen, Swift seems to be asking her unfaithful lover to give her a reason for the infidelity, a reason she could accept to stay in the relationship. On second listen, a more devastating interpretation suggests itself: Swift is standing on the cliffside, asking for a reason not to jump, a reason to go on.

What makes love so valuable that we are desperate for reasons to hold on to it even when the love in question is toxic? Or are we simply so overtaken by love that we cling to love even when it isn't valuable? With songs like "Picture to Burn," "Mr. Perfectly Fine (Taylor's Version)," and "Dear John (Taylor's Version)," Swift's early work earned her a reputation of using her songwriting to put exes in their place, rather than reflecting on philosophically interesting questions like the role of love in living a good life.[1] Lyrics like "So watch me strike a match on all my wasted time / As far as I'm concerned, you're just another picture to burn," from "Picture to Burn," capture the teenage angst of early heartbreaks that seems all too appropriate for an artist launching her career at age thirteen. We might, then, read "hoax" as yet another portrait of angst rather than a reflection on love and its role in our lives.

Swift's early reputation may have been for diaristic responses to breakups. But in this chapter, I want to explore how Swift's work philosophically answers the question of why love plays such a central role in living a good life, and why the value of love makes it so difficult to leave even toxic relationships. Beginning with her debut album, Swift seems to identify three different reasons why love is so valuable in our lives. First, love has the power to bring us out of ourselves by heightening our sensitivity to

Taylor Swift and Philosophy: Essays from the Tortured Philosophers Department, First Edition. Edited by Catherine M. Robb and Georgie Mills.
© 2025 John Wiley & Sons, Inc. Published 2025 by John Wiley & Sons, Inc.

the values and interests of our beloved, a distinctively *moral* role that love plays in our lives. Second, love brings us out of conditions of alienation, a role that love is uniquely well-positioned to play in our lives. Third and finally, we find partners in making sense of ourselves and the world in our loving relationships. Our loved ones help us to make sense of what we value in ourselves and in life.

Although a younger Swift might respond to the unfaithful lover in "hoax" by seeing them as "just another picture to burn," the appreciation for what makes love valuable that we find later in Swift's oeuvre can help us understand what reasons there are for continuing a relationship even when it is harmful (and even if those reasons are ultimately defeated by other considerations). When our loved ones harm us, we can still find ourselves valuing their particularities and invested in their well-being. Moreover, the important role our loved ones play in helping us make sense of ourselves and our world can persist even when the relationship itself is tumultuous. What "hoax" helps us to understand, then, is the real conflict we face when we must choose between losing our footing in the world by losing a lover, and leaving ourselves vulnerable to harm by holding on to a relationship with someone who is careless with our well-being. Whatever choice we make, we lose something that we have good reason to value.

"For You, I Would Ruin Myself": Love and Selflessness

In the chorus of "I'm Only Me When I'm With You," Swift describes not simply the butterflies, excitement, and infatuation of a teenage crush, but rather a profound investment in her lover. Swift writes, "I'm only up when you're not down / Don't wanna fly if you're still on the ground." As she describes, her own well-being is intimately connected to the well-being of her beloved. If her loved one is down, so is she. Moreover, her *interest* in her own well-being is dependent on how her beloved fares. She does not *want* to do well—to fly—when her lover fares poorly.

In "New Year's Day," we find another story of Swift's investment in the well-being of her loved ones through the highs and lows of life. In recounting the memories of a past New Year's Day, Swift writes, "I'll be there if you're the toast of the town, babe / Or if you strike out and you're crawling home." Similarly, in "seven," Swift describes a childhood friend whose struggles at home she could not fully process as a child, but who she nevertheless imagined running away with to facilitate escape from the friend's "haunted house." Even as time passes, even as she forgets the look of her friend's face, Swift recalls her desire to provide solace and reflects on the persistence of her investment in her friend's well-being through time, distance, and the obscurity of childhood memory.

Philosopher Harry Frankfurt (1929–2023) described this investment in the interests of one's loved ones as a kind of "selfless" devotion to the other.[2] One way we might care about the interests of our beloved is through a concern for how their satisfaction indirectly affects our own well-being. When our loved ones suffer, we can suffer in virtue of their unpleasant companionship. When our loved ones succeed, we can be uplifted by their celebrations. But in love, what we care about is how our loved one fares "for their own sake." We care about their interests and work to promote their interests not because of how we will indirectly benefit, but rather because we are invested in our loved one faring well. When our loved one succeeds, then, we celebrate their successes regardless of how their success affects how our lover behaves toward us or regards the relationship. Likewise, when our loved one suffers, we suffer not through some sort of emotional contagion whereby we become infected by their bad mood, but rather because we care that our loved one is free from suffering.

In our adoption of the interests of our beloved we not only take on the interests of our loved ones as our own, we also become motivated to subordinate our own, separate interests to promote the interests of our beloved. In "illicit affairs," for example, Swift writes, "For you, I would ruin myself." Swift's "peace" also tells a story of a lover who would do anything for their beloved, who would "die for you in secret," even amid worries that the relationship could never survive. The investment in the other person that Swift describes is not dependent on Swift's benefit or even the benefit of the relationship, the investment in the lover is simply for the lover's own sake.

So, what makes this not just a characteristic feature of love, but also a characteristic feature that is particularly *valuable* in our lives? Why shouldn't we simply understand this "selfless devotion" as an obsessive, and perhaps self-destructive, infatuation? Contemporary philosopher J. David Velleman argues that love should be understood as a *moral* emotion, an emotion that improves our moral character.[3] Rather than viewing others with an eye toward how they promote or inhibit our own needs, love involves an appreciation for the value of others, and so heightens our sensitivity to their needs. Philosopher Iris Murdoch (1919–1999) motivates this understanding of the relationship between love and morality, calling this morally valuable attunement to the interests of others "loving attention." Loving attention transforms what might be a morally deficient orientation toward others, where we view others through the distorting lens of self-interest, and turns it into something morally valuable, making us better people.

We find expressions of Murdoch's loving attention throughout Swift's catalogue. In "Ours (Taylor's Version)," for example, Swift sees the beauty others overlook through her loving attention to the beloved. As Swift describes, "people throw rocks at things that shine." We emotionally protect ourselves from others, refusing to let ourselves be affected by them and refusing to see what is so affecting about them. When we see what is valuable in others, we might, after all, find something that we cannot find in ourselves. But Swift embraces the vulnerability of looking at another with a view to what makes them shine. As another example, Swift writes of the gap between her lover's teeth, and ignoring her father's criticisms of her lover's tattoos. What might otherwise be perceived as threatening, imperfect, or as flaws when viewed through the distorting lens of self-interest, Swift sees as reflections of what makes her lover valuable because of her loving attention. As a consequence, Swift is better positioned to recognize what is valuable in the world beyond what serves her own self-interest.

"I'm Only Me When I'm With You"

So far, we have seen how Swift's lyrics express a number of related philosophical views about the nature of love: as selfless, as a moral emotion, and as loving attention. Following on from philosophical discussion of love as a kind of moral attention, the contemporary philosopher Vida Yao discusses how the attentiveness of love enables our escape from what she calls "the problem of alienation."[4] As Yao describes, love ideally fosters connection and communion, rather than estrangement between lovers. But when we attend to others, or others attend to us, we may recoil. When we are seen for who we are, we may worry that our beloved will not love us for who we are. They might, for example, not find the gaps between our teeth so endearing. As a consequence, we may withdraw to conceal what we find to be shameful about ourselves. In seeing others for who they are, we might also find that we wish to see less of them. We may wish we never learned of their callousness or their impatience. The attentiveness that makes for ideal love, then, can make us withdraw from others, obstructing opportunities for communion and connection, leaving us alienated or estranged from the other.

In embracing attentive love, as described by Yao, we become vulnerable by exposing those parts of ourselves that we are ordinarily too ashamed to reveal. All of our imperfections are on full display for the lover's attention. But when we are graced by attentive love, an attentiveness that is paired with love for *all that we are*, we can let our guard down and let another in. This vulnerability enables us to escape the problem of alienation and find connection, communion, and intimacy. We can be with another as we really are, without reservation.

As its title suggests, "I'm Only Me When I'm With You" speaks to this important role of love in our lives: it is through love that we can feel secure in being seen for exactly who we are. Swift writes, "And I know everything about you / I don't wanna live without you ... And I don't want to hide my tears / My secrets or my deepest fears / Through it all, nobody gets me like you do ... / When I'm with anybody else / It's so hard to be myself / And only you can tell." Through these lyrics, Swift describes how, in loving, she escapes the condition of alienation and estrangement she finds elsewhere in the world, where she is not seen or loved for all that she is. And she offers this love in return when she sees her lover for all that they are, and still wouldn't want a world without them.

We can see this role of love emphasized throughout Swift's catalogue. In "Enchanted (Taylor's Version)," for example, Swift describes forcing laughter and sitting in the same old tired, lonely place, only for that loneliness and insincerity to vanish when her loved one graced the scene. In "Dress," Swift describes how her lover sees the best of her, the truth in her, even in her worst times, her worst lies. In "Sweet Nothing," Swift describes how, in the world of celebrity where more is always demanded of her, she can find in her lover a safe place to confess that she is "just too soft for all of it." In all of these works, Swift describes being seen and loved for all that she is, the good and the bad, without pretension. We can understand from Swift, then, the important role that love plays in our lives in facilitating our escape from profound loneliness, just as Yao has argued. We live in a world where we are so often seen only for how our strengths and weaknesses benefit another. In love, however, we can be seen, loved, and valued for all that we are, just because of who we are.

Secret Languages and Sense-Making

In discussing Swift on the value of love, we have seen how love can help us overcome self-interest and escape alienation. Yet another reason love is so valuable in our lives is that in our loving relationships, we find partners who help us make sense of ourselves and the world we share. Swift helps us to understand this valuable feature of love by reflecting on the absence of a partner in sense-making. Throughout her work, she reflects on the loss of modes of self-understanding and expression when she loses a lover. In "illicit affairs," for example, Swift writes, "You showed me colors / You know I can't see with anyone else ... You taught me a secret language / I can't speak with anyone else." And in "Question ...?" Swift writes, "We had one thing goin' on / I swear that it was somethin' / 'Cause I don't remember who I was before you / Painted all my nights / A color I've searched for since." The languages we speak and the colors through which we see the world affect how we can make sense of the world. When we translate a sentence from one language to another, our concepts do not always translate, affecting what we can communicate with our words. And when we paint with different palettes, we have to reimagine what it is that we are painting. What languages and colors we have available are then profoundly important for what we can communicate and create. When losing a lover means losing a language or losing a color, how we can make sense of ourselves and the world can fundamentally change.

Contemporary philosopher Benjamin Bagley describes this role our lovers play in helping us make sense of ourselves and the world as a kind of "mutual improvisation." Bagley compares the way lovers collaboratively make sense of themselves and the world to the way musicians make sense of a musical idea through improvisation. As Bagley describes, musical partners work together to communicate a musical idea that is not yet fully articulated. What that musical idea is, or could be, is dependent on the contributions of the particular musical partners. The goals that lovers share go beyond the goal of communicating a musical idea. For lovers, the goals they share and work out together "constitute fundamental values with which they identify."[5] They are our ultimate goals and ambitions in life, such as the professional accolades we care to pursue, or what kind of person we want to become. For example, we may be in the process of working out if we want to be the sort of person who uses their art and social capital to inspire political change, and so we may look to our partner to help us make sense of our aspirations and how they fit in with what else we value in life. Identifying and articulating those values becomes a joint activity, rather than an isolated personal project.

Because we are in the process of working out an idea *together* with our partner in sense-making, we cannot make sense of the world in the same way without that same person. Once again, we can see this in Swift's discussion of what languages and colors we lose when we lose a lover. We cannot paint the same work of art or communicate the same concept without the shared resources found in the relationship. We can also understand the importance of our partners in sense-making when we look to Swift's own musical partnerships. Swift could not create the same musical idea she creates through collaboration with Jack Antonoff when she partners with Aaron Dessner, and vice versa—we could not have "cardigan" without both Swift and Dessner, and we could not have "mirrorball" without both Swift and Antonoff. The music they collaboratively produce is dependent on how they work out the particular musical idea they envision *together*. What we value in both our musical and loving partnerships, then, is the *particular way* in which our partners help us make sense of our ideas, ourselves, and the world. Our understandings of ourselves and the world are fundamentally informed by that collaborative vision to the point where, as Swift writes, we lose sense for who we were before the collaboration.

When No Other Shade of Blue Will Do

As illustrated in Swift's work, love can be understood as valuable for at least three reasons. First, love is morally valuable. Love takes us outside of our self-interest through our attention and investment in the value of another. Second, love helps us escape the problem of alienation and brings us connection, communion, and intimacy. Third and finally, we find in our loving relationships partners in making sense of ourselves and the world.

But while love brings a variety of values to our lives, we also become fundamentally vulnerable to our loved ones in loving. Our own well-being and interests become inextricably linked with and shaped by the well-being and interests of the beloved. Our points of reference for making sense of ourselves and our world become dependent on our relationship to our loved one. This brings us back to "hoax." When a loving relationship no longer serves us, the values the love makes possible render us fundamentally vulnerable to harm by our loved ones.

In "hoax," Swift speaks to the intimate knowledge possessed and exploited by her lover. She writes, "You know I left part of me back in New York ... You knew it still hurts underneath my scars ... You knew the password, so I let you in my door." What facilitates our communion and wards off alienation—sharing intimate details with another, like the sharing of a password—is precisely what makes us vulnerable to harm by another. Because our loved ones know us intimately, they can hurt us more deeply than anyone else.

The heartbreak of violated trust haunts Swift's lyrics, such as her second verse in "The Great War," where she sings, "I drew curtains closed, drank my poison all alone / You said I have to trust more freely." Swift describes here the foreclosure of vulnerability to protect oneself from future violation. And we find this again in "hoax," where Swift describes the violation of her trust as having frozen her ground. In making ourselves vulnerable through love, violations of that vulnerability can haunt us by compromising capacity for loving in the future. As a consequence, the violation can compromise our capacities for pursuing the variety of values that are distinctively realizable through love.

One reason why love makes us fundamentally vulnerable to harm is that the vulnerability we offer through love can be exploited. However, love can also make us fundamentally vulnerable to harm even when our vulnerability is honored by our loved ones. When we lose that particular other, we lose one source of sense-making. We cannot co-create our ends with the other, we cannot draw on their particularities to make sense of the world (just as what music Swift can create is dependent on her particular collaborative partners). In losing the particular other, we also lose a means of escaping alienation and someone in whom we have invested ourselves. We lose someone who we can share our whole selves with and for whom we would, as Swift puts it, ruin ourselves.

Reflecting on the values realizable through love, we can better understand why it can be so difficult to leave a loving relationship, even when that loving relationship is ultimately at odds with our own well-being. The souring of a relationship does not always or even often void our valuing of the other or their role in our lives. The lover is still the person we see as valuable for all that they are and as the particular person with whom we can make sense of ourselves and the world. As Swift writes, "Don't want no other shade of blue / But you / No other sadness in the world would do."

Even when the relationship is not salvageable, it is still the only context in which one can speak in the secret language or see the world with the unique colors of the lover. Of course, we may be able to create *new* languages and see *new* colors, but what is lost by leaving the relationship behind—the *particular* language or the *particular* shade—is itself irreplaceable.

In reflecting on the values realizable through love and the vulnerabilities we face in realizing those values, we can also understand what makes "hoax" so haunting, yet hopeful. "Hoax" is not a story of an angsty teenager dramatizing the heartbreak of their first experience with infidelity. And "hoax" is not a story of someone whose rational faculties are so clouded by infatuation that they overlook the faults of their lover. Instead, "hoax" tells a story of someone who has embraced what makes love valuable and, as a consequence, faces the harms we are made vulnerable to in loving. However, the harms do not erase what made, or still makes, that love so valuable in our lives or the value we find in the flawed people we love.[6]

Notes

1. This is a reputation that Swift explicitly rejects when she is asked about it in interviews, although lyrics from "invisible string" might contribute to this reputation: "Cold was the steel of my axe to grind / For the boys who broke my heart."
2. Harry Frankfurt, "Autonomy, Necessity, and Love," in *Necessity, Volition, and Love* (Cambridge: Cambridge University Press, 1998), 135.
3. J. David Velleman, "Love as a Moral Emotion," *Ethics* 109 (1999), 351.
4. Vidao Yao, "Grace and Alienation," *Philosophers' Imprint* 20, no. 6 (2020), 1–18.
5. Benjamin Bagley, "Loving Someone in Particular," *Ethics* 125 (2015), 502.
6. Many thanks to Catherine Robb and Georgina Mills for their helpful guidance and comments on an earlier draft. Thanks to my Spring '23 PHIL 890 students for indulging my Taylor Swift digressions, and thanks to Elle Townsend for inspiring my appreciation for *folklore*.

16

"Every Scrap of You Would Be Taken from Me"
Taylor Swift on Grief

Jonathan Birch

Taylor Swift's songwriting is notable for its direct, clear, and powerful expressions of grief.[1] "marjorie," "Bigger Than the Whole Sky," and "epiphany" are especially striking in this regard. In fact, the lyrics of these songs can be connected to contemporary philosophical discussions of grief in ways that not only heighten appreciation of the songs but also deepen our understanding of grief, a notoriously complex emotional state.

Grief and Memory

In "marjorie," Swift reflects on what, if anything, of our loved ones survives death. The song is about Swift's maternal grandmother, Marjorie Finlay, a singer who often performed in opera and with symphony orchestras. Details of Marjorie's life are scarce. Her Wikipedia page relies heavily on a few newspaper clippings that briefly mention a childhood in St. Charles, Missouri, followed by marriage, then moving with her husband's career to Havana, Caracas, and Puerto Rico, where she had her own TV show for a time.[2] These cannot have been ideal conditions to pursue stardom. Those frequent moves cannot have left much time to forge a career in any single place, and they took Marjorie far away from the major centers of gravity in the music industry. Swift alludes in the song to Marjorie's "closets of backlogged dreams."

Marjorie died in 2003. What remains of Marjorie after her death? A disordered set of memories. In the verses, Swift relates some pieces of advice inherited from her grandmother. When she calls the advice to mind, she thinks "If I didn't know better / I'd think you were talking to me now … / What died didn't stay dead / You're alive, so alive." Some other fragments rise to the surface in the song's bridge, which describes "Long limbs and frozen swims / You'd always go past where our feet could touch."

Taylor Swift and Philosophy: Essays from the Tortured Philosophers Department, First Edition. Edited by Catherine M. Robb and Georgie Mills.

Part of what makes the song so poignant is that these scattered and partial memories are tinged with regret. Swift was not as close to her grandmother as she now wishes she had been. The memories don't form a complete or coherent picture. A little selfishly, she wishes Marjorie had imparted more advice on how to live. But there is more to it than that: Swift also longs for physical contact, material continuity, hard evidence that Marjorie existed. The line where Swift laments that she "should've kept every grocery store receipt" hits particularly hard.

The song ends on an ambiguous note, by first suggesting, "If I didn't know better," but then taking it back and beginning again, to say: "I know better / But I still feel you all around / I know better / But you're still around." Swift acknowledges that the idea of a person literally surviving by means of a patchwork of memories and snippets of advice is fanciful. It *feels as though* they are still there, that's all. But she also reminds us that, through curating these personal memories, she is securing a legacy for her grandmother, granting her an enduring place in our shared cultural memory.

Swift's lyrics fit well with ideas put forward by Michael Cholbi in his excellent book, *Grief: A Philosophical Guide*.[3] Cholbi's powerful insight is that grieving is a process that *transforms*, but does not end, our relationship with the deceased. When someone dies, our relationship with them is not simply terminated: just as we continue to be related to people who are separated from us in space, we continue to be related to people who are separated from us in time. The past is real and we are related to it, but the nature of the relationship changes fundamentally. This process of transformation is exactly what "marjorie" describes.

Memory and Transformation

What is the nature of this transformation? When we grieve a person's death, it is because we had a significant relationship to that person: a relationship that mattered. That relationship can take many forms, and it need not be a close family relationship or friendship (for example, relationships of rivalry, collegiality, or fandom can also lead to grief). But the depth of our grief is related, Cholbi suggests, to how central the deceased person was to our *practical identity*: our sense of who we are, as it arises in the context of making decisions and choices.

Your practical identity has many aspects: you may think of yourself as a pop star, singer-songwriter, film director, daughter, granddaughter, and more. None of these would apply to me, but I have my own list: lecturer, scholar, policy advisor, mentor, father, husband, brother, son, and so on. We can all think of a list like this. When I make decisions, I try to be true to these aspects of myself and the expectations and commitments they bring, and which aspects matter most will depend on the context. Any aspect of my practical identity can be rocked by the loss of the people who help me sustain that aspect. In 2007, I grieved the loss of my first academic supervisor, Peter Lipton, even though I never really knew him as a friend—and I think that was because my initial identity as a scholar of philosophy was built around my relationship to him. Grief can strike us gently or severely, depending on how much a person mattered to our identity, and why. Grief hits us hardest of all when a central plank of our practical identity falls away. We lose our sense of who we are and how to live. This is often, but not always, associated with losing a relative or friend.

The process of grieving is one of trying to *rebuild* that practical identity as best we can. This helps explain why grief takes as long as it does, and why the process is so variable from one person to the next. Some rebuild fast, whereas for others the experience is long and slow, often characterized by ups and downs as early attempts unravel. Sadly, some people succumb to grief, never succeeding in rebuilding a practical identity.

When we think about grief in this way, it becomes clear that "marjorie" describes a late stage in the process of grief. We might even call it a "post-grief" song, because it captures Swift's relationship to Marjorie many years *after* the process of transformation triggered by her death. And the song aptly illustrates Cholbi's point: it is not that Swift no longer has any significant relationship to Marjorie, and it is not as though Marjorie has dropped out completely from Swift's practical identity. Rather, the nature of the relationship is transformed. Marjorie continues to be a source of advice, though the advice now comes in the form of remembered maxims, not actual conversations. Swift cannot turn to Marjorie with new problems, but can take the advice she offered at a general level ("Never be so polite you forget your power …") and apply it to her current situation.

Marjorie also features in the way Swift conceptualizes her plans and goals. Indeed, securing a legacy for Marjorie now features among those goals—a common way in which those we have lost continue to shape our choices, though certainly not the only way. By performing the song on the Eras Tour (even though it is not, musically, a natural choice for a stadium tour), Swift has left fans in no doubt as to Marjorie's continuing relevance to her life.[4] Moreover, Swift's goals include fulfilling the "backlogged dreams" (presumably, of stardom) that went unfulfilled in Marjorie's case, and that Swift sees herself as having inherited.

We see in this song the result of a *successful* grief process, and we can learn something from this about the value of grief. People often reflect that, although grief is one of the worst forms of suffering in the moment, they would not take an "anti-grief pill" that completely destroyed it.[5] It feels like something important, something valuable. Cholbi proposes that the value consists in the *self-knowledge*—the knowledge of who we are— that grief brings. Through grieving, we can learn about the significance of our relationship to the deceased. We can learn *why* they mattered to us— and (often) why they mattered so much more than we thought they did.

We learn about how our practical identity is structured, who it depends upon, and why. This knowledge helps us to live better from there on. "marjorie" exemplifies this achievement, demonstrating how Swift has recognized and preserved the significance of Marjorie to her practical identity. If Swift had taken an "anti-grief pill" in 2003, she might never have achieved the self-knowledge about Marjorie's significance to her own life and identity that the song beautifully crystallizes.

There are several points of convergence, then, between Swift's songwriting and Cholbi's philosophy of grief. Both highlight our continuing but transformed relationship to those we have lost, grief as a process of reconstruction, and the value of grief in promoting self-knowledge. Is it more than just convergence—does Swift add something new? I think something important is added by the mode of expression. Critics of Cholbi have argued there is something problematically self-centered about this way of thinking about grief—a way that brings it back to *you* and *your* practical identity. Should grief not center on the person you have lost?[6] One reply is that when we successfully grieve we center on the person we have lost by reconstructing our practical identity in a way that preserves their significance to us. But merely saying this will not persuade a critic that it can really happen. Swift's song *shows* it.

Grief and Myth

Let's turn to another song, "Bigger Than the Whole Sky." This one is harder to listen to, because it concerns unresolved grief. In it Swift sings "You were bigger than the whole sky / You were more than just a short time / And I've got a lot to pine about / I've got a lot to live without / I'm never gonna meet / What could've been, would've been / What should've been you." The song seems to express grief about the loss of a person Swift has never met and who may never even have fully existed. Many fans have interpreted the song as a crushing and unflinching description of the aftermath of a miscarriage—and have drawn comfort and solace from it.[7] On this interpretation, the song is especially courageous, and is helping to break the pernicious and pervasive culture of silence around this issue.[8]

Swift has not said anything to favor this or any other interpretation, though, and of course people may find the song just as applicable to other kinds of loss. There is no need to speculate on whether the lyrics refer to a real or imagined event. It's enough to say that this is not a "post-grief" song in the way that "marjorie" might be: it describes a much earlier stage, a raw reaction very close in time to a loss. The chorus is mild in comparison with the verses, which contain imagery that is frankly gut-wrenching: "Every single thing I touch becomes sick with sadness / 'Cause it's all over now, all out to sea ... / Did some bird flap its wings over in Asia? / Did some force take you because I didn't pray? / Every single thing to come has turned into ashes."

The second verse ends, surprisingly, with what sounds like a self-admonition: "So I'll say words I don't believe." In context, these words appear to be the words of the song's chorus. The version of Swift singing in the verses is seemingly admonishing the version of her singing in the chorus, a chorus which seems to entertain the supernatural, drawing consolation from the idea that there might have been far more significance and duration to the life of the deceased than there seemed to be.

The wordplay around appearance and reality, central to "marjorie," is repeated here in "Bigger Than the Whole Sky," but in a darker hue. In both songs, a narrator who wants to believe in miraculous life beyond death vies for supremacy with a narrator who "knows better." This time, the skeptical narrator seems to land a decisive blow in the second verse, stating that it's "all over." But the song rolls on for another minute, initially creating hope of a third verse or bridge that might offer some counterpoint. But this does not happen, and catharsis is withheld in favor of simply repeating the "words I don't believe" (the words of the chorus) over and over again.

Should Swift really criticize herself for saying "words I don't believe," or believing things that are false? Let's return to the idea of grief as a process of reconstruction. Your practical identity has been shattered, and you are trying to heal it. False beliefs about the deceased can sometimes be a valuable part of this process. We might tell ourselves we left things on a better note than we really did, or that a person's death involved less suffering than it really did. Healthy grieving need not take the form of a brutal confrontation with the unvarnished truth. Indeed, while there's no evidence of this in Swift's case, grieving people often report experiencing full-blown delusions and hallucinations: while Marjorie's voice in Swift's head is clearly a memory, for some grievers, the voice of the deceased appears very vividly, and they genuinely struggle to distinguish appearance from reality.[9]

This part of the grieving process is often stigmatized and pathologized. But the contemporary philosopher Lisa Bortolotti and her collaborators have long argued for the value of delusions in some circumstances. They propose that delusions can sustain the sense of "meaning and purpose" in the life of the griever. You might, for example, derive a sense of purpose from instructions you think the deceased person is giving you. This can add "coherence, directedness and belonging" to the grieving process. Instead of finding yourself alone and adrift, you feel as though a communication channel remains open, a literal connection persists.[10] This can lead to problems, of course. But it suggests we should not rush to judgment when someone seems in the grip of false beliefs following a loss. As with other kinds of grieving, this may have good or bad outcomes, depending on the situation. There is no "right way" to grieve.

There are many responses to bereavement that do not involve delusion but fall in the much broader category of "confabulation," or (to give it a more generous name) "mythmaking": telling ourselves stories that we believe to be true, at least in the moment we tell them.[11] Relatives visiting an unconscious patient in the hospital will sometimes tell a story of how they were able to communicate with them—about last words faintly heard—even when the medical evidence makes this incredibly unlikely. When Swift talks of "saying things I don't believe," she is clearly recognizing this to be part of the grieving process, for better or worse.

Mythmaking does have the potential to make grieving harder, especially if the myths create ways in which we spuriously blame ourselves, as with Swift's bleak thought that perhaps "a force [took] you because I didn't pray"—entertaining the possibility that she is to blame for what happened, in a way that seems unlikely to help the grieving process. But mythmaking can also aid the process, if it allows us to more easily bring about the changes to our practical identity that need to happen. If the imagined last words of an unconscious patient were in some way comforting or consolatory, there is no reason to think the grieving process would go better if the griever's false belief were to be uprooted.

There is a trade-off, though. The idea (from earlier) that grief can be a valuable source of self-knowledge helps us see this. Knowledge is only achieved when we accept the truth—the way things really are. If too many false beliefs take root, the self-knowledge that makes grief so valuable will be put at risk. A few embellishments or exaggerations about the deceased are likely to be inconsequential, but if we confabulate a whole alternative life for them (such as a life in which Marjorie achieves all her dreams) we risk ending up with a false picture of why they mattered to us. So, if we think about grief in the way Cholbi urges, and that Swift implicitly seems to endorse in "marjorie," we should be mindful of the risk of allowing false beliefs to persist right through the process. They may be necessary at the earliest stages, but we should ultimately try to move beyond them.

Collective Grief

Collective grief is the grief *we* feel as a group about losses that have befallen *us*. We might feel this for many reasons—wars, terror attacks, natural disasters, pandemics. I have so far mostly escaped these tragedies, with one exception: the COVID-19 pandemic. That experience was bleakly revelatory, in that it showed me how little we talk about collective grief and how impoverished our resources are for processing it. Taylor Swift's song "epiphany" shows unusual sensitivity to the problem—and hints at ways of solving it.

For all of us, the pandemic was a time of massive disruption, fear, exasperation, and isolation. Yet for Swift it was also a period of explosive creativity: almost unimaginably, she managed to record two entire albums in these conditions. The first of these, *folklore*, was released from nowhere in July 2020, about four months after its conception, achieved entirely though remote collaborations (mainly with Aaron Dessner and Jack Antonoff), with vocals recorded at home in Swift's personal studio. On most tracks, Dessner would send an instrumental, to which Swift would then add a melody and lyrics, often working at unbelievable speeds.

Together with *evermore*, released just five months later, these albums find Swift at her most spontaneous and exploratory. Something about that moment of appalling global crisis brought out the best in her. What is most impressive about both albums, and *folklore* in particular, is that they succeed in capturing something of the emotional texture of that strange and awful time. This is exemplified by the song "epiphany," inspired by Swift's paternal grandfather, Dean, who fought in the Pacific campaign in World War II:

> He never talked about it, not with his sons, not with his wife. Nobody got to hear about what happened there. So I tried to imagine what would happen in order to make you never be able to speak about something. I realized that there are people right now taking a 20-minute break between shifts at a hospital who are having this trauma happen to them that they will probably never want to speak about.[12]

This description doesn't quite do justice to what Swift achieves in the song: by drawing parallels between World War II and the COVID-19 pandemic, she powerfully evokes the collective grief felt by survivors in relation to both events. In the song, Swift gives us a masterclass in restraint and taste. She knows she is a bystander in both cases, as far from the frontline of the pandemic as she is from the battle of Guadalcanal. She knows the imagery she uses is impressionistic, gesturing obliquely in the direction of suffering she cannot represent. The repeated line "some things you just can't speak about" is an expression of humility, a recognition that it is impossible for a songwriter, looking in from a great distance, to capture experiences too traumatic for the people living them to put into words.

The lyrical techniques used in this song are comparable with those used eight years earlier in "Ronan," a song in which the lyrics are quotations from the blog of a bereaved mother, Maya Thompson, used with her permission. Here too, Swift acknowledges that only those with direct experience of a loss can convey its significance. The effect in "Ronan" seems somewhat incongruous because a grieving mother's words are spoken in Swift's voice. In "epiphany," Swift found a way to speak in her own voice about the personal grief of others, and its wider effects on all of us, in a way that still respects the primacy of personal experience.

The song's bridge is a display of Swift's gift for meaning-inverting lines, as the title takes on an unexpected significance: "Only 20 minutes to sleep / But you dream of some epiphany." There is no epiphany in the song. It's rather that the soldiers and doctors, in their twenty-minute breaks, dream of an epiphany. This is exquisitely ambiguous between two meanings: perhaps an epiphany comes to them in the dream, or perhaps they merely dream of having an epiphany, in the sense that they long for one. They *want* to be able to make sense of the suffering around them—but cannot. Their proximity to suffering has not brought with it any special understanding.

Collective grief is an elusive state, even less studied than individual grief and perhaps even harder to understand.[13] But we have all felt it, and struggled with it at some point in our lives, especially if we have lived through the COVID-19 pandemic. Unfortunately, we have also seen a great deal of *denial* of collective grief—little willingness to face up to what it means to have lost so many people to the pandemic. To focus for a moment on the British case, my own case, where we lost over 200,000 people in a country of 67 million. There have been few efforts to reckon with this. One exception is the National Covid Memorial Wall in London. This wall—like "epiphany"—seeks to represent the collective grief of Covid on the model of the world wars, implicitly drawing connections between the two kinds of collective trauma. It bears a clear resemblance to the poppy-adorned World War I memorials that can be found all over Britain.

How does collective grief relate to individual grief? This is a topic on which there is not yet a substantial philosophical literature. Philosophers have analyzed collective emotions (such as the emotions felt by crowds and teams), but without a focus on the special complexities of grief.[14] However, some of the points made earlier about individual grief extend to the level of the collective. Collective grief, like individual grief, is an active process. Our *collective* practical identity is broken, and we need to rebuild it. But what is a "collective practical identity"? There are, I suggest, certain self-conceptions that regulate the ways we act together, just as individual practical identities shape our individual actions. And, like individual practical identities, they can be rocked by loss.

In Britain, we conceived of ourselves as a country prepared for emergencies, and one in which the elderly and vulnerable are treated with dignity. When we grieve together for the more than 200,000 people lost, we at the same time reel from the loss of these parts of our identity. We will need to find new ways of rebuilding the self-conceptions we once had, or else form new ones. Our collective relationship to those we have lost—the fallen of the world wars, or of the COVID-19 pandemic—is not terminated but rather transformed. For many of us, there is a strong feeling that we *owe it to them*, collectively, to remember and memorialize their lives, so that their memory is situated at the center of our attempts to rebuild our shared practical identity.

I'm not suggesting *all* of this is encapsulated in "epiphany." The great value of this song consists not in providing a philosophical analysis of collective grief (it does not attempt this), but rather in finding a way of recognizing and expressing—rather than silencing and denying—the grief that pandemics, wars, and other great disasters induce in all of us, even those a long way from the frontline. Songs are not enough, of course. But they can be part of the process by which we move together through collective grief.[15]

Notes

1. I'll be focusing on the kind of grief that comes with the death of those we love. I don't deny we feel forms of grief about many other kinds of loss. Heartbreak at the end of a relationship might be considered a form of grief, and then a huge number of Swift's songs would count as songs about "grief." But I will be using the term more narrowly, exploring the form of grief evoked by the death of a loved one.
2. "Marjorie Finlay," Wikipedia, at https://en.wikipedia.org/wiki/Marjorie_Finlay (accessed April 18, 2024).
3. Michael Cholbi, *Grief: A Philosophical Guide* (Princeton, NJ: Princeton University Press, 2021).
4. Stephanie Soteriou, "Emotional Taylor Swift Honored Her Late Grandma's Dreams by Including Her Vocals in the Setlist for Her Sold-Out 'Eras' Tour," Buzzfeed News, March 22, 2023, at https://www.buzzfeednews.com/article/stephaniesoteriou/taylor-swift-tears-tribute-grandma-marjorie-eras-tour.
5. Michael Cholbi, "There Is Consolation in a Philosophical Approach to Grief," Psyche, July 18, 2022, at https://psyche.co/ideas/there-is-consolation-in-a-philosophical-approach-to-grief; Troy Jollimore, "Meaningless Happiness and Meaningful Suffering," *Southern Journal of Philosophy* 42 (2004), 333–347.
6. Jordan MacKenzie, Review of "Cholbi, Michael. *Grief: A Philosophical Guide,*" *Ethics* 133 (2023), 610–615.
7. Wyndi Kappes, "Taylor Swift's New Song Sparks Conversation around Miscarriage," The Bump, October 25, 2022, at https://www.thebump.com/news/taylor-swift-song-about-miscarriage.
8. Clare Moriarty, "I Was Blindsided by How Upset Saying the Words 'I've Miscarried' or 'I Need a D&C' Out Loud Made Me," Image, September 17, 2023, at https://www.image.ie/self/health-wellness/i-was-blindsided-by-how-upset-saying-the-words-ive-miscarried-or-i-need-a-dc-out-loud-made-me-576511.
9. Anna Castelnovo, Simone Cavallotti, Orsola Gambini, and Armando D'Agostino, "Post-Bereavement Hallucinatory Experiences: A Critical Overview of Population and Clinical Studies," *Journal of Affective Disorders* 186 (2015), 266–274.
10. Rosa Ritunnano and Lisa Bortolotti, "Do Delusions Have and Give Meaning?," *Phenomenology and the Cognitive Sciences* 21 (2022), 949–968.
11. Lisa Bortolotti, "Confabulation: Why Telling Ourselves Stories Makes Us Feel OK," Aeon, February 13, 2018, at https://aeon.co/ideas/confabulation-why-telling-ourselves-stories-makes-us-feel-ok.

12. Quoted in Liam Hess, "5 Things We Learned Watching Taylor Swift's Surprise New *folklore* Documentary," *Vogue*, November 26, 2022, at https://www.vogue.com/article/taylor-swift-folklore-documentary-5-things-we-learned.

13. Dorothy P. Hollinger, "The Collective Grief We Must Face," The Hill, February 22, 2021, at https://thehill.com/changing-america/opinion/539918-the-collective-grief-we-must-face.

14. For example, Bryce Huebner, "Genuinely Collective Emotions," *European Journal for Philosophy of Science* 1 (2011), 89–118; Mikko Salmela, "Shared Emotions," *Philosophical Explorations* 15 (2012), 33–46; Nina Trcka, "Collective Moods: A Contribution to the Phenomenology and Interpersonality of Shared Affectivity," *Philosophia* 45 (2017), 1647–1662. On collective grief, see John Danaher, "Pandemics and Collective Grief," *Philosophical Disquisitions*, April 20, 2020, at https://philosophicaldisquisitions.blogspot.com/2020/04/pandemics-and-collective-grief.html.

15. Many thanks to Eline Kuipers for her comments and to the editors for all the work they have put into this volume.

17

"What a Shame She Went Mad"

Anger, Affective Injustice, and Taylor Swift's "mad woman"

Erica Bigelow

Taylor Swift's reputation precedes her, as was the premise of her 2017 studio album, *reputation*. The tour for this album opened with a montage of reporters' voices reading headlines about Swift, eventually blurring into a simpler repetition—Taylor Swift, Taylor Swift, Taylor Swift—before she took the stage. It's Swift herself—not the men she's dated—who has become a popular media boilerplate, who's had to salvage her reputation time and again. It's Swift who has been cast as a crazy ex-girlfriend, victimizing men by daring to give voice to her anger toward them.

Perhaps the popularity of this narrative around Swift's dating history stems from the way that she subverts a cultural preference for linearity—you date someone, you break up, you're angry, sad, betrayed, and then you move on, and no one has to hear about it anymore. Perhaps, though, it's something a bit more sinister: the tendency for women (and members of other marginalized social groups) to have their anger interpreted as "Madness." I use a capital M here, along with contemporary writers like La Marr Jurelle Bruce, to invoke the sense of madness as so-called insanity and craziness.[1] The similarity between anger and madness might make it seem natural to interpret anger as Madness, but there are reasons to be worried about classifying anger as being Mad. This not because being Mad is a necessarily bad thing, but because being *treated* as Mad means that your anger is not being taken seriously.

To the chagrin of her critics, Swift is in on the anger-as-Madness "jokes" made at her expense. Many of her songs play on the crazy ex-girlfriend stereotype that she's been written into. In this chapter, we'll explore how Swift represents and experiments with this trope of the "Mad" woman, especially in the song with that title, though decapitalized as "mad woman." As we'll see, the philosophical concept of "affective injustice" can help us understand Swift's feminist message, showing how the sexist trope of a Mad woman works.

Taylor Swift and Philosophy: Essays from the Tortured Philosophers Department, First Edition. Edited by Catherine M. Robb and Georgie Mills.

"No One Likes a Mad Woman"

Throughout her career, Taylor Swift has shown a pointed awareness of how people talk about a woman in the aftermath of a breakup or someone else's wrongdoing. This theme is explicit in "mad woman," written from the perspective of a scorned woman, a woman who has, in some sense, been done wrong. More than that, it's about a woman who is *angry* about the wronging.

The song "mad woman" begins with a rhetorical question: "What did you think I'd say to that?" The specifics of what "that" in this lyric refers to are not elaborated on, but it's clear that it refers to some general wrongdoing the subject of the song has experienced. The rhetorical question suggests that the anger the song goes on to describe can only be thought of as a natural response to this wrongdoing. Why *wouldn't* she be mad about that? Anything else would be illogical.

This sentiment is echoed in the song's bridge, where Swift writes that some other *she*—perhaps some other woman who's been similarly wronged by the same perpetrator—"should be mad / Should be scathing like me / But," she can't be, because "no one likes a mad woman." Let's analyze how this lyric portrays anger by breaking it down into two parts. First, Swift claims that there is an imperative to being angry. It isn't just that the anger in this situation would be a "logical" or "acceptable" response, but that it's something that someone "should" or "ought" to have or feel. She *should* be mad, she *should* be scathing. As the contemporary philosopher Macalester Bell highlights, that anger in this kind of situation is the *right* feeling to have, and so it would be wrong not to feel it.[2] The second half of the lyric hints at one of the repercussions mad women face; no one likes them, so no one will like you once you've been portrayed as one of them. The contemporary philosopher Kristie Dotson has claimed that the threat of repercussions like these function as a kind of "silencing," as a way of ensuring that the anger never becomes public.[3]

In the chorus, the song explores the rhetorical transformation of anger into Madness, and so of an angry woman being turned into a Mad woman. Because "no one likes a mad woman," it becomes "a shame she went mad." The use of the word "mad" here is ambiguous. It might be that the "mad" woman is just angry. But in the second part of the lyric, the woman is described as *going mad*, which invokes craziness, insanity, and Madness with a capital M, rather than just madness understood as anger. Swift gestures in the song toward a sort of snowballing effect: "Every time you call me crazy / I get more crazy / … And when you say I seem angry / I get more angry." This demonstrates the slipperiness between anger and Madness, and how easily the anger can be morphed into craziness, and a mad woman morphed into a Mad woman.

The song also pokes fun at this mad-to-Mad transformation by occupying both subjective and objective positions with respect to it. In "mad woman" Swift both speaks self-referentially, writing in the first person, *and* takes on the third-person viewpoint of someone else talking about her. Most of the song is written from the former perspective; the verses, the buildup to the chorus, and the bridge use words like "I," "me," "my," and so on. The chorus itself, though, comes in the third person: "What a shame *she* went mad / No one likes a mad woman / You made *her* like that." By adopting both the first-person "I" and the third-person "she" in such close proximity, Swift shows she's aware of the public conversation about her, and about women more generally. Moreover, she succeeds in illustrating the internalization of such conversations, showing how the demeaning way people have talked about her—and women in general—becomes part of our own stories and identity. As the contemporary political theorist, Farah Godrej, has argued, the shame that is experienced by those who are treated in this way becomes part of their own sense of self, as they "come to identify with the values and perspective of one whose gaze has shamed" her.[4]

None of this is to say that Swift endorses the sexist tropes embodied by the mad-to-Mad transformation. On the contrary, the song is clear that whatever "craziness" the Mad woman displays isn't squarely (or at all) her own fault. The chorus further shows that Swift is fully aware of the manipulative tactics that create the Mad woman: "you'll poke that bear 'til her claws come out / And you find something to wrap your noose around." The point is that anger (the claws coming out) is a natural response to certain forms of mistreatment, and that those who cause the anger are, perhaps ironically but no doubt intentionally, often the ones who then wield the power to punish for it. Swift skillfully reclaims the narrative with regards to the Mad woman in a way that is similar to how disabled people have reclaimed the word "crip."[5] This word—usually in the longer form "cripple"—was originally used as a derogatory term to shame and stigmatize those who are disabled. But now it is used by some who are disabled to describe themselves and disability justice more generally. But as Alison Kafer says, the use of "crip" often leads those who are not disabled to "wince," making them feel uncomfortable, perhaps with the realization that the word they have been using for so long has had negative connotations. Swift does likewise in "mad woman." If the self-deprecating comments about herself as the crazy ex-girlfriend come off as confronting, grating, hard to stomach, then perhaps she's accomplished exactly what she wanted to. By reclaiming the phrase "mad woman," Swift subverts her naysayers by becoming—through her use of the first person—precisely that which they criticize her for being.

Affective Injustice and Mad Women

The analysis of anger and madness in "mad woman" can be further explored with a relatively new philosophical concept, "affective injustice." The term was first coined by Shiloh Whitney and Amia Srinivasan in separate papers published in 2018.[6] Affective injustice is an injustice that harms or wrongs someone in their capacity as an affective person, that is, in the way that they have or feel emotions. The paradigm example of affective injustice is an instance of someone's emotions not being taken seriously, or not being taken as seriously as they ought to be due to some form of discriminatory injustice. We can keep things simple by considering "affect" as the same as an emotion or a feeling. Because Whitney and Srinivasan wrote separate papers about this concept, their formulations differ slightly. What's interesting though, is that both of the different formulations of affective injustice are complemented and exemplified by Swift's portrayal of anger and madness in "mad woman."

According to Whitney's definition, affective injustice "damages the weight afforded one's feelings,"[7] which is to say that one's emotions or feelings are not given the appropriate credibility or seriousness. An emotion is intentional, which means that it has a purpose, and there is always a reason why you will feel that emotion. For example, you are sad because you didn't get tickets to the Eras Tour, or you are angry because your lover has cheated on you. Because of this, emotions also can guide people in how they respond to you. If you are sad for example, then I might try to cheer you up by buying you some Taylor Swift merchandise, or if you are angry at your cheating lover, then they might try to appease your negative feelings by apologizing. Emotions have meaning and purpose, and they can guide our actions.[8] Affective injustice occurs when other people do not take your emotion to be something that merits a response or action, because it is not taken seriously and not responded to accordingly. Responding to someone's sadness with laughter, or to their anger with accusations of insanity, would thus be an affective injustice.

It's clear that "mad woman" expresses this understanding of affective injustice, with its exploration of how anger leads to accusations of craziness, and so not being taken seriously. Whitney also writes about an "affective economy" in which an emotion isn't given proper weight or significance by others, and so can pile up until it becomes "toxic."[9] This is represented by the snowballing effect that Swift describes in "mad woman." When anger isn't appropriately legitimized, it grows and warps into "craziness" or Madness. It's cyclical— the Mad woman is angry in the first place, which is the basis on which she's described as Mad, but then she harbors further (righteous) anger about being treated as Mad. The Mad woman herself becomes angrier, and thus "crazier," until her anger and craziness begin melting together, becoming fundamental parts of who she is.

The toxicity is twofold. First, anger-Madness is bad for the Mad woman herself because of its emotional cost—there is a reason why the woman is angry in the first place, and anger itself is a difficult emotion to feel. Second, the anger that is felt becomes externally toxic, because it changes others' perceptions of the Mad woman by making her out to be unstable and unreliable. She becomes someone—and her anger becomes something—to be dismissed, rather than taken seriously, because seriously engaging with her Madness would be fruitless, a waste of time. The rhetorical transformation of anger into Madness—the transformation that undergirds the formation of the Mad woman—is an example of affective injustice, because it's a matter of an affect (anger) being misread (as Madness), and thus receiving the wrong kinds of reception.

Anger and Injustice

Amia Srinivasan, the other contemporary philosopher who coined the term "affective injustice," has taken a slightly different approach to understanding the concept. Srinivasan defines affective injustice as "the injustice of having to negotiate between one's apt emotional response to the injustice of one's situation and one's desire to better one's situation."[10] In other words, affective injustice results from having to decide between responding aptly (that is, appropriately or understandably) to injustice by expressing the "negative" emotions it provokes, and being able to actually address that injustice; never both. For example, Srinivasan recognizes that anger, no matter how appropriate it is, might not serve the angry person's best interests. It can make them vulnerable to the "counterproductivity critique": the idea that anger is counterproductive because it might alienate would-be allies by making them less sympathetic to our cause. Anger might also be counterproductive because there could be some reason not to get angry, for example, because you might be shamed or you know it will be held against you.[11] Even if anger is appropriate and warranted by the circumstances, you might try to refrain from getting angry if you know that it'll be held against you in some way. This, Srinivasan contends, is unjust.

The Mad woman from Swift's song seems to encounter this understanding of affective injustice, as explained by Srinivasan. Swift's Mad woman is forced into a problem without a clear solution. On the one hand, she can swallow her anger, declining to name her poor treatment for what it is, and risk appearing as though she's endorsing it. On the other hand, she can express her anger, and risk being taken as Mad, risking again all of the poor treatment that Madness entails. To be clear, neither of these options should be viewed as doing something morally wrong. The self-preservation instinct often involved when trying to swallow or ignore one's anger, and registering injustice by displaying the anger, are both morally appropriate responses to a relevant situation. The conflict that

Srinivasan describes arises because neither of the Mad woman's options are clearly right or wrong.

In both Whitney's and Srinivasan's accounts, affective injustice is an injustice experienced next to some other injustice. The paradigm examples used by both authors take anti-Black racism as the primary injustice, with emotional responses as secondary. Racism is the reason for affective injustice because it is often on the basis of race that individuals are either denied adequate affective uptake (as in Whitney's theory) or forced into dilemmas (as in Srinivasan's theory). Both philosophers, however, recognize that race is not the sole ground upon which individuals are subjected to affective injustice. If we consider Swift's "mad woman" as an example of affective injustice, the relevant primary injustice would be sexism or misogyny, based on the fact that women's emotions are often not taken seriously, often forcing women into difficult dilemmas.[12]

Sexism and Stereotypes

Contrary to both Whitney and Srinivasan, Swift's "mad woman" shows us that affective injustice is not just a secondary injustice that comes from a more primary injustice, like racism or sexism. Getting to this conclusion requires a clearer working definition of sexism. That sexism involves discrimination or ill-treatment on the basis of sex or gender seems like a given. But our definition should go further. We could add, like the contemporary feminist theorist Sara Ahmed does, that sexism is not only poor behavior or treatment, but the enabling and rewarding of that behavior and treatment.[13] This would mean that even if we are not directly engaging in the ill-treatment of someone based on their sex, if we enable that behavior or reward it, for example, by giving that person a prize, or by failing to implement policies that inhibit this kind of behavior, then we would also be contributing to the sexism. We can also draw from philosopher Marilyn Frye's feminist work, and add that sexism lies in the very forces that compel us to acquiesce to a sex binary. For Frye, sexism is a series of "structures which create and enforce the elaborate and rigid patterns of sex-marking and sex-announcing which divide the species, along lines of sex, into dominators and subordinates."[14] Sexism, then, also is a name for the structures and forces that make this binary seem natural or fated, and that therefore make it even more difficult to resist.

Taken together, these definitions allow us to view affective injustice as something that makes up and is part of sexism, and does not simply follow from it as a symptom or consequence. The figure of the Mad woman and the affective injustice that occurs, doesn't just follow from sexist depictions of femininity, but in fact helps to reinforce them. Part of what makes sexism itself seem natural is that women are haunted by stereotypes such as the Mad woman, and so such figures actually precede any instance of sexist treatment. If the Mad woman represents affective injustice, and if affective injustice is one way that sexism is instantiated, then sexism consists partly in experiencing affective injustice.

Taylor Swift's exploration of gender, stereotypes, and sexism in "mad woman" highlights that when a woman's anger is interpreted as a crazy Madness (with a capital M), this is a case of affective injustice, where your emotions are not taken seriously and you are forced you into a dilemma. But it is more than just an after-effect or symptom of sexism; the stereotype of the Mad woman that Swift so skillfully portrays represents the very core of sexism, and represents another way in which society is able to discriminate against and stigmatize the experiences of women. So, there are very good reasons that Swift's mad woman "should be mad / Should be scathing like me."

Notes

1. La Marr Jurelle Bruce, "'The People inside My Head, Too': Madness, Black Womanhood, and the Radical Performance of Lauryn Hill," *African American Review* 45 (2012), 371–389.
2. Macalester Bell, "A Woman's Scorn: Toward a Feminist Defense of Contempt as a Moral Emotion," *Hypatia* 20 (2005), 85.
3. Kristie Dotson, "Tracking Epistemic Violence, Tracking Practices of Silencing," *Hypatia* 26 (2011), 236–257.
4. Farah Godrej, "Spaces for Counter-Narratives: The Phenomenology of Reclamation," *Frontiers* 32 (2011), 113.
5. Alison Kafer, *Feminist, Queer, Crip* (Bloomington: Indiana University Press, 2013), 15.
6. See Shiloh Whitney, "Affective Intentionality and Affective Injustice: Merleau-Ponty and Fanon on the Body Schema as a Theory of Affect," *The Southern Journal of Philosophy* 56 (2018), 488–515, and Amia Srinivasan, "The Aptness of Anger," *The Journal of Political Philosophy* 26 (2018), 123–144.
7. Shiloh Whitney, "Affective Intentionality and Affective Injustice: Merleau-Ponty and Fanon on the Body Schema as a Theory of Affect," *The Southern Journal of Philosophy* 56 (2018), 495.
8. Whitney, "Affective Intentionality," 496.
9. Whitney, "Affective Intentionality," 497.
10. Amia Srinivasan, "The Aptness of Anger," *The Journal of Political Philosophy* 26 (2018), 135.
11. Srinivasan, "The Aptness of Anger," 125.
12. There is also a compelling case to be made about the ableism that the mad woman might face once it's been determined that she's "Mad."
13. Sara Ahmed, "Sexism: A Problem with a Name," *New Formations* 86 (2015), 9.
14. Marilyn Frye, *The Politics of Reality: Essays in Feminist Theory* (Freedom, CA: The Crossing Press, 1983), 38.

18

I'm Fine with My Spite
The Philosophy of Female Anger in the Work of Taylor Swift

Amanda Cercas Curry and Alba Curry

Taylor Swift embodies all-American femininity: she is beautiful, poised, and articulate, speaks with a soft voice, sings about kisses in cars and football games. And yet her tears are bullets, they ricochet ("my tears ricochet"), and there is nothing she does better than revenge ("Better Than Revenge (Taylor's Version)"). This spite deviates from the good deportment we expect from a woman. To her predominantly female audience, Swift's scathing lyrics are a sort of feminist manifesto—there are countless playlists of her angry songs, including "no body, no crime," where she leans into the trope of a vengeful, murderous woman. But for non-Swifties, her anger is nothing short of a tantrum from a spoiled brat.[1]

In this chapter, we'll look through the lens of Taylor Swift's lyrics to examine anger, how it's gendered, and its ethical value for women. In Swift's words, we'll make the value of women's anger "fade into view" ("Style (Taylor's Version)").

"I Can Feel the Flames on My Skin"

When you think of anger you might think of shouting, clenched teeth, tight fists, or maybe even breaking stuff. But whose anger is that? Have you ever been so angry you simply cried, or quietly left a room? Part of the reason we don't associate anger with "Taytay" is the fact that she has described herself as "imaginative, smart, and hard-working," as opposed to "sexy, cool, and edgy."[2] She is virtuous, thoughtful, measured, unlike angry people—at least some might think.

And yet, anger features prominently in Swift's songs. Why is that? Well, because many of her songs are about the wrongs that have been done to her, how she feels about them, and her desire to right the wrong. According to the philosopher Aristotle (c. 384–322 BCE), anger has three key characteristics: (i) it is a response to a perceived injustice; (ii) it is a desire for revenge or

Taylor Swift and Philosophy: Essays from the Tortured Philosophers Department, First Edition. Edited by Catherine M. Robb and Georgie Mills.
© 2025 John Wiley & Sons, Inc. Published 2025 by John Wiley & Sons, Inc.

payback, and (iii) it involves pleasure and pain.[3] The fact that Swift cares so much about doing the right thing makes her a great source for investigating what, if anything, is good about anger. In other words, Taytay and Aristotle have quite a bit in common. Just picture Aristotle getting ready for revenge.[4]

The Problem of Eternal Anger

Anger, as Aristotle says, is your response to perceiving that you, or someone you value, has been wronged. Anger, in other words, is about injustice. This is why virtuous people can also get angry. A virtuous person gets angry for the right reasons, at the right time, and to the right degree. Anger can be empowering because it involves the desire for payback, or revenge—which is pleasurable. This is a key difference between feeling sad and being angry— and remember what Swift tells us: "don't get sad, get even" ("Vigilante Shit"). The desire for revenge signals our desire to reestablish our worth in the face of someone who has disregarded us, made us feel insignificant or devalued. She did just this in her 2016 Grammy speech by (very publicly) calling out Kanye's lyrics, claiming he made her famous for undercutting her success. She got the award, got the Grammy, and reestablished her worth.

But what happens when you can't right the wrong? What does it mean to get even? Sometimes justice in the form of an eye-for-an-eye is not available or attractive. There is nothing you can do to undo the infidelity, the betrayal. Should you stay angry forever? Agnes Callard, a contemporary philosopher, reminds us that, while it is easy to understand why someone got angry, it is harder to understand why they stopped being angry. In other words, if you had a reason to be angry, if you really were wronged, you have a reason to be angry forever. This is what Callard calls the problem of eternal anger.[5]

Taytay and Agnes offer the same solution. You can never undo the other person's wrong; it will always constitute a violation of the relationship and therefore a devaluation of the relationship. Sometimes it might be appropriate to forgive the other person. But when forgiveness is not the right thing, you can simply stop caring about that relationship and why the other person devalued it to begin with. This is why "you don't have to forgive, you can just move on," as Swift suggests in "I Forgot That You Existed."

"Crimson Red Pain(t) on My Lips"

Being angry doesn't feel good; when we're angry we are in pain. In fact, Aristotle distinguishes between wanton aggression and anger by stating that anger is always accompanied by pain.[6] Anger isn't just bad for our minds but for our bodies as well, raising cortisol levels and potentially damaging our health. This observation has been used to argue against anger and in favor of other emotions or attitudes, such as meekness.[7] It has also been used to show the undue burden on victims of injustice. Consider this: when you suffer injustice you are doubly wronged because you are left to also suffer the consequences of experiencing anger.[8]

Aristotle had not thought this far—he didn't even know what cortisol was, and systemic injustices were not a topic of conversation in ancient Athens. For him, the pain of anger did not mean it should be avoided. Swift often refers to the bodily sensations of anger through gruesome but evocative language: blood and bruises, bones snapping, bullet wounds, burning skin. Why would anyone choose to lean into this torment? In contrast with Aristotle, Swift (and other women) has no choice but to deal with the injustice of sexism. Not all anger is created equal. Anger is gendered, meaning that people express and respond to anger differently depending on their gender. Tellingly, history has made little room for virtuous female anger.[9] Even within the general trend of the dismissal of women's emotions, anger is singled out as particularly inappropriate.[10] As Swift says, "No one likes a mad woman" ("mad woman").

Anger demands respect. Sexists and misogynists don't like an angry woman because they think that to be a woman means to yield to the control of others.[11] A slave should not get angry at her master. British philosopher John Stuart Mill (1806–1973) was ahead of his time when he said:

> All women are brought up from the very earliest years in the belief that their ideal of character is the very opposite to that of men; not self-will, and government by self-control, but submission, and yielding to the control of others.[12]

Moreover, Mill emphasized that men do not simply want obedient women, they want full control over women's emotions. Men don't just want a slave, but a willing one. As Taytay says, "Ladies always rise above / Ladies know what people want / Someone sweet and kind and fun" ("Vigilante Shit"). Femininity has been constructed to be conceptually incompatible with anger. An angry woman must grieve forgoing her female virtue—remember in "my tears ricochet," the specter must let go of her grace, one of the most important qualities of femininity.

There is a long history of injustice around the way in which women express their emotions—women have been unable to be angry. In philosophy this kind of injustice is called "affective injustice," where the *affective* refers to emotions. As Amia Srinivasan points out, women have been burdened with a double bind: if they are angry they are accused of lacking prudence or not wanting to actually better their situation, but if they fail to get angry they are failing to register an injustice.[13] Swift herself has faced this. She addressed the Kanye West controversy with sympathy and forgiveness in "Innocent," but was then accused of being condescending. Then she faced backlash when she called Kanye out during her Grammy speech.

In *folklore: the long pond studio sessions*, Swift discusses female rage in the context of "mad woman."[14] The song cleverly plays with the double meaning of *mad*—an angry woman is a crazy woman—to refer to the way female anger is dismissed and gaslit away while women are expected to "silently absorb whatever a guy decides to do." Swift's powerful imagery—a scorpion fighting back, a bear's claws coming out to defend itself—suggests that female anger is a direct response to a stimulus, something natural and of this world.

These natural creatures contrast strikingly with the trope of the witch, something hideous, evil, and supernatural that needs to be burned away. Just think of the Salem-like witch burnings in "I Did Something Bad." A picture emerges of madness as disenfranchisement: female anger, a display of agency and self-worth, is something punishable by death. So, the response to injustice is as offensive as the offense itself (or perhaps more) because in order to warrant anger you must first be of value, and women are not.

Glitter Gel Pen Anger

Correcting history with her portrayals of appropriate female anger, Swift has her very own signature variety of anger, "Glitter Gel Pen Anger." Swift has proposed a pen-themed categorization of her songs according to the moods they evoke: fountain pen songs ("modern, personal stories ... about moments that you remember in screaming detail"), quill pen songs ("Like you're a 19th century poet crafting your next sonnet by candlelight"), and glitter gel pen songs ("make you want to dance, sing and toss glitter around the room").[15] While many of the glitter gel pen songs deal with themes of youth, obsession, and crushes, the category also includes angry songs such as "Karma," "I Forgot that You Existed," "We Are Never Ever Getting Back Together (Taylor's Version)," and "Bejeweled." These songs don't represent anger in the way we often picture it, but they do touch on themes of being wronged and devalued.

Swift says glitter gel pen songs "remind you not to take yourself too seriously."[16] She doesn't mean you shouldn't take offenses seriously, but rather that they should not stop you from enjoying life. In contrast to other angry songs, in glitter gel pen songs she does not fantasize about revenge. Instead she walks away from the wrongdoing, rendering the wrongdoer beneath contempt, and *that* is revenge—they are as insignificant to her as they made her feel. "And by the way, I'm going out tonight," she declares offhandedly in "Bejeweled." Swift's lyrics act as open letters of resentment, expressing and protesting the wrong for the world to see. This, in turn, allows her to move on without forgiving, without forgetting, but also without being consumed by resentment.

Aristotle thinks you need revenge (in the right measure) to bring the person back down to your level, but Swift leverages community to pull herself up. By calling out misbehavior, her value has already been reestablished within her community and that is enough—the public shaming of the wrongdoer is cathartic. This echoes Swift's statements in the documentary *Miss Americana*: "you don't have to forgive, you don't have to forget, you can just move on."[17] And this resonates with Callard's solution to the problem of eternal anger: you may never be able to right a wrong, but you can stop valuing the relationship you had with the wrongdoer. The wrong will not be undone, but you will be able to move on with your life.

However, we might criticize Glitter Gel Pen Anger as not being widely available. After all, not many of us can hope to be called "the music industry."[18] Swift is privileged to deal with her anger this way, and she has the support of all her fans. Of course, for something to be good it does not need to be available to everyone in the same way. Swift is still showing her fans that you do not need to simply turn the other cheek, or forget, or be angry forever. You can feel supported by Swift and her fans when you listen to "Karma," learning to stop valuing what you had with the person that wronged you, as Callard suggests. Furthermore, given that Aristotle was interested in how we ought to live as a community, he would tell us that even if not everyone can pen anger like Swift, her anger serves the important function of reestablishing the worth of women and highlighting the actions of others that are worthy of condemnation.

"So, Light Me Up"

Audre Lorde (1934–1992), a Black lesbian poet, professor, philosopher, feminist, and civil rights activist, argues in her famous speech "Uses of Anger" that anger ought to be part of female virtue. The personal is political. Anger is not just about individual wrongs, but also about social justice, about institutional oppression. Lorde's focus was on the importance of women's anger against racism and against sexism. She tells us that, "every woman has a well-stocked arsenal of anger potentially useful against those oppressions, personal and institutional, which brought anger into being."[19] Lorde was what today we call an "intersectional feminist," which means that her account of feminism understood that we cannot think of sex and race in isolation. For example, what it is like to be a woman is influenced by other factors that *intersect*, such as your skin color, economic demographic, and geographical location. Lorde warns us against dismissing anyone's anger: "Mainstream communication does not want women, particularly white women, responding to racism."[20]

Lorde might have found fault with Swift for not doing enough against racism. Racism is not just a problem for Black people and people of color. Swift has been criticized for her lack of engagement with the racial equality movement, for having limited herself to following social media trends, and for her relationship with Matty Healy, who made racist comments on a radio show.[21] And yet, Lorde would still encourage us to ask who profits from silencing Swift's own anger. It isn't women's anger that makes us lock our doors at night, Lorde says, but the systemic racism and sexism found in the street—it is hatred. Whereas anger aims at change, in Lorde's language, hatred aims at destruction. Anger is about change because it identifies wrongdoings and works toward ensuring that those wrongdoings are not repeated. It both considers the past and looks to the future.

For Lorde, anger, used with precision, can become a powerful source of energy serving progress and change. There are two key lessons about female anger: (i) anger has *conative* power, which means that it motivates us to act; and (ii) anger is of epistemic value, meaning that we can learn things from anger. This is because anger is loaded with energy and information. Saying that anger has energy, or conative value, is another way of saying that anger involves a desire for something. Desires motivate us to do things, not just righting personal wrongs but also societal or political wrongs. Lorde tells us not to be afraid of anger but to use anger with precision for growth. As Swift sings, "Never be so polite / You forget your power / Never wield such power / You forget to be polite" ("marjorie").

It might seem that Swift only talks about personal wrongdoings. But if we look more closely, Swift often uses the language of romantic relationships to talk about the broad spectrum of social relations, perhaps as a way to connect more personally with injustices at every level. She often discusses unequal relationships—whether romantic, professional, or societal—where one partner gives it their all only to come up short when "graded on a curve" ("Bejeweled"). As further examples of this, "mad woman" deals explicitly with female rage, "Miss Americana and the Heartbreak Prince" is about "disillusionment with our crazy world of politics and inequality, set in a metaphorical high school," and "tolerate it" calls out inequality.

As Lorde reminds us, anger's essential value lies in its ability to reveal our own values, the values of those in our immediate vicinity, and wider society. We learn about our own values because often we do not know we care about something until it is taken from us. For example, you may not have known you had a certain expectation from a relationship until your loved one breached that expectation, triggering anger. In fact, your loved one may not have known either until you expressed your anger. As a wider society we can learn a lot about your anger, and how your loved one chose to respond to it. This is what Lorde means when she says anger is loaded with information. For example, in both "mad woman" and "Vigilante Shit" we find wives who know about an infidelity. In "mad woman," the wife cannot show her anger, and in "Vigilante Shit," Swift gives her "cold hard proof," allowing the wife to walk away from the marriage with everything, including pride. These two songs tell us a lot about anger in Swift's world: infidelity is worthy of anger, female anger is often gaslit and shamed away, and only women whose anger is substantiated with cold hard proof can walk away with their lives and pride intact.

Anger is also educational for Swift herself. She was criticized for homophobic and misogynistic lyrics on some of her earlier albums, particularly in her song "Better Than Revenge." In her recent rerecording, she changed the lyrics, showing growth and an acknowledgment of feminist values. Swift seems to have learned from her fans' anger at an injustice. This change, and Swift's open expression of anger also tell us something about the world: attitudes toward female agency and sexuality are changing.

Go, Fight, Win

In swooping, sloping cursive letters, Swift writes a thesis in Glitter Gel Pen Anger. This anger, like Swift herself, is packaged as happy and palatable, but beneath the surface there is a more progressive message of self-worth and agency. For Swift, anger is a powerful tool that highlights injustices to you and the larger world. Anger reminds you of your worth, and of what matters. Swift's philosophy of female anger tells us that the first thing women need to be angry about is the fact that female anger is often not well received. The responses from her critics ("isn't she wealthy and white, what could she have to be angry about?"[22]) are just another form of silencing. Swift's anger speaks to her fandom, urging us to go, fight, and win for all we are worth ("Miss Americana and the Heartbreak Prince").

Notes

1. For example, that she is a "defensive monster who will not hesitate to play any -ism card if and when her brittle sensibilities are rattled by even the most minor of transgressions" (Vinay Menon, "Just Because Taylor Swift Can't Take a Joke Does Not Mean Netflix Is Deeply Sexist," The Star, March 22, 2021, at https://www.thestar.com/entertainment/opinion/2021/03/02/just-because-taylor-swift-cant-take-a-joke-does-not-mean-netflix-is-deeply-sexist.html.
2. CBS Mornings, "Taylor Swift: I'm Not Naturally 'Edgy, Sexy or Cool,'" YouTube, October 29, 2014, at https://www.youtube.com/watch?v=Rux 5LZ1IU1Q&ab_channel=CBSMornings.
3. Aristotle, Rhetoric, 1378a29-3. All translations of Aristotle's Rhetoric are indebted to C.D.C. Reeve trans., Rhetoric (Indianapolis: Hackett Publishing, 2018).
4. Aristotle is important in debates about anger because for better or worse much of the debate in the West is still defined in his terms.
5. Agnes Callard, "The Reason to Be Angry Forever," in Mysha Cherry and Owen Flanagan eds., The Moral Psychology of Anger (London: Rowman & Littlefield, 2018), 123–138.

6. Aristotle, *Nicomachean Ethics*, 1149b2123.
7. Glen Pettigrove, "Meekness and 'Moral' Anger," *Ethics* 122 (2012), 341–370.
8. Lisa Tessman, *Burdened Virtues: Virtue Ethics for Liberatory Struggles* (Oxford: Oxford University Press, 2005).
9. There are exceptions outside the Western tradition, such as in *Lienüzhuan* 《列女傳》 of Liu Xiang 劉向 (77–6 BCE).
10. Susan Campbell, "Being Dismissed: The Politics of Emotional Expression," *Hypatia* 9 (1994), 46–65.
11. Kate Manne, *Down Girl: The Logic of Misogyny* (Oxford: Oxford University Press, 2017), 77.
12. John Stuart Mill, *The Subjection of Women*, vol. 1 (London: Transaction Publishers, 1869).
13. Amia Srinivasan, "The Aptness of Anger," *Journal of Political Philosophy* 26 (2018), 123–144.
14. *folklore: the long pond studio sessions*, dir. Taylor Swift (Taylor Swift Productions, Big Branch Productions, 2020).
15. Jessica Nicholson, "Taylor Swift Accepts Songwriter-Artist of the Decade Honor at Nashville Songwriter Awards: Read Her Full Speech," *Billboard*, September 21, 2022, at https://www.billboard.com/music/country/taylor-swift-nashville-songwriter-awards-full-speech-1235142144.
16. Nicholson, "Taylor Swift Accepts Songwriter-Artist of the Decade Honor."
17. *Miss Americana*, dir. Lana Wilson (Tremolo Productions, 2020).
18. Devin Leonard, "Taylor Swift *Is* the Music Industry," Bloomberg, November 14, 2014, at https://www.bloomberg.com/news/articles/2014-11-12/taylor-swift-and-big-machine-are-the-music-industry.
19. Audre Lorde, *Your Silence Will Not Protect You* (London: Silver Press, 2017), 110.
20. Lorde, *Your Silence Will Not Protect You*, 112.
21. Emma Specter, "Why Are Fans So Angry About Taylor Swift's Rumored Relationship with Matty Healy?" *Vogue*, May 18, 2023, at https://www.vogue.com/article/taylor-swift-rumored-relationship-with-matty-healy-controversy.
22. See, for example, Hadera McKay, "Is Taylor Swift Revolutionary or Is She Just White?" The Berkeley Beacon, November 11, 2021, at https://berkeleybeacon.com/is-taylor-swift-revolutionary-or-is-she-just-white.

"I SHOULD'VE KNOWN": TAYLOR SWIFT'S PHILOSOPHY OF KNOWLEDGE

19

"Summer Love" or "Just a Summer Thing?"
Feminist Standpoint Epistemology and the *folklore* Love Triangle

Lottie Pike and Tom Beevers

In the three *folklore* tracks "betty," "cardigan," and "august," Taylor Swift introduces us to three fictional characters: James, Betty, and Augustine.[1] In these songs, each character voices their unique perspective on the same tumultuous high-school love affair. "Betty" is sung from the perspective of the male love interest, James, and is a desperate attempt at an apology toward his former high-school sweetheart, Betty. In "cardigan," Betty gives her own retrospective outlook on the relationship between herself and James, which was corrupted by his "summer thing" with Augustine, whose perspective is described in "august." By giving us first-person insight into each side of this love triangle, Swift allows us to empathize with each character's emotions.

Now, situations of this kind (boy likes girl, boy cheats on girl, boy realizes his mistake and asks for forgiveness from girl) are often narrated with various underlying biases at play. Typically, the "other woman" in these affairs—here, Augustine—is portrayed as a callous homewrecker bent on stealing the poor impressionable man from his one true love. The difference with Swift's love triangle is that the listener is given access to every standpoint in this situation. As a result, the traditional perspective of the "other woman" is put into the foreground and is considered in a more sympathetic and realistic light.

There is something puzzling about this, however. By inhabiting the standpoints of Betty, James, and Augustine, we feel their emotions and let them inform our perceptions of the world. But from a certain perspective, it seems like this emotional empathy should make our perceptions less objective, not more. After all, to be objective, we are told we should be unemotional and indifferent—the very opposite of how we feel when we empathize with Betty, James, and Augustine. In this chapter, we will show how Swift's *folklore* love triangle challenges this notion of objectivity and

Taylor Swift and Philosophy: Essays from the Tortured Philosophers Department,
First Edition. Edited by Catherine M. Robb and Georgie Mills.
© 2025 John Wiley & Sons, Inc. Published 2025 by John Wiley & Sons, Inc.

viewing the world from a singular perspective, and will do so by drawing on some insights from an area of philosophy known as "feminist standpoint epistemology."

What Is Feminist Standpoint Epistemology?

Let's begin by defining our terms. First up, "epistemology" refers to anything to do with the philosophical study of knowledge—what knowledge is, how we get our knowledge, and why knowledge is valuable for all sorts of reasons. Here, we're specifically interested in how knowledge is valued and judged depending on who it belongs to. A "standpoint" is a distinct viewpoint, informed by features of one's social background (such as being a woman, being young, being a Taylor Swift fan, being a philosophy professor). To bring these two terms together, "standpoint epistemology" refers to the study of how we acquire knowledge through our unique standpoint. When we add the word "feminist" into this mix, we refer to the study of how we come to know certain things through experiencing the world through the unique standpoint of being a woman. What could we gain from looking at the world through this standpoint?

What's really valuable about feminist standpoint epistemology is that it encourages us to consider how knowledge is socially situated. A good example of socially situated knowledge is "what it is like to be someone." Only you can know what it is like to be yourself. This can be expanded to certain social groups: only members of a given social group can know exactly what it is like to belong to this group. Only Taylor Swift fans know what it is like to be a Swiftie, for example. Though some of this knowledge can be communicated—you can tell me what it is like to be you, and Swifties can tell their non-Swiftie friends what it is like to be a fan of Taylor—others will never understand our subjective experiences in full.

Despite there being a vast array of different perspectives in the world, it is an unfortunate fact that certain social groups are better represented in academic and public discourse than other social groups. For instance, in 2021, women held only 26 percent of full professorship positions, and made up just 33 percent of academic researchers.[2] Due to these differences in representation, the more dominant social group (that is, the group that is most represented in society) sets a "norm" of what counts as the kind of experiences we all have. In this way, mass subjectivity is tuned into an *assumed* objectivity—what is actually just a perspective of one social group is taken to be *the* perspective that we all have.[3] It then becomes difficult to engage with the perspectives of the social groups that aren't taken to be part of this norm. Feminist standpoint epistemology aims to address these problems. By intentionally investigating the perspectives of women, a group that has been historically underrepresented in social discourse, we may uncover truths that are obscured by traditional "objective" social narratives.

What underlies this exciting theory of epistemology is that it encourages us to move away from an understanding of knowledge as objective, which assumes that knowledge comes from a detached observer with no personal standpoint. As we are going to explore in this chapter with the help of Taylor Swift, so-called "objective" standpoints are actually not objective at all, as they often betray a perspective that is biased with particular values and ideas. By striving for a detached point of view, we run the risk of ignoring important ways of understanding the world. Since each perspective brings distinctive knowledge of the world, it is only by empathizing with a variety of perspectives that we can achieve true objectivity (although this notion of "objectivity" is understood differently than how we use it in everyday life). This is exactly what Taylor Swift helps the listener to achieve with the *folklore* love triangle. By inviting us to consider the emotionally charged perspectives of two women on opposing sides of a relationship, Swift helps us consider the dynamics of relationships in a less biased, more holistic way. Ultimately, Swift's narrative allows us to find true objectivity by taking into account different people's standpoints, perspectives, and emotions about a shared situation.

The View from Nowhere

Emotion can often get the better of us. It can lead us to act in ways we regret. It can also cause us to process information and make decisions in biased ways.[4] We have all been guilty of this at some point. Just think of the way we often react to the disappointment of losing at a game—it can't be that our opponent played better, they must have just been lucky! Or think of how we can let our emotions justify purchases—$500 for an Eras Tour ticket, what a bargain! In the *folklore* love triangle, James is guilty of this biased reasoning when he pleads to Betty, "I'm only 17, I don't know anything" ("betty"). By appealing to his youthful naiveté, he deflects the blame from himself and onto factors beyond his control. This, after all, is much easier than admitting that he knowingly hurt someone he loves (and in front of all of her "stupid friends," no less).

Given that emotions can cause biased responses, it makes sense that we might associate emotion with a lack of objectivity, and any beliefs that are influenced by our emotions—such as anger, fear, and love—we consider as biased. For example, the fact that you believe *1989 (Taylor's Version)* to be Taylor's best studio album might be because of the way you feel when you listen to it. This would indicate that your emotions and feelings are getting in the way of your belief about which of Taylor's albums are the best. Many philosophers believe that this kind of judgment, influenced by our emotions, does not count as objective reasoning. Ernest Nagel (1901–1985), for example, pioneered the claim that engaging in objective reasoning, or holding an objective belief, is to make judgments "from the view from nowhere." This view transcends any one person's or group's perspective, and requires us to stand outside of ourselves and see reality uncontaminated by human interests and desires. When you judge that *1989 (Taylor's Version)* is Taylor's best studio album, it should not be because it makes you feel certain emotions, or anything else to do with who you are and your personal likes and dislikes, but because it is objectively the best.

This idea that we can achieve objectivity by "standing outside of ourselves" has been criticized by many philosophers, who believe that achieving this viewpoint is difficult, perhaps even impossible.[5] As Susan Stebbing (1885–1943) highlights: "It is persons that think, not purely rational spirits."[6] Even if we accept that it's possible to embody this purely disinterested perspective for the objects of science, it's far from clear we can attain it when thinking about relationships. The idea of a relationship seems to be an essentially interest-relative notion, and closely connected to who we are as individuals and how we uniquely experience the world. When Taylor sings of her relationships, she will often sing from the first-person perspective: "I lived in your chess game" ("Dear John (Taylor's Version)"), and "I can read you like a magazine" ("Blank Space (Taylor's Version)").

"No One Likes a Mad Woman"

When we consider more closely what this "view from nowhere" really is, we see that its claims to objectivity often mask a biased partial perspective.[7] Many readers might have experienced first-hand the perspectives of women being diminished or not taken seriously by others—often men, but not always (as Taylor reminds us in "mad woman," "Women like hunting witches too," after all). Proponents of feminist standpoint epistemology argue that what might underpin this "delegitimization" (not being taken seriously) is the stereotypical view of the role that emotions have to play in how women form their beliefs. Men's beliefs are stereotypically considered to be unemotional, hence rational and superior, and women's beliefs are usually considered to be impaired by emotion, hence irrational and inferior.[8] As a result, male beliefs and views are considered as objective, and so what constitutes "the norm"—something that we all should strive for, and are considered deviant if we do not conform to. These sexist biases are seen throughout public discourse, and often justified by allusions to an "objective" science. For instance, in ancient Greece, male philosophers attempted to explain female mental illness as "female hysteria" caused by a "wandering womb," essentially reducing the mental state of women to the state of their uterus.[9]

In her lyrics, Swift highlights this connection between femininity, emotion, and irrationality. In "mad woman," she writes, "there's nothing like a mad woman / What a shame she went mad / No one likes a mad woman / You made her like that." This line plays on the double meaning of "mad" (angry or crazy) to demonstrate the tendency for heightened female emotions to be construed as demonstrations of hysteria, or madness. Feminist standpoint epistemology encourages us to identify the origins of these sexist associations, so that we can identify them as belonging to the perspective of a specific social group, as opposed to simply masquerading as extensions of what has been considered the "norm."

We can also see that the claims to disinterested objectivity—these so-called "views from nowhere"—correspond to a traditionally masculine way of thinking, and mask their own emotions and vulnerabilities. Swift highlights this point in her *folklore* love triangle. By giving us a glimpse into James's first-person perspective in "betty," Swift lays his emotions bare, and we can begin to see glimpses of his jealousy: "I hate the crowds, you know that / Plus, I saw you dance with him." We also see James's fears of being rejected: "But if I just showed up at your party / Would you have me? / Would you want me? / Would you tell me to go fuck myself?" In these lyrics, Swift gives us a valuable insight into James's emotions and fears, devoid of any pretense of being indifferent, unemotional, or objective. Although James is a man, he is not inhabiting a "view from nowhere."

Augustine and the Power of Emotions

Far from being something to avoid when forming our knowledge and beliefs, emotions can give us valuable insight. As the contemporary philosopher Michael Brady has pointed out, emotions often enhance our ability to know things about the world, and tell us important things about the way the world is.[10] We see Swift drawing on the insightful power of emotion throughout her discography, but in *folklore* she is at her most effective in employing emotions to challenge the way we tend to reduce people into heroes and villains—particularly when it comes to relationships. Swift tells us that this was one of her explicit intentions when writing "august," attacking the "total myth" of the bad villainous girl who "takes your man."[11] By experiencing the emotional anguish of Augustine, Swift allows us to realize that "everybody has feelings and wants to be seen and loved ... Augustine, that's all she really wanted."

How exactly does Taylor achieve this feat? In "august" we encounter Augustine at a delicate moment in her life when she is bridging the gap between innocence and womanhood, as demonstrated through careful lyrical choices. "Whispers of 'Are you sure?' / 'Never have I ever before'" alludes to the childhood game "Never Have I Ever," while also hinting that Augustine may have lost her virginity to James during this summer romance. Instead of viewing Augustine as an evil villain scheming to take Betty's man, we are invited to see her as a vulnerable young woman "living for the hope of it all" and "lost in the memory" of her summer romance. The conflicting testimonies of Augustine and James in "august" and "betty" show us the heart-wrenching contrast between how they describe their short-lived love affair. For Augustine it was "summer love," for James it was "just a summer thing." Now we see Augustine not as a callous homewrecker, but as someone who was deeply in love, chasing someone who was never really hers.

Even if this underlying narrative was not evident to all listeners, the true nature of Augustine would have been transparent to women who have been in similar situations. In this way, our experiences make it easier for us to know certain things, but not others. One way in which feminist standpoint epistemologists account for this association between knowledge and experience is with the idea of a "social location." Analogous to a physical location, a "social" location refers to an individual's background and place in society. This can be determined by a number of factors, including race and gender. For example, Augustine's social location might involve factors such as her being young and being a woman.[12] According to feminist standpoint epistemologists, our social location impacts our capacity for knowledge by giving us opportunities to know certain things, while withholding others. Being placed in a woman's social location, for instance, gives you the opportunity to know the way in which men can mistreat women (as Betty and Augustine sadly come to learn). Conversely, being a man may provide some distinct opportunities for knowledge as well, such as the pressure to remain unemotional in times of hardship.[13]

As well as imposing limitations on what we can know, our social location can also affect how our knowledge is treated. Women's viewpoints have traditionally been unfairly disregarded due to the social location they inhabit. The same can sometimes be true of young people, particularly when love is involved. It's easy for older people to forget the importance with which we regard our young relationships, and the deep lasting impact they have on our lives. In *folklore*, we see Swift giving pride of place to the perspectives of young people and asserting the validity of their emotional experiences. We are thus able to see the wisdom in each young person's testimony, and their fears of how their emotions will be regarded while confessing them. In "cardigan," Betty laments the fact that "when you are young they assume you know nothing," but rebuts, "But I knew you / Dancing in your Levi's / Drunk under a streetlight," and then, "I knew you'd linger like a tattoo kiss / I knew you'd haunt all of my what-ifs." All of these demonstrations of knowledge work to support her final claim, that "I knew everything when I was young," powerfully reclaiming her status as a woman, as young, and as someone who *knows*.

How Can We Inhabit a Standpoint?

So far in this chapter we have made the following two claims: one, that our knowledge is constrained by the social location we inhabit, and two, that we can understand other people better by putting ourselves in their shoes. This might seem puzzling. There is a tension here between the idea that our social location is inescapable, and the fact that empathy allows us to gain knowledge possessed by people of backgrounds different to ours. If we are really stuck with our own standpoint, how can we go outside of this to also understand the perspectives of others? Because of this apparent tension, feminist standpoint epistemologists have been criticized for creating "barriers to knowledge." This means that they are seen as carving out a special category of knowledge which only women can know, or only someone who shares the same standpoint could know. Critics claim that by excluding others from being able to know certain things, feminist standpoint epistemology underestimates our capacity to empathize with people different from ourselves.

By analyzing Swift's *folklore* love triangle, we can see that this criticism of feminist standpoint epistemology is mistaken. Feminist standpoint epistemologists can consistently claim that social location influences what we can know, *and* that we can expand our knowledge by empathizing with those different from ourselves. How so? Well, to say that there are limits on what we can know about other people's experiences is not to say that such knowledge is completely impossible to come by. Similarly, by empathizing with others we do not suddenly escape all constraints on what we can know. Our capacity for empathy will always be incomplete—there are always facts that we will miss, details that will be obscured by our own perspective, and we often make mistakes about what other people are thinking and feeling.

By empathizing with Augustine, even though we do learn something about her experience and come to know a little more about her experiences, we cannot learn all the complexities of being a young woman in her position. Our social background and our past experiences in life will also influence the way we empathize with her. Some people might listen to Augustine's testimony and misinterpret her as being cruel and manipulating. Some people might hear their own experiences in Augustine's testimony and deeply understand the subtle emotions she expresses as if they were their own. Some might listen and fail to understand what the song is about, because the situation is so far removed from their own experiences that they can't quite make sense of it. So, while the limits of our social location can be expanded with empathy and reaching out to understand the perspectives of others, it cannot be escaped.

By giving us access to the first-person testimonies of Betty, James, and Augustine, Swift challenges the traditional narratives of relationships and the biases that accompany them. By delving into the emotional content of each character's experiences, we are encouraged to relinquish the typical villain–victim dichotomy in favor of a more nuanced approach to the people we encounter.

Swift's storytelling clearly demonstrates the extent to which emotions shape our lives, and that paying attention to the emotions of others can help us to fully understand their perspectives. Thinking that emotions are irrational, and that we ought to instead associate knowledge with detached objectivity—a "view from nowhere"—inevitably leaves something out of the story. On a detached and objective view, Augustine becomes the silenced "other woman," trapped forever in the summer that meant nothing to anyone but her. James becomes the classic teenage boy who made a mistake but is forgiven, because "boys will be boys." And Betty becomes just another ingénue who has her heart broken by her high school boyfriend.

But this is not how Swift portrays them in *folklore*. Instead, Augustine is the naive young woman who fell for the wrong guy at the wrong time, yet held out hope nonetheless. James is the boy who did the wrong thing and knows it, and won't stop until he sets it right again. And Betty is the girl who grows into a woman, but is still haunted by the echoes of a long-lost love. Each character materializes as a complex individual, and we fully appreciate this by inhabiting each of their standpoints, one by one. Swift's songwriting demands that we put emotion in its rightful place in epistemology, demonstrating the power of empathy to unveil the intricacies and complexities of the human experience. If we only see one side, we will never get things quite right.[14]

Notes

1. "Augustine" is the unofficial fan name given to the unnamed voice in "august," adopted by Swift herself when referring to the character. See *folklore: the long pond studio sessions*, dir. Taylor Swift (Taylor Swift Productions, Big Branch Productions, 2020).
2. European Commission, Directorate-General for Research and Innovation, "She Figures 2021—Gender in Research and Innovation—Statistics and Indicators" (Publications Office, 2021).
3. Sally Haslanger, "On Being Objective and Being Objectified," in her *Resisting Reality: Social Construction and Social Critique* (New York: Oxford University Press, 2012), 35–82.
4. See, for example, Ziva Kunda, "The Case for Motivated Reasoning," *Psychological Bulletin* 108 (1990), 480–498. See also, Nicholas Epley and Thomas Gilovich, "The Mechanics of Motivated Reasoning," *Journal of Economic Perspectives* 30 (2016), 133–140.
5. Indeed, it's not clear if the "view from nowhere" is ever obtainable. Some philosophers claim that the way we understand reality is always mediated through our values and interests. See Hilary Putnam, *The Collapse of the Fact/Value Dichotomy and Other Essays* (Cambridge, MA: Harvard University Press, 2004).
6. Susan Stebbing, *Thinking to Some Purpose* (New York: Taylor & Francis, 2022).
7. As Sandra Harding highlights, historically the "[c]ommitment to an objectivity defined as maximizing social neutrality was not itself socially neutral in its effects." See "Introduction: Standpoint Theory as a Site of Political, Philosophic, and Scientific Debate," in Sandra Harding ed., *The Feminist Standpoint Theory Reader* (New York: Routledge, 2004), 5.

8. Teresa J. Frasca, Emily A. Leskinen, and Leah R. Warner, "Words Like Weapons: Labeling Women as Emotional during a Disagreement Negatively Affects the Perceived Legitimacy of Their Arguments," *Psychology of Women Quarterly* 46 (2022), 420–437.

9. Christopher A. Faraone, "Magical and Medical Approaches to the Wandering Womb in the Ancient Greek World," *Classical Antiquity* 30 (2011), 1–32.

10. See, for example, Michael Brady, *Emotional Insight: The Epistemic Role of Emotional Experience* (Oxford: Oxford University Press, 2013).

11. *folklore: the long pond studio sessions.*

12. As a fictional character, Augustine's social location seems indeterminate in certain respects. It seems indeterminate whether Augustine is tall, or brunette, for instance. For an accessible introduction to the philosophy of fictional characters see Stacie Friend, "Fictional Characters," *Philosophy Compass* 2 (2007), 141–156.

13. Some contemporary philosophers, such as Sandra Harding, have argued that the *dominated* group has a superior epistemic position to the *dominant* group. This is because the dominated group is typically forced to see the perspectives of the dominant group as well as their own. The dominant group, on the other hand, often has the luxury of only seeing things through their own privileged viewpoint. See Sandra Harding ed., *The Feminist Standpoint Theory Reader* (New York: Routledge, 2004), 21.

14. Lottie Pike is the lead author of this chapter and is responsible for the main ideas, as well as drafting and editing. Tom Beevers helped with drafting and editing.

20

The Trouble with Knowing You Were Trouble

Eric Scarffe and Katherine Valde

When Taylor Swift sings, "I knew you were trouble when you walked in" ("I Knew You Were Trouble (Taylor's Version)"), what exactly does she know? And how does she know it? In this chapter, we will consider three possible interpretations of how to answer these questions about what Swift knows. As we'll see, she tells us something important about how we know things, in a way that goes beyond the philosophical accounts of knowledge, and can help to improve them.

The Simple Claim

When Swift claims to know "you were trouble when you walked in," let's take her at face value to be claiming to know something about *you*. This is the simplest interpretation of the claim, but it is also the most morally problematic. If we understand Swift to be claiming to know something about someone else based on nothing more than a first impression, then she might be unfairly assuming that all people who share some particular characteristic are the same. This is a stereotype. For example, we might assume on first impression that all handsome male celebrities are going to break her heart and cause her trouble just because they are handsome, male, and a celebrity. The simple interpretation of the claim in "I Knew You Were Trouble (Taylor's Version)" (we'll shorten this to IKYWT) is to conclude that Swift is engaging in a type of stereotyping or profiling of the guy who just walked through the door and she has just met.

Of course, this isn't entirely out of character for Swift. Many of her lyrics straightforwardly embrace stereotypes and well-worn social scripts as a way of understanding her world, and in particular her romantic relationships. For example, in "Love Story (Taylor's Version)," in the same breath Swift claims she "knew it when [she] met him," and also casts their story into a social script by referring to her partner as "Romeo." On this reading, Swift's claim that she *knew* it when she met him likely wouldn't pass the smell test for what counts as genuine knowledge. In philosophical

Taylor Swift and Philosophy: Essays from the Tortured Philosophers Department,
First Edition. Edited by Catherine M. Robb and Georgie Mills.

accounts of knowledge, genuine knowledge is considered to consist of a justified and true belief—justified because it has evidence to back it up, and true because it turns out to actually be the case. This means that for Swift to genuinely know something, she must believe with good reasons that it's true, and the thing she believes must really be true. In this example of "Love Story," she is claiming to know the other person was "the one" having just met him. However, she only knows this because she is casting this person as her "Romeo" and assuming they are similarly destined to be star-crossed lovers.

The problem, of course, is stereotyping and profiling like this tends to lead us to false beliefs about the world. Swift doesn't have good reasons for believing that this Romeo is the one if she's just met him, and so down the line it might end up being a false belief. She might be optimistic about a potential relationship. She might know she was attracted to him when she met him, but referring to this potential romantic partner as "Romeo" demonstrates the way in which she doesn't genuinely know anything about this partner. Rather, she has cast this new person into a stereotypical romantic social script.

We might accuse Swift of being naive about the potential for this new romantic relationship, but who is she really hurting by forming this belief on nothing more than a first impression? To see why the simple version of the claim in IKYWT is morally fraught, let's consider a made-up example. What if the context for Swift's lyric wasn't about a romantic partner, but was a barista seeing a Black man walk into their coffee shop? If the barista were to say they "knew he was trouble when he walked in," how would we respond?

First, we would likely say that the barista didn't actually "know" anything in this case. As the contemporary philosopher John Finnis notes, "knowledge" is an "achievement-word."[1] When someone *believes* something it can be true or false, but when someone *knows* something that means it's true. When someone has knowledge, they have a belief that accurately represents reality—that they don't just have *a belief*, they have a *true* belief. Flat earthers, for example, might claim to know the earth is flat, but according to Finnis they don't have knowledge because this belief isn't true. In the case of our imagined barista, they concluded *this* Black man was trouble based on the false assumption that *all* Black men are dangerous. Beliefs formed on illegitimate or false evidential grounds are not genuine instances of knowledge because they fail to accurately represent reality. Our imagined barista may form the belief that this man is dangerous, but this wouldn't constitute a genuine knowledge claim. Their conclusion that this man is dangerous is derived from a false assumption that does not represent the way the world really is.

Perhaps more importantly we would also say the barista committed a *moral* wrong in drawing this conclusion about their customer. The barista is irresponsible for how she formed her beliefs, because she claimed to know something that wasn't true. But the barista is also morally culpable, because forming these sorts of racist beliefs about *all* Black men further perpetuates and enables the ongoing oppression of Black persons.

Of course, there may be important differences between forming a racist belief about someone else through stereotyping or profiling, and forming a belief that someone is or is not a suitable romantic partner for you. However, at the very least, it seems Swift would be on shaky ground to claim she *knew* you were trouble based on nothing more than a first impression. For that reason, we should dismiss this first interpretation out of the "principle of charity." This principle tells us that when someone makes a claim or argument we should interpret it in the best possible light. So, if there is a way to interpret what Swift means that doesn't commit her to saying something false or morally problematic, then we should adopt that alternative interpretation.

The Self-Knowledge Claim

Let's turn to the second way we might interpret Swift's claim to know "you were trouble when you walked in." The second way to interpret this claim, which avoids some of the problems with the simple claim we discussed above, is to take her claim as a "self-knowledge claim."

Swift's claim to *know* you were trouble is not literally to have knowledge about you (another person). Rather, her claim to *know* you were trouble is shorthand for knowing something about herself: recognizing her own patterns and proclivities to behave in certain ways. We call this a "self-knowledge" claim because, on this interpretation, the target for the knowledge claim is reflexive (it interprets Swift to be claiming to have knowledge about herself) even though the literal reading of the statement is other-regarding (on face value she is claiming to have knowledge about another person). This interpretation takes her claim to "know you were trouble" to have a hidden part—what she knows is that you're "trouble *for her*."

But how does she know this? Well, interpreting this as a self-knowledge claim we could say that she has observed herself in past relationships and knows that she has a tendency to invest her time or emotional energy into persons or situations that resemble the one she has just encountered. In the past, these situations have ended in "trouble." The inference is that she has not changed herself and is likely to find herself in a similar situation again now.

While this interpretation seems less morally problematic as it's not making any profiling claims about someone else, nevertheless, it also has its problems. For instance, one issue with interpreting the lyric as a kind of self-knowledge claim is that this is unsupported by the lyrics of IKYWT. As Swift sings "Once upon a time / A few mistakes ago / I was in your sights /

You got me alone / You found me ... / 'Cause I knew you were trouble when you walked in / So shame on me now." Taken in its full context, therefore, Swift seems to be suggesting that while she *should* have known better (due to her past mistakes), she did not, in fact, know. The lyrics to IKYWT suggest Swift didn't actually know much about herself.

However, elsewhere in Swift's discography we can find more evidence that she does know a fair bit about herself. For instance, if we look to a song like "Blank Space (Taylor's Version)" we can see her in a more self-empowered state that is supportive of a "self-knowledge" reading. As Swift sings in this song, she "Saw you there and I thought / 'Oh, my God, look at that face / You look like my next mistake / Love's a game, wanna play?'" Unlike IKYWT, the agency in these lyrics is firmly with the singer. Swift knows the "trouble" she might get into by pursuing this relationship. Instead of being in someone else's sights (as was the case in IKYWT), here she unambiguously understands how these sorts of situations operate for her, and (at least in this case) she is prepared to act on her knowledge, even if the outcome isn't any different in the end, as it goes "down in flames."

So, there is at least some evidence that Swift's claim to *know* something may actually be an indication that she knows something about herself. Although our knowledge of ourselves may not be undisputable (who hasn't had a friend or loved one point out some of our less-than-healthy patterns or behaviors?), such claims seem easier to justify than *knowing* something about someone you've just met. In the case of knowing ourselves, we have evidence in the form of past behavior, as well as (at least somewhat) privileged access to our inner monologues. For Swift to claim that a situation is trouble *for her*, then, is, at least on face value, a more plausible claim to "know" this.

Still, there is a lurking issue. The self-knowledge interpretation appears to result from a kind of "faux-feminism," and ultimately might not be the most mature version of the IKYWT claim that is possible. To explain, Swift certainly seems to *know* herself better in "Blank Space (Taylor's Version)" compared to IKYWT, but if we look beneath the surface we worry that this interpretation would mean Swift has fallen victim to false empowerment, by trying to capture morally problematic elements of male privilege.

For example, in "The Man" Swift sings about sexual conquest and opulent spending that makes her "the man," implying that such behaviors ought to be as empowering for women as they are for men: "They'd say I played the field before I found someone to commit to ... / Every conquest I had made would make me more of a boss to you." However, as contemporary philosophers such as Amia Srinivasan have pointed out, encasing oneself in the values of the male privilege does not offer true liberation, but merely perpetuates the system that will continue the very oppression that oppressed persons are seeking to destroy.[2] Enslaving a former master does not correct for the injustice of being held in slavery, it merely perpetuates a system that treats human beings as objects to be bought and sold.

When it comes to IKYWT, instead of engaging with the person who just walked in as a human being, it might be that Swift is treating him as an object of potential romantic interest. In doing so, the self-knowledge interpretation of the line in IKYWT appears to inadvertently perpetuate the patterns of objectification and sexualization that feminism seeks to dismantle. As such, the principle of charity tells us that if an interpretation exists that wouldn't commit Swift to a morally objectionable claim on feminist grounds, then we ought to adopt that different interpretation. Let's have a look at another interpretation.

Women's Intuition and Epistemology

This brings us to the last way we could interpret Swift's claim to "know you were trouble." Like the simple interpretation, this final interpretation has the virtue of taking the lyric at face value: it takes Swift to be claiming to know something about *you*. In contrast to the simple interpretation, however, this interpretation does not presume she is misrepresenting reality by engaging in stereotyping or profiling. Rather, this final interpretation takes seriously the possibility that Swift is drawing valid inferences from sources of evidence that have been used by women and people from other vulnerable minority groups to keep themselves safe.

For example, body language communicates vast amounts of information to others. As Alex Hitchens, the main character from the movie *Hitch*, infamously claims, "Sixty percent of all human communication is nonverbal, body language; thirty percent is your tone. So that means that 90 percent of what you're saying ain't coming out of your mouth."[3] Although these exact percentages have not been proven true by any scientific studies, neuroscientist Christine Tipper and her team have concluded that "[i]n the course of our everyday lives, we pick up information about what people are thinking and feeling through their body posture, mannerisms, gestures, and the prosody of their movements."[4] And so, a lot of information is communicated beyond the actual words a person says. From this, it would seem to follow that Swift *could* know something important about you when you walk in, by paying attention to your body language and a host of other behavioral and nonverbal social cues.

But what (if anything) is different about Swift's knowledge claim in IKYWT from other forms of racist or sexist stereotypes and profiling? After all, isn't stereotyping just forming beliefs based on body language or other social cues? How can we claim that Swift is making a justified knowledge claim when the racist barista isn't? Turning to a bit of philosophy can be helpful here.

One common view put forward by contemporary philosopher Tommie Shelby (yes, he does share the name of the famous character from the show *Peaky Blinders*), is that racist beliefs misrepresent reality and perpetuate or enable ongoing oppression and injustice.[5] Racist beliefs don't merely go wrong at the level of belief formation, by relying on false information and misrepresenting reality. They also do harm to others by perpetuating or enabling oppression and injustice.

And so, with this philosophical distinction in mind, one difference between Swift's claim in IKYWT and the racist barista is a difference in the moral harm generated by the claim. The belief that "you are trouble" doesn't perpetuate oppression or injustice in the same way that sexist or racist beliefs do. Like all women, Swift does not owe anyone her attention or a chance to get to know her better. Any "harm" which befalls the person walking in, therefore, is a harm only if we accept the mistaken belief that men are entitled to the attention and consideration of women. Swift might not genuinely "know" something about you, but insofar as her claim to know you were trouble doesn't perpetuate oppression and injustice, she doesn't have to be cancelled for unfairly stereotyping or profiling you.

However, Swift may have more credible evidence for drawing the conclusion that you are trouble. For example, as a woman she faces social oppressions that have conditioned her to be more sensitive to situations that might be dangerous for her. Common tropes about women carrying their keys between their fingers or pretending to be on a phone call while walking alone, or about Black parents teaching their children to be deferential to cops, highlight how social power can attune members of different oppressed groups to different elements of situations. The unfortunate reality of social oppression means that members of oppressed and vulnerable groups are socially trained (often implicitly) to read evidence in order to protect themselves from acts of violence (physical or otherwise). Swift's claim to "know you were trouble" could be based on a socially trained and epistemically reliable form of "women's intuition."

Interpreting the lyric as a kind of claim about women's intuition may seem unsupported by the lyrics of IKYWT. However, in other songs Swift draws attention to the manipulation and gaslighting that are consequences of failing to take this sort of "women's intuition" seriously. For example, in "mad woman," Swift sings that "Every time you call me crazy / I get more crazy / What about that? / And when you say I seem angry / I get more angry." Similarly, in "Nothing New (Taylor's Version) (From The Vault)," she laments that society's relationship to women in the entertainment industry is rife with changing standards. As she sings, "How can a person know everything at 18 but nothing at 22?" The answer, it would seem, is that society listens to the testimony of women only when they fit a particular set of shifting standards and expectations, dismissing the genuine knowledge, stories, and experiences of women and other historically marginalized persons when they step outside the socially accepted mold that is made for them.

Not only is Swift's claim to "know you were trouble when you walked in" importantly different than racist, sexist, or other stereotypes, it also highlights an "epistemic injustice" committed against women and other vulnerable minorities. "Epistemic injustice" is a term coined by the contemporary philosopher Miranda Fricker to explain how injustice can occur in relation to knowledge. Fricker argues that "epistemic injustice" occurs when the words and testimony of people are discounted or discredited unfairly or unjustly.[6] While this complaint itself may not be present in IKYWT, Swift clearly demonstrates an understanding of the difficulty of making claims to know things from vulnerable or oppressed social positions in songs such as "mad woman" and "Nothing New." So, this third interpretation is the most charitable and strongest interpretation of Swift's claim in IKYWT. The third interpretation preserves the simplicity of having her claim be about "you," but it also allows us to understand her as making an important point about what counts as "legitimate" sources of evidence for knowing.

Swift's Epistemology

There are some general lessons we can take away from the discussion about Swift's epistemology (understanding of knowledge) in IKYWT. First, what it means to "know" something is attached to a particular context. For example, what it means to "know" something in mathematics is different from what it means to "know" something in biology, and what it means to "know" something in biology is different from what it means to "know" something about your friend, yourself, or about morality. It's not that one of these forms of knowledge or ways of knowing is the true form, and the others just false copies or imperfect replications. Rather, whatever we mean by the term "know" is context specific. Being aware of these differences can help guard against pernicious introductions of doubt and uncertainty, which have been used to undermine the lived experiences of women and other marginalized persons. Swift "knows you were trouble" in the context of her position as a woman in a male-dominated society. The way she "knows" this may look different from the way we know facts about biology or chemistry, but that does not make this form of knowledge less worthy of our consideration.

This leads to the second general lesson—Swift's lyrics reveal a need for more work to be done in philosophy to understand nonlinguistic sources of knowledge, such as body language. It seems almost self-evident to point out that body language communicates information that is at least as valuable to understanding our social world as language and speech. It is also apparent that our social world is laced with racism, sexism, ableism, and all sorts of different 'isms' we have a moral obligation to combat. It would be a mistake, however, to draw the conclusion that because *some* of our social cues are racist, we should exclude *all* social cues as genuine sources of evidence. Pretending that women and other historically marginalized persons do not know important things about you when you walk in gaslights their experience of the world and discounts important sources of evidence and knowledge which should not be overlooked. We suggest taking seriously Swift's report to "know you were trouble when you walked in," just like the reports of countless other women and minorities.[7]

Notes

1. John Finnis, *Natural Law and Natural Rights*, 2nd ed. (New York: Oxford University Press, 2011), 59.
2. Amia Srinivasan, *The Right to Sex* (London: Bloomsbury, 2022).
3. *Hitch*, dir. Andy Tennant (Columbia Pictures, Overbrook Entertainment, 2005).
4. Christine Tipper, Giulia Signorini, and Scott Grafton, "Body Language in the Brain: Constructing Meaning from Expressive Movement," *Frontiers in Human Neuroscience* 9 (2015), 450.
5. Tommie Shelby, *Dark Ghettos: Injustice, Dissent, and Reform* (Cambridge, MA: Harvard University Press, 2018).
6. Miranda Fricker, *Epistemic Injustice: Power and the Ethics of Knowing* (New York: Oxford University Press, 2007).
7. This chapter is inspired by the memory of Adam Shmidt, PhD. Adam's endless enthusiasm for the overlap between ethics and epistemology, and love of Taylor Swift, formed the basis for much of this discussion. May his memory be a blessing.

21

"I Knew Everything When I Was Young"

Examining the Wisdom of Youth

Urja Lakhani

Taylor Swift's *folklore* features three songs—"cardigan," "betty," and "august"—written from the points of view of characters who find themselves entangled in a love triangle during their teenage years. Betty loves James, and James loves Betty, but James cheats on Betty with another girl, who also loves James. Reflecting on this situation, Betty and James express different views about whether older people have greater knowledge in comparison to younger people. Betty staunchly insists "I knew everything when I was young" ("cardigan"), while James appeals to his age and naiveté to excuse his behavior, saying: "I'm only seventeen, I don't know anything" ("betty"). Who is right? Can the young be wise? Or is youth synonymous with folly?

What Is Wisdom Anyway?

It's common to associate age with wisdom and youth with ignorance. As Swift sings in "cardigan"—"when you are young they assume you know nothing." The driving force behind this belief is the notion that certain knowledge comes with experience, and since the young have lived fewer years and have limited exposure, they potentially lack wisdom. This form of reverse ageism often leads to the dismissal of young people's beliefs, convictions, and feelings.

The question of whether or not the older are in fact wiser, and how this relates to Swift's work, cannot be answered until we take a closer look at what wisdom entails. Here is where philosophy comes in. After all, the word "philosophy" means the love of wisdom. Let's start with Aristotle's (384–322 BCE) understanding of wisdom from his best-known work, *Nicomachean Ethics*. Aristotle distinguishes between two types of wisdom: theoretical wisdom and practical wisdom. Theoretical wisdom is concerned

Taylor Swift and Philosophy: Essays from the Tortured Philosophers Department, First Edition. Edited by Catherine M. Robb and Georgie Mills. © 2025 John Wiley & Sons, Inc. Published 2025 by John Wiley & Sons, Inc.

with truth and requires extensive factual knowledge. This includes knowledge of the sciences, mathematics, history, philosophy, music, and other relevant disciplines.[1] This kind of wisdom is more about education than age. The second type of wisdom that Aristotle describes—practical wisdom—captures what we more commonly understand to be wisdom. It concerns making good decisions and judgments about how to live well, about what is good for ourselves and others.[2]

The philosopher Robert Nozick (1938–2002) expanded on this idea, highlighting that wisdom is not just one type of knowledge. Rather, the value of wisdom comes from its diversity; the content of what a wise person knows and understands is varied. It includes, among other things, knowledge of the most important values and goals in life, knowing the true and often implicit value of things, what leads to these goals without great cost, knowing when to take the long-term view, and how to cope with major dilemmas.[3] In light of Nozick's criteria, can we say that Betty was right, and that she was wise even though she was young? Did Betty really know "everything" when she was young, or did she know "nothing"?

Wisdom of the Young

Focusing on practical wisdom, we can make a compelling case that Betty was indeed wise. To start, Betty was aware of the important values and goals in life. In "cardigan," Betty shows that she knew her relationship with James—which made her feel seen and valued—was important and was worth preserving: "To kiss in cars and downtown bars / Was all we needed." In our culture, young romance is often perceived as frivolous in comparison to more "important" things such as career development or monetary gain, but Betty recognizes the true value of it.

Betty also indicates that she knows the means for attaining the goal of preserving her cherished relationship with James. Faithfulness is necessary, as she expresses when, as the narrator, she says: "A friend to all is a friend to none / Chase two girls lose the one" ("cardigan"). Betty further displays wisdom in taking a long-term view, recognizing that losing the relationship that she values deeply will lead to lasting regret: "I knew you'd linger like a tattoo kiss / I knew you'd haunt all of my what-ifs." Lastly, Betty displays her aptitude in coping with major dilemmas. Faced with the dilemma of whether or not to forgive James and take him back, Betty forgives James—he comes back to her, and they end up together.

When it comes to wisdom, Betty, and the young in general, may actually have an advantage. In our youth we possess a distinct ability to identify what truly matters, precisely because we have not yet been influenced by social expectations regarding what is deemed conventionally worthy or desirable. This lack of conditioning can allow us to recognize the true value of things. Plato (427–347 BCE) articulates a similar perspective in his dialogue *Meno*. In this dialogue, the character Socrates argues that all knowledge is innate rather than acquired and is accessed through the process of recollection.[4]

This view of knowledge—as innate, and equally available to all at birth—challenges the idea that knowledge is acquired through experience. And so, this weakens the strength of the idea that older individuals are wiser than younger ones. In fact, it opens the door to the opposite assertion—that the young may be wiser. This is because if one is born with all the necessary knowledge, and this knowledge is forgotten over time, it is reasonable to believe that the younger generation possesses a greater share of this knowledge, having had less time to forget it.

Plato's argument extends not only to theoretical knowledge (mathematics, science, philosophy), but also to morality and virtue, which play a central role in discerning what is important—the very subject matter of wisdom. This theme of losing knowledge of morality and virtue as we grow older is explored in Taylor Swift's song "seven," where the protagonist reminisces: "Before I learned civility / I used to scream ferociously / Any time I wanted." This lyric implies that when the protagonist was younger, she possessed a certain moral intuition and unwavering conviction in that intuition, which waned as she grew older and became more accustomed to societal norms. Reflecting on this song in the music documentary *folklore: the long pond studio sessions*, Swift remarks "when did I stop doing that when I was upset? When did I stop being so outraged that I would throw myself on the floor and throw the cereal at my mom? ... Obviously, you know, we can't be throwing tantrums all the time, and we learned that that's not the right thing to do, but there's something lost there too."[5] Swift alludes to the idea that as we age we often become more accommodating of problematic social norms, leading to a loss of the moral clarity and wisdom we possessed in our youth.

"Take the Moment and Taste It"

Another view that might explain why the young possess wisdom is the availability of the time required for careful deliberation on what matters to us. When we are young, we are unburdened by adult pressures and have the time to reflect on things that are important. Valerie Tiberius, a contemporary philosopher, claims that wisdom requires, among other things, that a wise person live the sort of life that he or she could sincerely endorse upon reflection.[6] This means that a wise individual should lead a life that, upon deep and honest introspection, aligns with their core values, beliefs, and principles. They should be able to look back on their life choices with a sense of authenticity and conviction, believing that the path they've chosen reflects their true self and what they genuinely consider to be worthwhile.

As we grow older, the mounting responsibilities that accompany adulthood demand our attention and often leave us with limited time for such deep reflection. This can lead us to merely go through the motions of life, conforming to societal norms and following the well-trodden paths of those who came before us. In contrast, the young, unburdened by the weight of these pressing responsibilities, possess more freedom to engage in introspection and careful deliberation. Betty, for instance, at the tender age of seventeen, demonstrates a remarkable capacity for self-reflection, leading her to recognize the value of her relationship with James.

Adulthood, with its increasing focus on career and other ambitions, can lead one astray. In "You're On Your Own, Kid," Swift writes, "The jokes weren't funny, I took the money / My friends from home don't know what to say," alluding to the potential loss of childhood friendships in the relentless pursuit of success. The lyrics suggest that a busy and demanding lifestyle left the narrator with little time for contemplation about what truly mattered. Nevertheless, when she finally slows down and engages in introspection ("I looked around in a blood-soaked gown"), the narrator comes to appreciate the significance of friendship and the importance of savoring the present moment: "So make the friendship bracelets / Take the moment and taste it."

Was James Wise?

Contrasting with Betty, James says that he didn't know anything because he was seventeen. James's admission of his lack of knowledge, reflected in his past reckless behavior, raises an interesting issue—the relationship between action and wisdom. Some philosophers reject the view that wisdom is a matter of knowledge alone, instead arguing that wisdom is reflected in action. John Kekes, a contemporary philosopher, argues that wisdom manifests in good judgment: "in good judgment, a person brings his knowledge to bear on his actions. To understand wisdom, we have to understand its connection with knowledge, action, and judgment."[7] Therefore, wisdom can't be solely assessed based on words and understanding—it must also be evident in one's actions. A similar perspective is shared by Valerie Tiberius, who suggests that a wise person's actions should reflect their core values, noting that actions are a means to express wisdom and reflect one's understanding of how to lead a good life. Reckless people, even if they are knowledgeable about life, are not wise.[8]

So, is James a reckless, unwise individual, or is he a wise person who made a mistake? I suspect the latter. Wisdom is not synonymous with perfect judgment—it's more about learning from one's mistakes. James's wisdom shines through in his acknowledgment of his error and his willingness to admit his folly and seek forgiveness. Furthermore, he doesn't merely dwell in regret, but takes action by showing up at Betty's door and confessing that his infidelity was "the worst thing" he ever did ("betty").

We could also interpret James's claim—"I don't know anything" ("betty")—as a reflection of his intellectual humility, which aligns with the Socratic understanding of wisdom. Socrates believed the essence of wisdom is the ability to recognize the limits of one's knowledge and be open to learning from others. If wisdom is understood as intellectual humility, we have even more reason to believe that it is often found in young people. As we age, we tend to become more confident in our beliefs, thoughts, and values, making us less open to admitting ignorance or mistakes. The pressure to live up to the notion of being "older and wiser" may lead us to hesitate to acknowledge when we lack knowledge or are wrong about something. Additionally with increasing age, we accumulate more power and status, which can inadvertently breed overconfidence in our own knowledge. So, regardless of the way wisdom is conceived—as knowledge of the important things, or as intellectual humility—we have reason to believe that the young may know something, after all.

"Don't Call Me Kid"

Clearly, the assumption that older people are wiser and more knowledgeable is unfair. To defer to someone who genuinely possess more knowledge or wisdom is reasonable. In fact, it is encouraged. However, we should not defer to someone and assume they are wiser simply because they are older, especially when gender dynamics are involved. The theme of deferring to an older and supposedly "wiser" man is prominent in the song "tolerate it" from the *evermore* album. The narrator is a young woman, who we can infer is married to a much older man, and who struggles to find validation in her relationship. She sees him as "so much older and wiser," while perceiving herself as "just a kid." Feeling infantilized, she asks for her partner to validate her feelings: "If it's all in my head, tell me now / Tell me I've got it wrong somehow." The song suggests that her partner may not be wise at all, given that he is unable to recognize her emotions and feelings toward him, leaving her feeling unheard and misunderstood. This dynamic results in the protagonist confronting a sense of insignificance, and loss of confidence, as if she's "taking up too much space and time." The song powerfully portrays the complexities of age-related gender power dynamics and how they can lead to unbalanced relationships.

Swift herself has experienced this dynamic of an older man in a romantic relationship with a younger woman, reflecting on such relationships in songs like "All Too Well (Taylor's Version)," "Dear John (Taylor's Version)," and "Would've, Could've, Should've." As Swift shows us in her lyrics, the association of epistemic authority with older age and male gender, can pave the way for problematic power dynamics in relationships, fostering environments prone to gaslighting and self-doubt. Contemporary philosopher Andrew Spear highlights this association, arguing that the effectiveness of gaslighting hinges on the gaslighter assuming epistemic superiority, asserting that they possess more knowledge than their victim, which influences the victim's experience.[9] As a consequence of this intellectual deference, the victim not only accords the gaslighter unwarranted credibility but also begins to question her own judgment, losing faith in her own experiences, thoughts, and judgments.[10] This internal turmoil results in confusion, uncertainty, and a troubling lack of confidence in the victim's own reality.

We find a fitting example of this in Swift's *All Too Well: The Short Film*, which depicts the protagonist having a conversation with an older partner regarding an uncomfortable experience she had at a dinner party with older people. The experience made her feel excluded and embarrassed, and when she communicates this to her partner, he fails to offer support, dismissing her emotions as if she had imagined things. His response, "I think you're making yourself feel that way," leads her to doubt her own experience.

The infantilization and gaslighting of women are pervasive issues that extend beyond intimate relationships—as Swift expresses in her songs, they also permeate our culture at large. In "mad woman," she highlights the gaslighting experienced by young women in society, which often leaves them questioning their own sanity, and making them feel "mad." In the *folklore* documentary, discussing the song with her collaborator Aaron Dessner, Swift says: "the most rage-provoking element of being a female is the gaslighting that happens when, for centuries, we've been expected to absorb male behavior silently."[11] In the song, Swift sheds light on the consequences for women who refuse to remain silent and start asserting themselves, showing that they are once again subjected to gaslighting, making them feel "mad," as though their emotions and concerns are unjustified.

Time to Run

These considerations about the systemic discounting of young people, young women in particular, have political significance. Young people are significantly underrepresented in political institutions and there are many obstacles that make it harder for them to vote.[12] This is particularly concerning given that many of our current political challenges disproportionately impact young people. As Swifts describes in a *Variety* interview: "young people are the people who feel the worst effects of gun violence, and student loans and trying to figure out how to start their lives and how to pay their bills, and climate change, and are we going to war."[13]

In response, Swift offers hope to the young, highlighting how political leaders may be corrupted by age, and encouraging the young to trust their wisdom to drive cultural and political change: "They aren't gonna help us / Too busy helping themselves / They aren't gonna change this / We gotta do it ourselves / They think that it's over / But it's just begun / Only one thing can save us / Only the young" ("Only the Young"). The young look forward and the old look back. Swift reminds us that it's time to look forward.

Notes

1. Aristotle, "Nichomachean Ethics," in Richard McKeon ed., *The Basic Works of Aristotle* (Oxford: Oxford University Press, 2011), particularly Book VI.
2. Sharon Ryan, "Wisdom," in *The Stanford Encyclopedia of Philosophy*, at https://plato.stanford.edu/archives/fall2023/entries/wisdom.
3. Robert Nozick, *The Examined Life* (New York: Simon & Schuster, 2006), 267–278.
4. Plato, "Meno," in John M. Cooper ed., *Complete Works* (Indianapolis: Hackett, 1997), 880.
5. *folklore: the long pond studio sessions*, dir. Taylor Swift (Taylor Swift Productions, Big Branch Productions, 2020).
6. Valerie Tiberius, *The Reflective Life: Living Wisely with Our Limits* (Oxford: Oxford University Press, 2008), particularly chap. 7.
7. John Kekes, "Wisdom," *American Philosophical Quarterly* 20 (1983), 277.
8. Tiberius, *The Reflective Life*, chap. 8.
9. Andrew Spear, "Epistemic Dimensions of Gaslighting: Peer-Disagreement, Self-Trust, and Epistemic Injustice," *Inquiry* 66 (2019), 68–91.
10. Spear, "Epistemic Dimensions of Gaslighting," 70.
11. *folklore: the long pond studio sessions*.
12. Alexandria Symonds, "Why Don't Young People Vote, and What Can Be Done About It?," *The New York Times*, October 8, 2020, at https://www.nytimes.com/2020/10/08/upshot/youth-voting-2020-election.html.
13. Chris Willman, "How Midterm Elections Inspired Taylor Swift's New Song, 'Only the Young,'" *Variety*, January 21, 2020, at https://variety.com/2020/music/news/taylor-swift-political-song-documentary-miss-americana-1203473948.

22

How Do We Know What Taylor Swift Is Feeling?

Neil Mussett

There is something special about the connection that Taylor Swift fans, or "Swifties," feel with Taylor and each other. On the second night of the 2023 Eras Tour in Philadelphia, thousands of fans who could not get tickets showed up to "Taylor-Gate" in the nearby parking lot, hearing what they could from the concert and enjoying some time with fellow fans.[1] The perks of being a Swiftie are clearly more than memorable music and inventive videos. Taylor has created a "tribe of like-minded people," whose community is meeting the need to be seen, understood, and validated by others.[2]

What is happening here? How can so many people feel that close to someone they don't see in their daily lives? How can an artist (or anyone else for that matter) share their inner lives in a way that lets us know their thoughts and feelings? How can we be sure of what we know about Taylor, especially when she talks about songwriting as "magical and mystical?"[3] We see Taylor performing the ten-minute version of "All Too Well" live on *Saturday Night Live* and we feel like we see her pain and regret, but also her resolve and hope. What does it mean to "see" that?

Doubt and Descartes

Any time you ask a "How do we know?" question around philosophers, they flash back to René Descartes (1596–1650), who freaked us all out so thoroughly that we're still not over it. Descartes invented analytic geometry,[4] was a rainbow scientist,[5] said "I think, therefore I am,"[6] and died when a twenty-two-year-old queen forced him to wake up too early.[7] (He would not have done well on tour with Taylor, considering her intense pre-tour training routine.[8]) Descartes is famous for being a skeptic (doubting what we can know), which is really sad, because his life mission was actually to fight against skepticism.

During the live performance of "Doubt" in 2015, Taylor Swift said, "Every single day, no matter what happens, I continue to doubt myself."[9]

Taylor Swift and Philosophy: Essays from the Tortured Philosophers Department, First Edition. Edited by Catherine M. Robb and Georgie Mills.
© 2025 John Wiley & Sons, Inc. Published 2025 by John Wiley & Sons, Inc.

Descartes felt the same way. His approach, called "methodic doubt," required that if we can find any way to doubt the truth of a claim, we should distrust it and set it aside as something unreliable. Adopting these standards would (and did) limit many philosophers to talking only about reliable things like math and language. It seems like we can never really be sure about what other people are thinking and feeling, and so methodic doubt would set such speculation aside.

The Wisest Woman Had to Do It This Way

This brings us to Edith Stein (1891–1942), who was a German feminist, a Jewish philosopher, a Catholic saint, and a Holocaust martyr. She could have escaped Auschwitz but didn't, saying "If I cannot share the lot of my brothers and sisters, my life, in a certain sense, is destroyed."[10] She wrote twenty-eight books, but the one that helps us here is her doctoral dissertation, "On the Problem of Empathy." Her topic? "The question of empathy as the perceiving of foreign subjects and their experience."[11] In other words, "empathy" is our ability to know ("perceive") the experiences of other people ("foreign subjects"). Stein asked the questions: Can we "perceive" the feelings of others like we see their faces? And how much access do we have to other peoples' inner lives?

Like any modern philosopher, Stein was worried what Descartes would say about her project, but she had a secret weapon—the "phenomenological method." Stein's mentor, the philosopher Edmund Husserl (1859–1938), had founded a new movement in philosophy called "phenomenology." Phenomenologists were a new breed of philosophers who felt that the way to do philosophy was to describe our experiences as best we can, before worrying about the possibility of deception and doubt. Phenomenologists thought that it would be silly to doubt that we experience the world as full of thinking, feeling people with minds of their own. People aren't robots or zombies. According to phenomenologists, if I encounter another person, they are "not given as a physical body, but as a sensitive, living body belonging to an 'I', an 'I' that senses, thinks, feels, and wills."[12] Every person we see has their "I"—their own point of view that has desires, thoughts, and feelings, and this experience is hard to doubt.

Not only do I experience other people as other selves, I also seem to know something about their inner lives. Taylor Swift's songs are filled with recognition of unspoken emotion. In "Only the Young," she writes about seeing her friend's fear: "It keeps me awake / The look on your face / The moment you heard the news / You're screaming inside." In "Let's Go (Battle) (Taylor's Version) (From The Vault)" she talks about the look on her frenemy's face as if it were a full conversation: "You're looking at me like I tried to take you down." In "Would've, Could've, Should've," she writes about her blush giving her away: "If I never blushed, then they could've / Never whispered about this." Our blushing body expresses our feelings to others, and Edith Stein writes that when we see someone blush after saying something awkward, we can "see" their realization and their shame.[13] We do this so naturally that we can even spot people who try to fake their feelings. So, what is this ability to "see" someone's feelings?

Our Endless Empathy

The ability to comprehend the experience and feelings of others is empathy. Stein uses "empathy" as a technical word (she knows it's been used to mean a lot of different things). Like a good phenomenologist, she compares empathy to similar experiences we have when trying to understand the world. Stein claims that empathy is similar to sense perception (the perception of the world we have when using our five physical senses) because what we experience is present in front of us. However, Stein also claims that empathy is not physical in the same way that sense perception is. I see your face and I see your pain, but unlike your face, I don't see it as a physical object. When I see your emotion, it comes to me as something I see *in* your face. Taylor Swift's lyrics are full of seeing emotion in the face of the other. In "willow," she regrets missing the smug dishonesty in someone else's face: "Guess I should've known from the look on your face / Every bait and switch was a work of art." Similarly, "Afterglow" speaks of a face accusing her: "Why'd I have to break what I love so much? / It's on your face, and I'm to blame, I need to say." Guilty intentions are evident in someone's face in "Babe (Taylor's Version)": "And it's strange how your face doesn't look so innocent / Your secret has its consequence and that's on you, babe."

My empathy has your experience as its content, and this experience is presented to us *in* physical expressions. In "You're Losing Me (From The Vault)," Taylor sings, "Every morning, I glared at you with storms in my eyes." You can imagine it was you she was singing about. You imagine her looking at you like that and can read the hurt and anger in her face. You try to understand more about this hurt, and it naturally directs you toward the reason for her mood (she has fallen out of love). You can look again at her face and feel her pain. This pain is felt, not known like some neutral fact. However, it is felt as the pain of another person: you don't experience it as you experience your own pain, and you are not confused about whose pain it is. Stein would describe this as your experience of empathy being "led" by Taylor's pain.[14]

Stein contrasts her idea of empathy with that of her former teacher, Theodor Lipps (1851–1914), or as the hip-hop community knew him, "T-Lipps."[15] He was a pioneer in the study of boredom[16] and empathy.[17] Lipps described empathy as an "inner imitation" of someone else's experience, so that when

I feel empathy for you, it is because my mind mimics your actions or facial expressions and I have a similar experience as you. For example, we see Taylor on stage in a sold-out stadium, and we put ourselves in her place, "moving" with her as we watch her actions. If we see her experiencing the thrill of performing, we feel thrilled, too. Lipps says this is what we mean by empathy. If we see that Taylor is thrilled, but we don't feel thrilled ourselves, then this is "an incomplete, preliminary level of empathy." Stein understands empathy differently; she claims that we can empathize with someone even when our own emotions do not match the other's.[18]

We Have More Than Your Sympathy

Stein contrasts "empathy" (perceiving someone else's emotions) with "sympathy" (feeling the same as someone else). Stein says there's a tendency for "fellow-feeling" or "sympathy," but it's not the same as empathy. Let's say you managed to get backstage passes to the next Taylor Swift concert. I see how happy you are (empathy), and I'm happy for you (sympathy). Sympathized joy and empathized joy aren't the same. Your joy is probably more intense than mine. This is especially true with "negative empathy": if you got a backstage pass and I did not manage to get a ticket, we won't feel the same. I can see just how happy you are, and as much as I would like to feel that way, too, I wouldn't be able to. On Lipps's account, you would be failing to have empathy, but Stein would say that this just highlights the difference between seeing someone's emotions (empathy) and feeling the same way with them (sympathy).

Stein and Lipps also differ concerning the relationship between empathy and a feeling of being "one" with the other. Lipps argues that empathy is a feeling of unity and oneness such that it erases the distinction between my own "I" and the other's "I." We would have to step out of empathy to regain our own identity and sense of self. Stein says this isn't really how it works: as thrilling as it is to watch a skilled acrobat fly through the air, as much as I feel his ups and downs, "I am not one with the acrobat, but only 'at' him."[19] When I was with my daughter at Taylor Swift's Speak Now Tour, Taylor flew directly over our seats in a cloud of glitter. We felt each other's joy, but did the barriers separating us break down? Stein would say that as much as I felt my daughter's joy, it's real to me as *her* joy, which I am feeling. Her joy is alive in me, which makes it possible to experience it as a "we." And so, even though empathy is not the same as the feeling of oneness, we couldn't feel oneness without it. Empathy makes it possible to feel with others (sympathy) and feel united to others (oneness).

Taylor Swift ties these three moments of empathy, sympathy, and oneness together in "Long Live (Taylor's Version)." The song attempts to freeze a moment of victory for a couple in love: "I said remember this moment / In the back of my mind / The time we stood with our shaking hands / The crowds in stands went wild." Taylor recognizes the triumph in her lover and screams, "long live the look on your face." Telling him to "remember this feeling," Taylor identifies the feeling as singular and shared, not worrying about any distance between them.

You're Not Sure and I Don't Know

So now that we're clear on what empathy is and how it works, Descartes has been in the corner with his hand raised the whole time just waiting to ask one question: How can you be sure? Can we find a way to doubt our experiences of empathy? Is it possible to make a mistake or be deceived about what the other person feels? If so, do we have to throw out our account of empathy, sympathy, and oneness?

Sure—sometimes we're surprised, confused, and even deceived about what other people think and feel. For example, if you've had a terrible accident and your leg is mangled, but I look in your face and you're smiling, I wouldn't know what to make of that. Or, you could see your friend's red face without knowing whether they are embarrassed, angry, or just flushed from working out. Someone might tell you that they really care about you, but their eyes are cold, and the facial expression just doesn't seem to match up with what they're saying. These are all Stein's examples, and she asks a simple question: How can you be more accurate with your empathy, and figure out what people are feeling? The answer: use more empathy! You use your senses to explore the world around you; you use empathy to do the same with people. You can use context to interpret your friend's red cheeks, and you can see their embarrassment because they have just said something that might be considered cringey or awkward. Well-trained empathy lets us spot fake smiles and dramatic sadness. It can even help us understand strange new reactions in other people like angry laughter or relieved tears.

Still, it's possible to have doubt and deception in empathy. Many of Taylor Swift's most poignant songs are about misunderstanding and confusion in relationships. That is the most painful part of a song like "The Story of Us (Taylor's Version)," where Taylor writes, "Now I'm standing alone in a crowded room / And we're not speaking and I'm dying to know / Is it killing you like it's killing me?" To wipe the smile off Descartes' face, Stein makes two points. First, the case of deception is not the normal case. How often are you genuinely deceived about how someone is feeling? If your friend snarls when they are actually relaxed, or cries when they are hiding inspiration, that's not the standard case. Our everyday experience is usually of people who at least have some coherence between what they express and what they feel. Second, confusion about other people's experiences is only removed again by empathy. You might mistakenly assume that your friend has the same love of a Taylor Swift song as you do, but your mistake will disappear the minute you blare it and turn around and see boredom in their face. In this example the problem was not that your empathy was mistaken, but that you made a false inference—you were reading your emotion of enjoyment into someone else, when it clearly was not there in your friend's own emotional reaction.

To avoid getting fooled, we need to use our eyes and ears. Paying close attention to people's body language will help us avoid most errors. Our original naive attitude is true, as Stein writes: "We love and hate, will and act, are happy and sad and look like it."[20] The unity between our body language and our emotions is so strong that it reveals who we are more than we realize. Over time, our experiences of empathy either confirm or correct our understanding of a person's character. Our closest friends may even know us better than we know ourselves. That is what Taylor means in "You Belong With Me (Taylor's Version)" when she says, "You say you're fine, I know you better than that ... / Can't you see that I'm the one / Who understands you?"

She Is Somebody That We Don't Know

We know what Taylor is feeling by using empathy. But there's a problem: we have been discussing empathy in terms of in-person interactions. Unless you are Andrea Swift, for example, you can't really count on seeing Taylor Swift in person on a regular basis. Instead, you see her in videos and concerts, which are merely performances. You see her in interviews, which are edited and leave out a lot of information about Taylor's private life. You might read her Instagram posts, but these are all limited glimpses into a much fuller life. Her songs are emotional, but how much do they tell us about her own feelings?

Explaining the songwriting process for *folklore*, Taylor says that "I found myself not only writing my own stories, but also writing about or from the perspective of people I've never met, people I've known, or those I wish I hadn't."[21] Does this mean that Taylor may never have felt any of the feelings associated with these stories? What can we actually learn about Taylor from these songs?

I Know Your Favorite Songs

The philosopher R.K. Elliott gives a good description of what's going on when we listen to songs (and perceive other works of art).[22] Songs express the thoughts and feelings of the author—we can perceive the feelings expressed by a song with a kind of artistic empathy. Elliott's explanation is a type of "Expression Theory," which claims that songs have qualities that include not only things like length and key, but also affective (emotional) qualities like anger or regretfulness. Much like Edith Stein's account of empathy, Elliott claims that we have the ability to perceive aesthetic qualities along with the outward appearances of artistic works. For example, when you hear a song like "Ronan," the sadness of the song is given along with the lyrics and melody. You don't have to be sad yourself to know it is sad, even though the full experience of the song would include feeling sad yourself.

On Elliott's view, a song is an expression of thoughts and feelings. When I listen to a song, I can think of it as just sounds—loud, soft, repetitive, long, short—or I can think of it as the speech or thought of another person. I can even try to make the expression my own, as if I'm the one who wrote it. I can use my imagination to adopt the perspective of the songwriter, placing myself in the situation described by the lyrics. Elliott calls this experiencing the "from within."

For example, in "Clean (Taylor's Version)," Taylor writes "When I was drowning, that's when I could finally breathe / And by morning / Gone was any trace of you, I think I am finally clean." The "I" in this lyric can be interpreted as an invitation for you to put yourself in the singer's place. Someone who doesn't know Taylor Swift's music may not take up that invitation, and so hear it as just another calm pop song. However, if you are a Swiftie you can use imagination to invest yourself with Taylor's situation, and experience her expression and the song's emotion from her perspective. You may not have the exact same experience of slowly moving to a more peaceful place after a breakup, but that emotion is somehow present in you when you use your empathy. Elliott says the emotion is "present in me … but not predicable of me."[23] In other words, you can feel Taylor's peace in the song even though it would not be exactly true to say that you are peaceful, or you feel peace. You can be there together with Taylor, as if you inhabited the same body and she were speaking with your voice. That experience can feel quite intimate and allows you to form a sort of relationship with the version of Taylor that has written the lyrics and is singing the song.

And so, given Elliott's account of artistic expression, really understanding a song is about using artistic empathy to go deeper into this experience. When we first hear a song, we may just hear the sounds and the rhythm. As we get more familiar with it, we experience certain passages as if they came from inside us instead of coming from the outside. This experience allows us to contribute the element of our own feeling, which makes a difference in how we evaluate the song: people who haven't experienced a song this deeply may not fully appreciate its aesthetic qualities. Elliott argues that some of our deepest disagreements about the value of music depend on whether we hear it as "just" sounds or as an expression of the artist.

With empathy, we can perceive the emotion of other people. With artistic empathy, we have a way to perceive emotion in songs. This helps us understand how we might know what Taylor is feeling, given the emotion that she expresses in the lyrics and music of her songs. But there are limitations. We know for a fact that Taylor Swift writes some songs from perspectives other than her own. For instance, Taylor said that her song, "betty," was written from the perspective of a seventeen-year-old boy.[24] It's a song full of longing, anticipation, and fear. A high-schooler wrongs a girl named Betty, but then regrets it and shows up uninvited to her party hoping for a reconciliation. Do we know that Taylor Swift has had this experience? If we take her at her word, then we have to conclude that this experience is not her own. Can we say for sure that she hasn't felt the emotions expressed by the song? Certainly artists use their own experiences to write, but they also use imagination, and as fans who do not have a personal relationship with Taylor, we are not in a position to easily distinguish between the two.

Even though there are limitations, there is hope. Taylor's wide array of interviews, her performances, and her social media posts give us opportunities for empathic experiences. Like Stein says, empathy allows us to get a sense of the unity behind someone's individual experiences and actions, and Elliott says that our experience of art has the potential to be deep and vivid, if we use our artistic empathy. Even if the emotions in some of Taylor's songs are the product of her imagination, they came from somewhere inside Taylor, and this makes the connection between the expression and the emotions in the song feel powerful. So Swifties can feel confident when we say that we know what Taylor is feeling, most of the time.

Notes

1. Emily Bloch and Kasturi Pananjady, "For Every Three Taylor Swift Attendees, One Came Just to Hang in the Parking Lot of Her 'Eras Tour' in Philly," *The Philadelphia Inquirer*, August 3, 2023, at https://www.inquirer.com/entertainment/music/taylor-swift-eras-tour-philadelphia-lincoln-financial-field-20230803.html.

2. Tasha Seiter, "Why Taylor Swift's Fans Love Her So Much," Psychology Today, July 17, 2023, at https://www.psychologytoday.com/us/blog/mindful-relationships/202307/why-taylor-swifts-fans-love-her-so-much.

3. Caleb Triscari, "Taylor Swift Says Songwriting Remains 'Magical and Mystical' to Her," *NME*, June 10, 2021, at https://www.nme.com/news/music/taylor-swift-says-songwriting-remains-magical-and-mystical-to-her-in-award-speech-2965478.

4. Donald L. Wasson, "René Descartes," in *World History Encyclopedia*, at https://www.worldhistory.org/Rene_Descartes.

5. Bill Casselman, "The Mathematics of Rainbows," AMS – American Mathematical Society, February 2009, at https://www.ams.org/publicoutreach/feature-column/fcarc-rainbows.

6. René Descartes, *Discourse on the Method for Conducting One's Reason Well and for Seeking Truth in the Sciences*, trans. Donald A. Cress (Indianapolis: Hackett Publishing, 1998), 19.

7. The Editors of the Encyclopedia Britannica, "How Did René Descartes Die?," in *Encyclopedia Britannica*, at https://www.britannica.com/question/How-did-Rene-Descartes-die (accessed April 19, 2024).

8. Sam Lansky, "2023 Person of The Year: Taylor Swift," *TIME*, December 6, 2023, at https://time.com/6342806/person-of-the-year-2023-taylor-swift.

9. Mary J. Blige and Taylor Swift, "Doubt," YouTube, December 28, 2015, at https://www.youtube.com/watch?v=GZ0474w66uw.

10. Christian Bergmann, "Edith Stein's Catholic Feminism," Catholic Archdiocese of Melbourne, August 12, 2021, at https://melbournecatholic.org/news/edith-steins-catholic-feminism.

11. Edith Stein, *On the Problem of Empathy*, trans. Waltraut Stein (Washington, DC: ICS Publications, 1989), 1.

12. Stein, *On the Problem of Empathy*, 3.

13. Stein, *On the Problem of Empathy*, 5.

14. Stein, *On the Problem of Empathy*, 11.

15. Not really.

16. Theodor Lipps, "Arten den Gefühlen," in *Leitfaden der Psychologie* (Leipzig: Wilhelm Engelmann, 1906), 294–304.

17. Theodor Lipps, "Empathy, Inner Imitation and Sense-Feelings," in *A Modern Book of Esthetics*, trans. E.F. Carritt (New York: Holt, Rinehart & Winston, 1979), 374–382.

18. Lipps, "Empathy, Inner Imitation and Sense-Feelings," 12.

19. Lipps, "Empathy, Inner Imitation and Sense-Feelings," 16.

20. Lipps, "Empathy, Inner Imitation and Sense-Feelings," 88.

21. Will Richards, "Read Taylor Swift's New Personal Essay Explaining Eighth Album 'folklore,'" *NME*, July 24, 2020, at https://www.nme.com/news/music/read-taylor-swift-new-personal-essay-explaining-eighth-album-folklore-2714540.

22. R.K. Elliott, "Aesthetic Theory and the Experience of Art," *Proceedings of the Aristotelian Society* 67 (1967), 111–126.

23. Elliott, "Aesthetic Theory and the Experience of Art," 113.

24. Glenn Rowley, "Taylor Swift Confirms Who the 'Betty' Characters After [sic] Named After," *Billboard*, August 7, 2020, at https://www.billboard.com/music/pop/taylor-swift-inspiration-betty-characters-names-9430752.

"BACK TO DECEMBER": FATE, MEMORY, AND IMAGINATION

A Real Lasting Legacy
Memory, Imagination, and Taylor Swift

Christopher Buford

Memory is an important part of what it is to be human, and so it's not surprising that we find plenty of references to memories in Taylor Swift's songs. In fact, songs ranging from "Speak Now (Taylor's Version)," to "New Year's Day," to "Christmas Tree Farm," employ the concept of memory in different ways. As we'll see, Swift's use of memory in songwriting raises questions concerning imagination, identity, and responsibility. Are there different types of memories? Might memories help determine who we are, and what we are responsible for? Addressing these questions can help us further appreciate Swift's songs as an important commentary on who we are.

A Memory Garden

In the opening verse of "Christmas Tree Farm," Swift closes her eyes and is instantly transported somewhere else "like magic." But how does she manage to travel so easily? One explanation is that she relies on "episodic memory," the ability humans possess to engage in something akin to the mental re-enactment of events we have already experienced.[1] For many important events in our lives, we not only remember that they occurred, but remember aspects of what it was like to have that experience. The use of this capacity is certainly suggested by the video for "Christmas Tree Farm." The home-movie montage allows us to peer into Swift's mind as she recollects various scenes from her childhood, using memory as a way to re-enact what happened in the past.

Our ability to remember events in this way seems different from our ability to merely remember various facts about the world. Because of this, episodic memory has also been described as involving "mental time travel," allowing us to re-experience events from the past. This type of memory is often distinguished from remembering *how* to do something (which is called "procedural" memory), and is also different from remembering *that*

Taylor Swift and Philosophy: Essays from the Tortured Philosophers Department, First Edition. Edited by Catherine M. Robb and Georgie Mills.

something is the case (which is called "semantic" memory). Swift remembers how to play the guitar and this ability relies on procedural memory—remembering how to do something. She also draws on semantic memory to remember that she was born on the thirteenth of December 1989—as this is a memory that something is a fact.

Episodic memories, though, play an important role in our lives as individuals. Think about, for example, the decision to attend a Taylor Swift concert. Suppose I ask why you want to attend the concert. What reasons might you provide? You might point out that you want to hear your favorite songs live, see Swift in person, and enjoy the process of choosing the right outfit and making a friendship bracelet. But I bet one of the reasons extends beyond the time of the concert itself; you want to go to the concert because of the memories you will make at the concert. And this is a good reason. In fact, psychologists tell us that happiness is best promoted not by buying things, but instead by having positive experiences.[2] And the memories that you will cherish are going to be episodic in nature, because they are a recollection or re-experiencing of something that has happened, and the way that event made you feel. Attending a Taylor Swift concert will leave you with positive episodic memories. But episodic memories can also be negative and can negatively affect our well-being.[3]

We can see, then, that episodic memories can have significant effects upon our lives, both for good and bad. But might they play an even more important role? Perhaps such memories are responsible for making you who you are.

I Want to Be Defined By …

Some philosophers believe that there is a connection between episodic memories and our identities as individuals. According to the theory of "narrative" identity, who we are is closely tied to the stories that we form about ourselves. According to contemporary philosopher Marya Schectman, each individual creates a narrative by interpreting "individual episodes in terms of their place in the unfolding story."[4] So, the events we include in our narrative are indicative of who we really are. Some episodes might be more important to us and so play a starring role in our sense of who we are. Other episodes and events we might think of as not so important, so we will downplay their role in our narrative. What episodes we choose as being important enough to us to include in our narrative can have a genuine effect on our sense of self, and they help us to navigate important moments in our lives.

Episodic memories play a role in the construction of each individual's narrative, since what has happened to us, as well as how we experienced it, will often become part of our narrative structure—our own story of who we are. We see Taylor Swift in the process of creating her narrative, for example in "The Moment I Knew (Taylor's Version)," where she sings "People ask me how I've been / As I comb back through my memory." Here Swift can be seen as engaging in reflective assessment on her own narrative, and her songs can be seen as offering insight into the specific structure and content of her own story. The window offered into Swift's narrative through her music draws many fans to her, as we get a sense of who she is and what she considers important in her life.

Sometimes we might struggle with finding our narrative selves and figuring out what story we want to tell. Consider for example "All Too Well (Taylor's Version)," in which Swift sings, "Time won't fly, it's like I'm paralyzed by it / I'd like to be my old self again / But I'm still trying to find it." Here she admits to being unsure about certain aspects of her own narrative, since the nature of her "old self" is in part created by her self-narrative. Similarly, in "Mine (Taylor's Version)" she provides us with this characterization: "You made a rebel of a careless man's careful daughter." Here we see her signal a particular character trait as playing an important role in her own narrative and sense of who she is, with this particular story highlighting the difference between one's identity as rebellious or careful changing over time.

Mine

Another type of identity makes an appearance in Swift's lyrics—what philosophers call "personal" identity. Although it sounds like this type of identity would involve figuring out who you are as a person, don't be fooled by the name. Instead, this type of identity is used to refer to the survival of your "personhood" over time. That is, surviving some particular event in the future requires that you, the very same person, make it through this event. In other words, personal identity is the kind of identity that allows people to know that you are the same person throughout time, that Taylor Swift at five years old is the same Taylor Swift we saw on the Eras Tour when she was thirty-four years old. This identity is really important because, without it, no one would know who we are from one day to the next. In fact, some philosophers have argued that episodic memories are *essential* to our personal identity. As we'll see, the lyrics of "New Year's Day" suggest this essential relationship. To fully grasp this, we need to get into some more philosophical theory.

The philosopher John Locke (1632–1704) is usually interpreted as arguing that personal identity is intimately related to our ability to recall the past.[5] According to one interpretation of Locke's view, you can only be the same person as some individual in the past if you remember the experiences that they had at that time. This view has the consequence that you cannot have done what you cannot remember, and you cannot be a person if you do not have their memories. For example, for you to be the same person now as you were ten years ago, you need to have memories of what it was like for you ten years ago, and recall events from the past. Your friend might have some idea of what you were like at age ten, because you tell her about your memories, but your friend cannot be you, because she does not *have* your memories.

Taylor Swift presents this view of identity in "New Year's Day" when she sings, "Hold on to the memories / They will hold on to you." The first clause of this lyric is a standard cliché that we often use when we talk about memory, encouraging us to remember good times so that we can look back at them in future. But the second clause hints at Locke's view. What would it be for my memories to hold on to me? They cannot literally do so of course, but my memories might "hold" on to me metaphorically, by allowing me to continue to exist as the same person. If my memories hold on to me, then they are attached to who I am, and make me who I am over time.

However, this version of Locke's theory has been criticized. The requirement that we remember doing something in order to be the same person who did it seems too strong, because it would mean that if you don't remember something then you are not the same person that had that experience in the past. For example, if I forget that when I was five years old I went for ice cream with my father at the beach, then under this interpretation of Locke's view, I am not the same person who had that experience. This can't be true. Even though the theory seems wrong, Locke maintained it because he understood the notion of a person to be a "forensic" one. This means that it is a notion tied to legal responsibility and what a person can be held responsible for. Locke thought it was unfair to blame someone for an act that they cannot rec-ollect having done. So, Locke's view that we can't blame someone for what they can't recall, together with the view that personhood is a forensic notion, leads to the conclusion that personal identity over time requires memory.

The connection between memory and responsibility suggested by Locke seems too strong, but there is some part of the theory that seems plausible. Taylor Swift also seems to suggest that there is a close connec-tion between the two. For example, "Would've, Could've, Should've" includes the powerful line that "Memories feel like weapons." One way that memories might act as weapons is to force us to face our past actions—which can be difficult, especially when we are not happy with how we have acted. We might be pushed to deal with such memories by others or by ourselves, but in the end they are "weapons" because we have to take responsibility for the past actions that we re-live through our memory. In the same song, Swift sings of regret, and missing who she used to be. Wishing to be a different sort of person, and regretting how things are now, seems to imply a negative assessment of one's current character and situation. Our memories of the past also inform how we assess the way our lives are going now, and the responsibility that we take for who we are, and once were in the past.

Beautiful Ghosts

Swift seems to rely on memory to revisit the Christmas tree farm of her childhood, but humans also possess the ability to mentally travel using imagination. Her travel would be no less "magical" if she closed her eyes and imagined herself somewhere else, looking into the eyes of another as her duet partner does in "The Last Time (Taylor's Version)." In fact, some philosophers have argued that our ability to remember events and to imagine events comes from the same capacity. According to this view, we should understand memory as a type of imagination.

Philosophers who consider memory to be a type of imagination are known as "continuists."[6] Let's look at an example to make sure we understand how the continuist sees the relationship between imagination and memory. Imagine yourself visiting a Christmas tree farm on a snowy day in mid-December. Imagine the feel of the snow, the smell of the trees, and all the other details that are important for your mental picture. In doing so, you most likely entered a state that seemed much like a genuine memory. In fact, for those of us who have visited Christmas tree farms, we may have been inclined to return to a memory rather than engage in an act of imagination. Sometimes people confuse mere imaginings with genuine memories. This is called "confabulation." What the continuist claims is that there is no deep or fundamental difference between acts of imagining and remembering. The only significant difference is that memories are necessarily aimed at representing the past, while imaginings don't have to be based on past events.

In your image of the Christmas tree farm, you might have seen yourself in the imagined picture, so that you were part of the image. This perspective is called an "observer" memory, where you take a third-person perspective regarding the event recalled. This would mean that in our memory we look on to the memory as an external third person, seeing ourselves in the memory, as if we were someone else looking on. Some of the images from the video for "Christmas Tree Farm" suggest this perspective, with Swift looking on at herself as if she was an observer in the event rather than being in the event herself. As another example, imagine yourself being pulled up on stage by Taylor Swift. There are a few ways you might do this. You might imagine looking up at her as she approaches and reaches down to grab your hand. But you might also imagine from a different perspective, say of someone a few rows back, so you see yourself in the image too. If we were imagining from our own perspective, then we wouldn't be able to see ourselves. In this case, when you see yourself in the image of your mind, then you would presumably be able to see your own body and see how joyful and happy this moment makes you. In this case, you would presumably be imagining your physical manifestations of sheer joy.

Because continuists see memory as just a form of imagination, this implies that our memories could be about things that might not have actually happened. This is because imagination does not require a causal connection between a person and the scene that they imagined. For example, suppose you didn't get tickets to the Eras Tour, and you did not go to any of the concerts. I bet that you can still quite easily imagine going to one of the concerts—you might do so by watching the Eras Tour concert movie, and imagining yourself there in the crowd singing along during certain songs. And so, if you were a continuist, if you think imagination and memory are the same capacity, then you would claim that causal connections are not required for memory—you can have memories of something that did not actually happen.

This is a strange view, and it is inconsistent with some other facts about memory. To see this, return to your imagined Christmas tree farm. Suppose I ask you which Christmas tree farm you imagined. Your answer would probably be that there is no particular Christmas tree farm that you had in mind. You *imagined* it after all, so the farm was "made up." However, with memory things are different. There is a particular Christmas tree farm that Swift remembers. Swift remembers *her* farm. If memory requires causal connections, then this fact about memory makes sense, because it refers to something that has actually happened, or something that is real. Swift's memory is a memory of the particular Christmas tree farm that caused her episodic memory. However, if you are a continuist, and you don't believe that memory involves a causal connection, then it's hard to make sense of this. So this is a good reason *not* to be a continuist.

The good news is you don't have to choose whether or not you are a continuist to see that memories and imagination are intertwined in some way, and that memories play an important role in our lives. Our episodic memories make us aware of past events, not as disinterested observers, but as individuals starring in the event itself. This helps explain why sifting through memories, as we see Swift do in "The Moment I Knew (Taylor's Version)," can have such influence on one's narrative identity. The causal nature of memory also helps to explain the ways in which memory can influence our sense of self. She seems to regret a particular memory in "Maroon," at least in part because of the individual responsible for that memory and what it says about her. The memory was attached to something that actually happened and was significant in her life.

Ultimately, Swift's songs improve our grasp on how episodic memories are intimately intertwined with our sense of self, and how we live our lives. In "mirrorball," Swift details how the mirrorball possesses the power to show you "every version of yourself." Though our memories may not be this powerful, they are significant in how we construct and maintain different versions of ourselves that we judge, praise, blame, and identity with, or even imagine.

Notes

1. John M. Gardiner, "Episodic Memory and Autonoetic Consciousness: A First-Person Approach," in Alan Baddeley, John P. Aggleton, and Martin A. Conway eds., *Episodic Memory: New Directions in Research* (Oxford: Oxford University Press, 2002), 11–30.
2. Leonardo Nicolao, Julie Irwin, and Joseph Goodman, "Happiness for Sale: Do Experiential Purchases Make Consumers Happier Than Material Purchases?" *Journal of Consumer Research* 36 (2009), 188–198.
3. Sabine Schönfeld and Anke Ehlers, "Posttraumatic Stress Disorder and Autobiographical Memories in Everyday Life," *Clinical Psychological Science* 5 (2017), 325–340.
4. Marya Schectman, *The Constitution of Selves* (Ithaca, NY: Cornell University Press, 1996), 97.
5. John Locke, *An Essay Concerning Human Understanding*, ed. P.H. Nidditch (Oxford: Clarendon Press, 1975), chap. 27.
6. Kourken Michaelian, "Against Discontinuism: Mental Time Travel and Our Knowledge of Past and Future Events," in Kourken Michaelian, Stanley B. Klein, and Karl K. Szpunar eds., *Seeing the Future: Theoretical Perspectives on Future-Oriented Mental Time Travel* (Oxford: Oxford University Press, 2016), 62–92.

24

Stained Glass Windows in My Mind

Modality in the Imagery of Taylor Swift

Shoshannah Diehl

Can I ask you a question …? Have you ever grappled with the thought that only certain parts of your potential can be fully realized in a single lifetime? How often do you consider what your life would look like now if you'd done one thing differently or taken a slightly different path? If you've ever wondered about the unexplored possibilities of your life, you are in good company—the most lauded and successful individuals in the world are actively doing the same to attempt to understand who they are. This exploration of personal potential plays an especially significant role for artists like Taylor Swift, who is known for producing autobiographical content. For many, Swift's music provides a map for self-discovery and authenticity in a media-inundated world that tends toward entertainment and distraction.

Swift has made a brand out of growing with her fans, paving the road forward to a more authentic and fulfilling life as an example to young women everywhere. The glue that holds this creator–consumer relationship together is Swift's transparency, particularly when it comes to difficult subjects like loss of innocence, mistakes, grief, and regret. Over the years, the public has watched as Swift has stretched and extended past mere storytelling into thought experiments of what her life *might have been* at different junctures. This transparency is not only humbling for Swift, but creates a dynamic space where listeners are prompted to engage in the same kind of counterfactual modality to foster authenticity.

If One Thing Had Been Different

To understand what lies ahead, we must first settle on an understanding of counterfactual modality. Modal logic is reasoning that we use to qualify the truth of a statement—in short, it explores judgments that are *necessarily*

Taylor Swift and Philosophy: Essays from the Tortured Philosophers Department, First Edition. Edited by Catherine M. Robb and Georgie Mills.

true versus judgments that are *possibly* true. Modal logic, then, essentially refers to our understanding of potential. Which potentialities exist in our current reality?

Counterfactuals are conditional judgments that relate specifically to what is *not* true in the current reality—but perhaps *could have been* under different circumstances. Under the umbrella of modal logic, counterfactuals explore things that are *possibly* true but not *necessarily* true. Take, for instance, a commonly used example from the philosopher David Lewis (1941–2001):[1]

1. If Oswald did not kill Kennedy, then someone else did.
2. If Oswald had not killed Kennedy, then someone else would have.

In this example, (1) is indicative—if it is true that Kennedy was killed, and it is true that Oswald did not kill him, then it stands to reason that someone else did. This is a simple inference. In (2), we are given a counterfactual. It is *possibly* true that if Oswald had not killed Kennedy, then someone else would have. However, it is not *necessarily* true.

Take a similar example from the lyrics of Swift's "the 1":

1. If my wishes came true, it would have been you.
2. It would have been fun if you would've been the one.

In this instance, just like the previous example, both are conditional statements. Though the tone of (1) is wistful, it reflects a judgment that is *necessarily* true. Though the statement is set up as a conditional, the narrator is simply revealing that she once wished to form a lasting bond with her love. On the other hand, (2) is only *possibly* true. The narrator presupposes a happy outcome to a relationship that never actually came to fruition.

Not all the lyrics we'll consider under the umbrella of modal logic will be phrased as conditionals, so it's important to consider that modal logic can take many forms. In the case of Swift's discography, modal logic appears in the form of counterfactual conditionals, modal expressions like "would've," "could've," and "should've," metaphors of potential, and musings about possible worlds.

Consider again the opening track of Swift's *folklore*. In "the 1," our narrator reminisces on a failed relationship and how fulfilling that relationship might have been if it hadn't ended prematurely. Several images from this song showcase counterfactual thinking through metaphor. In one such instance, the narrator mourns the potential of the lost relationship, saying "you know the greatest films of all time were never made." The line evokes the image of a story that was never told and prompts listeners to consider its potential truth: Is it possible that some of the best art doesn't exist because the artist chose not to share it? Because they were too disenfranchised to reach public visibility? Because of budgetary problems?

This seed of potential is applied to the failed relationship and presents the question: What if we could have been the greatest story ever told? An actualist would argue that it doesn't matter: a dead relationship doesn't have potential, and a film that was never made isn't a film at all.

Swift, however, sets up camp in the tenuous space of possibility. Occupying this modal space is inextricably linked to existential anxiety, or what Søren Kierkegaard (1813–1855) calls "the dizziness of freedom."[2] If we are to acknowledge that our lives could have taken different paths under different circumstances, then we are forced to wrestle with questions of our own agency and whether we have made the "right" decisions at certain junctures of our lives. In "the 1," Swift touches on this existential insecurity when she asks, "If one thing had been different / Would everything be different today?"

Although wondering *what could've been* under different circumstances isn't likely to change the current reality, the inclusion of counterfactual thinking and modal language in Swift's lyrics can achieve other ends: namely, authenticity for herself and catharsis for her listeners.

I'd Be *das Man*

But what does it mean to be authentic? This is a question philosophers have considered from countless perspectives. For Martin Heidegger (1889–1976) "authenticity" refers to a kind of "ownedness" or the sense of being one's own. This process of aligning the self involves wrestling with *das Man* or "the They"—the social context and expectations around us that inform our lived experience.[3] An example of a schoolteacher can illustrate *das Man*. If you want to be a teacher, you "must adopt (and perhaps blend) some set of the ready-made styles of classroom presentation and of dealing with students laid out in advance by existing norms and conventions of professional conduct."[4]

Being a musician and a celebrity brings its own set of norms and conventions. Unlike a teacher, however, being a public figure means having a "brand identity" that goes beyond just acting the way you're expected to act. Add to this that the nature of celebrity life and the music industry is "performance," and you have a multilayered existence that could lend itself to an inauthentic life, which Kierkegaard argues contributes to a sense of "despair."[5] A glimpse of this struggle is present in songs like "mirrorball," which Swift has called a "metaphor for celebrity." At the same time, "mirrorball" relates on a deeper level to anyone who feels they must perform an inauthentic self for society.[6]

Authenticity is the remedy to this problem and is reached through coming to terms with who you are and the things you do—*apart* from the socially prescribed constraints of *das Man*. One way of coming to terms with who you are and what you do is to sort through the anxiety-inducing bevy of things you are *not* and perhaps things you *didn't* do. Making sense of one's current reality in a way that attributes meaning to the self must involve some consideration of other possibilities.

Just Like Leo?

Before delving into Swift's imagined possibilities and their implications, it's important to set a few more guidelines for what we mean by *possibility*. Questions of modal logic have often been conceptualized through the lens of possible worlds.

The theory of possible worlds considers what other possibilities exist outside of the current reality. Not every alternative to our world is a possibility, and the distinction lies in the logic of the statement. For instance, there may be a possible world where I, like Taylor Swift, am a multiplatinum musician and Grammy award winner. However, there is no possible world where I was born to different parents, because then I would not be myself, and the logic of the statement would refute itself. These limitations are referred to by Saul Kripke (1940–2022) as rigid designators.[7] In other words, simply stating something doesn't make it a possibility—think back on our discussion of modal logic and the difference between what is *necessarily* true and what is *possibly* true. When we say something is *possibly* true, then there may exist a world in which it is not true. Something that is *necessarily* true must be true in all possible worlds. This is the logic that determines what makes a rigid designator.

Swift explores some worlds that are possible and other worlds that are not possible. For instance, when she says, "If you would've blinked then I would've / Looked away at the first glance," she is considering a possible world where she does not enter a toxic relationship. When she says, "If I was a man / Then I'd be the man," she is positing a world that is not possible. While gender itself is not a rigid designator, if Taylor Swift was a cisgender man (which seems to be the hypothetical in question), she would not be the same Taylor Swift we know today. The question that muddles the logic in this case isn't whether Taylor Swift could be a man, but rather whether a man could be Taylor Swift.

"The Man" engages in this larger conversation with reflections like "They'd say I played the field before I found someone to commit to / And that would be okay for me to do" and "Every conquest I had made would make me more of a boss to you." Though Swift's imagination is extending into a world that is not possible, the lyrics demonstrate an awareness of this discrepancy—to be a man would be counterintuitive to the existence of Taylor Swift, the brand and the person.

If I'd Only Played It Safe

Three words are inextricably connected to counterfactual modality: "Would've, Could've, Should've." The so-titled Swift track from *Midnights* is aptly named, as it engages with some of the most explicit counterfactual thinking we see in her discography. This song, largely believed to be auto-biographical, considers a relationship in which the narrator was exploited at a young age. This narrator, looking back from a place of maturity, muses "If you'd never looked my way / I would've stayed on my knees / And I damn sure never would've danced with the devil." The image conjures a loss of innocence that could have been prevented. However, for the narrator, this might constitute a world that is not possible. This isn't presented as a counterfactual in which the narrator could have chosen a different path and achieved a different end. Though the lyrics are heavy-laden with regret ("If I'd only played it safe"), the onus is placed on the perpetrator of the exploitation to have chosen a different path. The repetition of "If you would've" and "If you['d] never" makes the man in this relationship the initiator of the conditional. The responding "I would've" suggests a corresponding possibility for her to then embark on a different path. The implication here is that she always would've reacted the same way to his advances. In other words, a different action from him would've solicited a different reaction from her. This dance of If → Then and Call → Response is what makes this reflection of *what might've been* a scathing indictment of older men who pursue young women and an anthem for young women who have been exploited. The narrator in this case toys with the idea of what might have been, but concedes that it was not in her power to change this at the time of her exploitation, when she was young and impression-able. These reflections mirror lyrics Swift penned more than ten years prior about the same situation. In "Dear John (Taylor's Version)" the narrator progresses from a refrain of "I should've known" to a final "You should've known."

It is important to note that our actions and decisions do not exist in a vacuum—they must comingle with the circumstances around us and the choices of others. In the case of "Would've, Could've, Should've," the original decision is made by the perpetrator to pursue Swift in an inappro-priate way, and every decision thereafter is part of that ongoing chain of events. Having the freedom to choose does not mean having equal power in a situation. Just as we said before that choices do not exist in a vacuum, part of the atmosphere our choices exist in is the social and cultural cli-mate we inhabit. Swift's indictments on grooming acknowledge these dif-ferences while still wrestling with the existential guilt that causes her to wonder if it was within her power to avoid the situation. Even in the earlier-written track, "Dear John (Taylor's Version)" her consideration of her own agency fluctuates. She likens herself to a pawn, saying "I lived in your chess game / But you changed the rules every day." Later, she rejoices that her agency removed her from a situation that could have been worse, delivering the empowering line "I took your matches before fire could catch me." This nuanced consideration of agency reflects the fluid and often confusing experience of victims as they attempt to make sense of their situation. Swift's powerful lyricism proves that explorations of modality and counterfactual conditionals can be useful tools for regaining this sense of agency and self after victimization.

More than ten years later, Swift supplies the image of a stained-glass window to describe this multifaceted reflection. In "Would've, Could've, Should've," the narrator laments, "The tomb won't close / Stained glass windows in my mind / I regret you all the time." While this image holds religious significance related to the song's theme of waning innocence, it also presents a metaphor for modality in Swift's art. Stained glass is a mosaic form of art—each pane is colored differently, but they combine to create a larger and more cohesive pattern or image. This art form mirrors Swift's artistic attempts to view events in her life through varying lenses and reach an authenticity that leads to a larger acceptance of her life and things as they are.

Help! I'm Still at the Restaurant!

In "right where you left me," Swift provides another potent image—this time of a woman who flat out refuses to let her life branch into varying possibilities. This story of a woman who sits in a restaurant for years, refusing to let her wounds heal, serves as a cautionary tale for those who resist the necessary journey to authenticity. The opening lines, "Friends break up, friends get married / Strangers get born, strangers get buried," show that the narrator is aware of the natural order of things but finds herself unable to progress through time and change in the same way ("But I'm right where you left me"). This hiccup in the natural order is further emphasized in the image "Pages turn and stick to each other." Though the story is moving forward, she is choosing to provide resistance.

This leads to reflections similar to those we saw in "Would've, Could've, Should've": How do we reconcile our understanding of personal agency with the regret and longing we feel for possible worlds? Though the narrator has chosen not to move forward, she is aware that the rest of the world is moving forward without her and even imagines how her ex-lover's path might have developed based on their own decisions ("I'm sure you've got a wife out there / Kids and Christmas").

In many ways, "right where you left me," serves as a cautionary tale for those who tend toward getting lost in counterfactual thinking to the point that they are in denial of the current reality. "The girl who lives in delusion" at the restaurant represents the dark side of reflecting on possible worlds without acknowledging its purposes for growth and forward movement. It is immediately followed by a sister track (so called because these are the only two deluxe tracks and represent two sides of the same coin). In "it's time to go," listeners are heartened again with an encouragement that they will "know when it's time to go." We are presented with decisions that seem counterintuitive to the natural path (like "giving up" and "running"), and Swift reinforces our own agency in the current reality in spite of the outside forces that have also had an effect on our lives. The assurance that an action like "walking away" at the right time will "find you the right thing" implies that there is a natural or true self that one must find and "own" in the myriad of possibilities—in other words, "it's time to go" is describing a state of authenticity.

These examples highlight the possible outcomes of reflecting on what our lives could be under different circumstances. At its worst, counterfactual thinking can create a sense of paralysis or even delusion. At its best, it can lead you to a place of greater authenticity, wherein your sense of self and identity is strengthened.

You're a Cowboy Like Me

Now, we've considered why engaging in this kind of personal reflection matters. The question is: Why does it matter that Taylor Swift employs counterfactual modality in her lyrics? And what makes her music an effective catalyst for engagement with our existential insecurities in the first place?

Albums like *evermore* traverse the dark, murky waters of existential doubt and "the dizziness of freedom," but they also show the artist emerging victorious on the other side and developing an image that is (presumably) closer to a place of personal authenticity. The panic of "right where you left me," is followed by the certainty of "it's time to go." The regret in "I should've known," is followed by a resolute, "*you* should've known." We are given the opportunity to watch Swift engage with these questions of agency and possibility in real time.

Swift's art goes further than a mere model for growth, however, as it creates an experience of catharsis for her listeners. You can't listen to an album like *folklore* or *evermore* or *Midnights* without being prompted to consider existential questions. Aristotle (384–322 BCE) first presented the idea of catharsis as it relates to depictions of tragedy in the arts. Catharsis is a process of purging or expelling negative feelings and experiences through engagement with art, which often imitates the darker parts of life.[8] When you watch a tragedy, you experience all the necessary negative feelings associated with tragedies like sadness, fear, and regret. However, when the show is over, you come out on the other side and return to a place of normalcy and closure.

Though not every story in a Taylor Swift song is a tragedy in the traditional sense, listeners are prompted to deal with all the same feelings.

In other words, *what might have been*—a loss of potential—constitutes its own kind of tragedy. By engaging with these negative feelings and following through to the resolution, we are experiencing catharsis. This kind of relationship between artist and audience is part of what makes the art timeless and accessible. It engages with the human experience in a way that transcends simple storytelling.

So, the next time you are lost in existential guilt or wandering the no-man's land of *what might have been*, put on Taylor Swift. She'll charge ahead of you into the dark with a lantern, providing the catharsis you need to deal with difficult emotions and come to terms with your authentic self. Things may not be what you thought they would be—the greatest films of all time may have never been made—but that's alright, because as Swift reminds us in "the 1," "if you never bleed, you're never gonna grow."

Notes

1. David Lewis, *Counterfactuals* (Oxford: Blackwell, 1973). Lewis cites Ernest Adams as the originator of the example, which has been adapted.
2. Søren Kierkegaard, *The Concept of Anxiety*, trans. Reidar Thomte (Princeton, NJ: Princeton University Press, 1980).
3. Martin Heidegger, *Being and Time*, trans. John Macquarrie and Edward Robinson (New York: Harper & Row, 1962).
4. Somogy Varga and Charles Guignon, "Authenticity," in *The Stanford Encyclopedia of Philosophy*, at https://plato.stanford.edu/archives/sum2023/entries/authenticity.
5. Søren Kierkegaard, *The Present Age*, trans. Alexander Dru (New York: Harper Torchbooks, 1962).
6. Interview from *folklore: the long pond studio sessions*, dir. Taylor Swift (Taylor Swift Productions, Big Branch Productions, 2020).
7. Saul Kripke, "Identity and Necessity," in Milton K. Munitz ed., *Identity and Individuation* (New York: New York University Press, 1971), 135–164.
8. Pierre Destrée, "Aristotle's Aesthetics," in *The Stanford Encyclopedia of Philosophy*, at https://plato.stanford.edu/archives/win2021/entries/aristotle-aesthetics.

25

"Take Me to the Lakes"
Transcendentalism and Ecology in Taylor Swift's *folklore*

Joshua Fagan

Even many of Taylor Swift's most ardent fans expressed shock when she released *folklore* in July 2020, at the apex of the COVID-19 pandemic. Part of that shock came from how she wrote and recorded the entire album in lockdown over the course of a few months. But the content and scope of the album were no less surprising. *folklore* crafts a mosaic of interlocking narratives, set in vibrant natural landscapes, domains of salt-soaked air and damp summer creeks. The wistful songs, by her but not directly about her, leave behind the world of fame and glamor, and instead embrace the wonder of the natural world, from the "purple-pink skies" of "invisible string" to the "sunlit room" of "my tears ricochet." The album cover art, which depicts Swift in the deep woods, surrounded by primordial trees, suits the wider, more sprawling perspective of the album. As the title *folklore* suggests, the songs have a dreamy, timeless quality, with striking images that evoke the sense of connection between people and the natural world, which the chaos of everyday life obscures.

Swift's decision to depart from autobiographical storytelling to this more ecological perspective was surprising because so many of her previous songs came from such an intensely personal place. The early albums were successful because of their sharp songwriting and infectious melodies, but they also made such a profound impression on her listeners because of their relatability. In Swift's blockbuster sophomore album *Fearless*, for instance, she sings that when "you're fifteen" and "somebody tells you they love you / You're gonna believe them" ("Fifteen (Taylor's Version)"). Such statements of romance and heartbreak expressed common experiences and created intimacy between her and her fans. Still, with her rising fame came increasing scrutiny of her public image, obsessive inquiries into minute details of her personal life, and the frantic examination of her lyrics for hints about her romantic relationships.

COVID-19 and the ensuing lockdowns forced a departure from the public eye, yet at the same time created an opportunity to leave behind the

Taylor Swift and Philosophy: Essays from the Tortured Philosophers Department, First Edition. Edited by Catherine M. Robb and Georgie Mills.

suffocating trappings of superstardom. Instead of focusing on managing her public image, meticulously deciding the most commercially successful strategy for marketing her next big single, Swift embraced the mystery and wonder of the deep woods, the leafy realm of nature and myth. As she wrote in an essay announcing the album, "In isolation my imagination has run wild and this album is the result."[1] That journey into the undiluted wilds transcends the artificial demands of an exhausting, superficial world.

An essay in the *New York Times* by Jeff Opperman correctly notes that, in *folklore*, "nature is not remote," and that it becomes "a place to bond, seek solace or just hang out."[2] Though serving as places of refuge and healing, the ecological landscapes Swift illustrates in the album are social. These natural havens, far from isolating, create a new feeling of community and closeness. From the stroll along the High Line urban park described in "cardigan" to the shared trip to the Windermere Peaks of England in "the lakes," immersion in nature is a way of creating and celebrating connections, not escaping from them. In the intro essay, Swift describes the songs as her "way of escaping into fantasy, history, and memory," but she also tells her audience that "it's up to you to pass them down."[3] These two ideas form a fascinating philosophical couple: Swift embraces escapism, departing from a cold and impersonal society, but at the same time, she encourages others to join her in sharing in the unity of these stories.

The Transcendental Attitude

This juxtaposition of escapism and unity calls to mind the British Romantics, the nineteenth-century writers who saw industrial society as destroying the connections between people, and between people and the environment. Romantic writers like William Wordsworth (1770–1850) and Samuel Taylor Coleridge (1772–1834) achieved widespread acclaim for their introspective reflections, their vibrant depictions of nature, and their valorizing of imagination and creativity. Fittingly, Swift heavily evokes the Romantics in "the lakes," even explicitly referencing the name of Wordsworth.

There is another group of writers that *folklore* seems to evoke—the American Transcendentalists, such as Ralph Waldo Emerson (1803–1882) and Henry David Thoreau (1817–1862). The American Transcendentalists were a group of writers who mostly lived in New England during the middle of the nineteenth century. Like the British Romantics, they praised the revitalizing power of imagination and the mystery of nature, and they sought to avoid the malaise of a commodified, judgmental world by abandoning society altogether. Emphasizing both the oneness of all living beings and the vitality of the individual spirit, Emerson and Thoreau argued that a conformist and materialistic society creates lonely and disconnected individuals who doubt themselves and view others with suspicion.

Even more than the British Romantics, the Transcendentalists addressed the duality Swift illuminates: how escaping into the distant woods, far from society, can be a path to establishing a deeper and more fulfilling sense of connection with others. In *folklore* Swift explores the Transcendentalist idea of how leaving behind the artifice and conformism of society can mean connecting with others in a fresh and profound way. Placing *folklore* in the context of Transcendentalist thinkers like Emerson and Thoreau illuminates how Swift advocates escaping from society in order to promote a sense of fellowship and community. She wants to be free, but she wants others to join her in that freedom.

The writer-philosopher Thoreau escaped to Walden Pond in Massachusetts to write the most famous text of the Transcendentalist movement, *Walden*, which emphasizes self-reliance and the need to abandon conformity. Thoreau proudly declares at the start of *Walden* that he "lived alone, in the woods, a mile from any neighbor, in a house which I built myself," asserting that this journey provided a release from the "fool's life" of commercial society.[4] Statements like these earned Thoreau a reputation as anti-social and disdainful of towns and cities. Such a reputation, while not wholly wrong, overlooks what Thoreau was really trying to say. He did not despise his fellow humans, but he expressed disappointment that they pursued empty materialism and ignored the wonder and strangeness of the world. The domain of nature heightened both that wonder and that strangeness.

In describing a night spent on Mt. Katahdin in Maine, Thoreau writes, "I stand in awe of my body, this matter to which I am bound has become so strange to me," in a passage that ends with him imploring the reader to think of "rocks, trees, wind on our cheeks."[5] For Thoreau, the stark beauty of the mountain causes the divide between his body and the natural environment to collapse. Both the trees on the mountain and his body lose their ordinary characteristics as separate material objects, and become manifestations of a singular, fundamental unity that exists in all things.

Searching through the strangeness and mystery of the natural environment, and in the retold stories and faded memories that folk storytelling entails, Swift finds a similar unity. The stories she crafts on *folklore* do not directly relate to her personal life, at least not to the same extent as the songs on albums like *Fearless (Taylor's Version)*, but she nonetheless presents them from her distinct perspective. There are songs in which she makes her connection with the subject matter clear, such as in "the last great american dynasty," where she sympathetically recounts the story of Rebekah Harkness, the unconventional Standard Oil heiress who previously owned the Rhode Island house Swift later bought. In other cases, such as with the forsaken lovers on "exile" or the frustrated teenagers on "betty," the connection is less immediately obvious. Still, in these songs Swift creates a connection to these vignettes by singing about them, by including them in her world of storytelling.

Swift takes stories that appear distant and dream-like and makes them intimate and vivid on an album that paints a vision of a rich natural setting. We see it in our mind's eye most clearly when listening to "the lakes," which creates a world of dazzling auroras and red roses emerging from the frozen ground, with Swift singing about wanting to "watch wisteria grow / Right over my bare feet." In *folklore*, vegetation and auroras do not belong to a distant universe, but to one singular ecosystem. A fundamental oneness contains everything from red roses to the High Line, from Rebekah Harkness to Swift's grandfather in "epiphany," to the muted, mundane reflections of "the 1." In true Transcendentalist spirit, Swift recognizes these experiences as externally different but linked together on a more profound, essential level.

Despite divisions between past and present or between the bustling city and the deep woods, the scenes Swift depicts belong to the same mosaic. By leaving behind the exhausting, alienating world of fame and celebrity, Swift reveals the obscured links between people, and between people and their environment. In *folklore*, every stroll through ancient forests and every childhood memory belongs to an interrelated whole. The tales Swift sings differ significantly in their subject matter—from the feminist protest of "mad woman" to the melancholic tale of infidelity of "illicit affairs"—but a greater similarity underlies them, as they all reveal the vibrant impressions too frequently obscured by the chaotic routines of ordinary life.

Merging into Folk Tales

The unseen unity between different images and narratives is a major component of folk narratives. Naming an album about escaping the confines of society *folklore* aligns Swift with the Romantic celebration of legends and myth. From the perspective of the Romantics, these old stories carry a timeless essence that reveals wisdom lost in the utilitarian modern world. Wordsworth wandered around the English Lake District that so captivates Swift, writing poems like "The Solitary Reaper," about a young woman singing as she works in the fields. Wordsworth and Coleridge named their most famous collection of poetry *Lyrical Ballads* because of their immense appreciation for rustic folk melodies. In his 1800 preface to *Lyrical Ballads*, Wordsworth wrote that these folk melodies represented the truest essence of what poetry should be: "there is no necessity to trick out or to elevate nature" and a true poet writes from the language that "real passion itself suggests."[6]

Folk songs and tales capture the earnest, organic desires of a pre-literate society. Such stories did not fade, because every generation decided they had value and significance, that they deserved to be preserved. They appeal to a fundamental unity between people across different regions and eras.

Trends fade, and even historical events become vague cultural memories, but the tales persist. For example, a story like "Cinderella" may appear simple, but it has a vast cultural history. Before it was written down by tale collectors like the Grimm Brothers, it lingered for centuries. Different villages and towns saw the tale as worthy of preserving, and talented storytellers emphatically told the story to the next generation. The persistence of folk tales is also expressed by Swift throughout *folklore*. In "seven," she sings, "Passed down like folk songs / The love lasts so long." A later line asserts, "And just like a folk song / Our love will be passed on." Swift prizes how folk songs endure, how they withstand the decay of time, and how they represent our deepest personal connections. In her release statement for the album, she writes that "A tale that becomes folklore is one that is passed down and whispered around."[7]

As far back as the first release of the album *Red* in 2012, Swift expressed a deep anxiety about how long her fame and acclaim would last, asking, "Will you still want me when I'm nothing new?" ("Nothing New (Taylor's Version)"). During the viscerally intense media backlash against her during the *reputation* era, these anxieties intensified, not helped by the relative commercial underperformance of the album *reputation*. In the documentary *Miss Americana*, recorded in the years immediately following *reputation*, Swift reveals her crippling fear that her career might be in decline. By escaping to the realm of folklore, this alleviated the expectations of celebrity.

"It's Up to You to Pass Them Down"

The world of folk tales is a world of endurance and unity, where listeners remember the stories they heard as children and ensure those stories survive by retelling them. Because these stories have psychological and emotional relevance, their influence never fades, and they connect individuals from different backgrounds and time periods. They appeal to primal feelings untouched by the falseness of social conformism. Our world is no longer a world of castles and princesses, like in "Cinderella," but the appeal of that story persists. In fact, it arose independently in different parts of the world, such as in China, where Cinderella is "Ye Xian."[8]

From the beginning of her career, Swift drew inspiration from the persistent appeal of fairy tales, a tendency exemplified by an early song literally called "Today Was a Fairy Tale." *folklore*, however, represents a different focus: not the world of Disney fairy tales, but the older and more primordial world of folk tales, where the wondrous and strange emerge from the expected and predictable. The natural world of "Cinderella," for instance, is mysterious but helpful, as many versions of the tale involve benevolent animals who attempt to help her. At their best, folk stories create the kind of awe Thoreau describes, overthrowing the misconceptions of an anxious, utilitarian world to reveal how seemingly isolated individuals are connected, and how all individuals are connected with the natural wilds.

Folklore endures, but every generation of new storytellers revitalizes it, as the contemporary folklorist and Harvard professor Maria Tatar describes. For Tatar, the magic of tales "derives from their mutability," and she argues that the constant revising and reinterpretation of these tales across different eras and countries demonstrates that "there is really no conflict between preserving traditions and creating them anew."[9] Swift similarly gathers stories together in order to entrust them to her audience, inviting that audience to make her stories their own. The stories are hers in the sense that she crafts them, but she does not claim restrictive ownership over them. In the release statement for *folklore*, she tells her audience explicitly: "I've told these stories to the best of my ability with all the love, wonder, and whimsy they deserve. Now it's up to you to pass them down."[10]

Watching Wisteria Grow

Throughout *folklore*, Swift dreams of a world beyond the distractions of modern technology. This wistful longing is expressed most directly in "the lakes," with its fantastical imagery of wisteria enshrouding Swift, who luxuriantly claims, "I haven't moved in years." she disdains "hunters with cellphones," explicitly making a distinction between the alienating, modern world of celebrity, and the nourishing, timeless world of the Lake District. Seeing the red rose, Swift celebrates that there was "no one around to tweet it." In opposition to the inane bits of information circulating on social media, Swift wishes to revel in "cliffside pools / With my calamitous love and insurmountable grief." Given that the rest of the scenario the song describes is almost utopian, the primary use of the words "calamitous" and "insurmountable" here is tonal. These elevated, multisyllabic words sound sophisticated and literary, like they belong in a Romantic or Transcendentalist poem. They fit the dream world about which Swift fantasizes: an elegant place of wild grandeur, surrounded by mountains and poetry.

The mountains convey, for Swift as much as for Thoreau, connection with the undiluted wonder of the natural world. Poetry, which for Swift includes songwriting, conveys connection with the undiluted wonder of human yearning in all its varied shapes. In her essay about *folklore*, Swift discusses writing from not only her perspective, but the perspectives of "people I've never met, people I've known, or those I wish I hadn't," and she describes a cascade of imagery: "Stars drawn around scars. A cardigan that still bears the scent of loss twenty years later. Battleships sinking into the ocean, down, down, down."[11] These stories, as different as they may be, emerge from the impulse to look beyond Swift's immediate life into a wider perspective, seeing all of these different tales as relevant to her, emotionally and psychologically, even though their external details differ substantially from her life as a successful musician. This wider perspective is healing, gliding through mountain peaks while surrounded by Romantic and Transcendentalist poetry and fragments of her own folkloric stories.

From a pessimistic perspective, the viewpoint of "the lakes" could be considered self-serving and fantastical. Not everyone, of course, has the financial capacity to escape from the stresses of modern society and live in a world of lush green mountains and the memories of great poets. Even for Swift, the image of staying still long enough for wisteria to slowly grow over her feet is only a fantasy. Between her intensive touring, the pace at which she relentlessly releases albums, and her passions for acting and directing, she gravitates toward art and interacting with an audience, not spending long stretches of time hidden in the wilderness.

In this way, Swift resembles the Transcendentalist writer Emerson, who combines a deep skepticism toward the bloodless conformism of society with a willingness to enter into society and combat that conformism. Emerson became the foremost spokesperson for the Transcendentalists, giving rousing lectures and writing popular essays. Beyond the divisions and separations that characterize everyday life, there exists for Emerson a profound oneness that, when understood, heals alienation and isolation. As he writes, under "all this running sea of circumstance" lies the "abyss of real Being."[12] This unity of real existence, or "Being," is everywhere, not only in the untouched woods, but in towns and cities as well. It's just that the chaos of everyday life obscures this beauty. Escaping into the woods matters for Emerson because it refreshes the mind to the unity of life, a unity that transcends superficial differences and exists even in humble sights. Emerson erupts into exhilarated wonder upon seeing an ordinary puddle, as he sees in that puddle the radiant oneness of the world that the disorienting chaos of modern society obscures.[13] Departing into the woods brings enlightenment, but Emerson responds to that enlightenment by returning to society and sharing what he has discovered. Swift's flight to the deep woods in *folklore* has a similar effect—she came out of the woods to share her art with us.

A Better Way to Escape

folklore is indeed an escape, as Swift noted, but such an escape does not mean abandoning others. It does not mean retreating to a self-interested or self-indulgent perspective. Rather, it means quite the opposite: *folklore* gave Swift a forested realm apart from the pressure of celebrity, the stress of her public reputation, and the practical challenges of managing grandiose tours and extensive album rollouts. Like the Transcendentalists, Swift revels in the paradox that physically escaping society can heal alienation.

This healing occurs in part through celebrating a connection to nature, from the "midnight sea" in "the last great american dynasty" to the cliffsides in both "the lakes" and "hoax." Even imagery like "love you to the moon and Saturn" on "seven" evokes the vast expanses of the universe, far beyond the utilitarian world of everyday life. As the Opperman *New York Times* essay notes, such an abundance of imagery provides relief to a culture that "has experienced a steady and dramatic decline in its connections to nature."[14] In true Transcendentalist spirit, *folklore* revitalizes these connections, not only for Swift's benefit, but for the benefit of her listeners.

In its songs, *folklore* acknowledges the differences between the rural Lake District and the urban High Line, as well as between Swift's era and that of Rebekah Harkness, but the album exemplifies how, on a deeper level, these apparent opposites are secretly similar. Swift, in her ecological perspective, celebrates nature not as an abstract ideal, but as an intimate reality to feel and touch. The wide, capacious perspective of the album allows Swift to escape the impositions of fame and reveal her personal stories as being only one component of a vast, unifying tapestry of tales old and new, extending far beyond her individual life.

Swift, like any great folk storyteller, maintains her own distinct artistic voice while inhabiting stories from different times and worlds. In *folklore*, these stories all belong together, united despite their external differences by wistful longing and the eruption of hidden, suppressed feelings. All seventeen songs and the worlds they create belong to a more expansive, organic whole. By escaping into the woods, Swift finds that whole, and she reveals it to us through her music and words. Escaping the confines of society is not an act of selfishness and division, but one of selflessness and connection.

Notes

1. Taylor Swift, quoted in Will Richards, "Read Taylor Swift's New Personal Essay Explaining Eighth Album *folklore*," NME, July 24, 2020, at https://www.nme.com/news/music/read-taylor-swift-new-personal-essay-explaining-eighth-album-folklore-2714540.
2. Jeff Opperman, "Taylor Swift Is Singing Us Back to Nature," *The New York Times*, March 12, 2021, at https://www.nytimes.com/2021/03/12/opinion/taylor-swift-grammys-nature-lyrics.html.
3. Taylor Swift, quoted in Richards, "Read Taylor Swift's New Personal Essay."
4. Henry David Thoreau, *Walden* (New York: Thomas Crowell & Co., 1910), 1, 4.
5. Henry David Thoreau, *The Maine Woods* (New York: AMS Press, 1968), 78–79.
6. William Wordsworth, "Preface to *Lyrical Ballads*," in *The Major Works* (Oxford: Oxford University Press, 2000), 604.
7. Taylor Swift, quoted in Richards, "Read Taylor Swift's New Personal Essay."

8. Arthur Waley, "The Chinese Cinderella Story," *Folklore* 58 (1947), 226–238.
9. Maria Tatar, "Introduction," in Maria Tatar ed., *The Cambridge Companion to Fairy Tales* (Cambridge: Cambridge University Press, 2015), 3.
10. Taylor Swift, quoted in Richards, "Read Taylor Swift's New Personal Essay."
11. Taylor Swift, quoted in Richards, "Read Taylor Swift's New Personal Essay."
12. Ralph Waldo Emerson, "Compensation," in Brooks Atkinson ed., *The Complete Essays and Other Writings* (New York: Modern Library, 1950), 185.
13. See Emerson, "Nature," in *The Complete Essays and Other Writings*, 6.
14. Opperman, "Taylor Swift Is Singing Us Back to Nature."

26

Wildest Dreams
Stoic Fate and Acceptance
(Taylor's Version)

David Hahn

Stoicism is a philosophy that calls for self-control, detachment, and acceptance of one's fate. When viewed retrospectively, it can be easy to claim that fate has decided things, but when viewed in the present, fate can be the source of anger and frustration. Accepting our fate can be a matter of struggle, effort, and pain, but it can also be the source of joy and ecstasy. Many of Taylor Swift's songs reflect this dichotomy. In some, a coming fate is lamented, for example "Wildest Dreams" and "Treacherous." In others, like "I Know Places" and "Blank Space," fate gives a momentary bout of excitement and happiness. In other songs, like "Cruel Summer," Swift sings of a sealed fate, and in "Karma" the hope is for fate to deliver justice. In yet other songs, like "Paper Rings" and "The Man," she considers the possibility that fate could have been different.

The Stoic philosophers believed that living a good life was achievable even if fate was aligned against us. Swift seems to agree. Even if the world is against her, she can not only survive, but flourish. This is especially true when most of the problems she faces are out of her control. Taylor Swift shows us that what fate has in store for us is not in our power to determine, but we can determine how we face it.

Emotions and Acceptance

Stoicism tells us we should accept the things in life that we cannot control. This is not easy, for the slings and arrows of life often occupy our minds, and only with discipline and training can we come to accept them. Taylor Swift knows this well. She recognizes the way our fate and life experiences can consume our minds, so that it's hard to accept the cards we've been dealt. In "I Forgot That You Existed" she sings, "Your name on my lips, tongue tied / Free, rent, living in my mind / But then something happened on a magical night / I forgot that you existed / And I thought it would kill

Taylor Swift and Philosophy: Essays from the Tortured Philosophers Department, First Edition. Edited by Catherine M. Robb and Georgie Mills.

me but it didn't / And it was so nice / So peaceful and quiet ... / It isn't love, it isn't hate, it's just indifference." These lyrics begin by telling of being tortured by an unshakeable feeling and emotional attachment, of the experience of a person who lives rent-free in your mind, even though you despise that person. The thought of that person controls you. Epictetus (50–135 CE), the enslaved Stoic philosopher, cautions against letting the thought of someone control you in this way: "If a person gave your body to any stranger he met on his way, you would certainly be angry. And do you feel no shame in handing over your own mind to be confused and mystified by anyone who happens to verbally attack you?"[1]

Anger at a person's words, their existence, and at our memory of them can feel like mental torture. The Stoics believed this was the worst possible state that a person could be in: unable to control the rational part of the mind wholly subject to wild emotion.[2] The use of reason to control emotion and guide our lives was crucial for the Stoics.[3] What Swift describes in the concluding part of the previous lyric from "I Forgot That You Existed" is a snow at the beach moment, a sudden onset of peaceful acceptance. By moving past the anger, frustration, and hatred to an acceptance, detachment, and ultimately an "indifference," she becomes the Stoic ideal.

Fate and Free Will

When we claim that something was "fated," this implies that we did not have a choice and that we are stuck with the consequences. Consider what Swift sings in "Getaway Car": "Don't pretend it's such a mystery / Think about the place where you first met me / Ridin' in a getaway car." The lyrics describe how past events created the meeting of two people. The meeting is a natural consequence of two people's past experiences—it is not a mystery. This idea implies that we carry our entire lives with us, and our past experiences create what we experience now. Standing in the audience at an Eras Tour concert is the result of your past actions of buying a ticket, of listening to someone suggest, "listen to this *1989* album," of how you became friends with that person in the first place, and so on. Becoming *TIME*'s Person of the Year is the result of so many factors that it would be impossible to list them all. The award does not just signify that Taylor Swift is influential. It's how she *became* influential, it's how her fans not only first encountered her music but their life stories that led them to become attached to it and her. It is the story of the editorial staff at the magazine that made the choice, the past editors that came up with the "Person of the Year" title to begin with, and so on.

Returning to "Getaway Car," Swift reminds the other person that they met her "on the run," and so they should not have expected a different outcome to their relationship. It was fate that their relationship would end up the way it did. Similarly, when we look back on the course of our lives it appears that the events of our lives could not have happened otherwise. The philosophical problem with this is that if things are fated, then we have no choice at all. It would mean that the words I am writing and that you are now reading are also the products of fate, and beyond our choice. It is impossible that things could have been different. It would mean that no matter what, you were fated to read this chapter in this book right now where you are. Everything would be the product of fate. Swift describes this in "Treacherous," singing, "I can't decide if it's a choice / Getting swept away / I hear the sound of my own voice / Asking you to stay." The song describes Swift becoming infatuated with a person who, for one reason or another (the lyrics never indicate), she would be "smart to walk away" from. She's aware that this feeling is happening but is unsure whether it is fate, or whether fate is the excuse she uses for her actions. In the song, Swift hears the sound of her voice asking the person to stay. It's an important detail that highlights fate's hand in this moment; she has no choice but to go along with what is happening. She's merely a bystander watching herself ask the person to stay. This is the core of the philosophical theory of determinism, which says that every event, act, and decision is the inevitable consequence of what comes before. Our choices and actions are the products of forces that we have no authority over. Swift is predetermined to be "swept away" even though she is aware that it would be better if she just let the person leave.

Many philosophers reject determinism and argue that we have free will, meaning not only that we have control over our actions but also that the future is not fated. Swift shows some sympathy for this side of the debate as well. Contra "Treacherous," she writes in "Blank Space," "I'm dying to see how this one ends / Grab your passport and my hand," and later, "So it's gonna be forever / Or it's gonna go down in flames? / You can tell me when it's over / If the high was worth the pain." These lyrics are ambiguous but could be interpreted as making a place for free will and an uncertain, un-fated future. Either the relationship goes well or ends, but her point is that even if it ends badly the experience will still be worth it. In essence she says, the breakup sucks, but the good times were worth it.

Fate Is Not Supernatural

To understand why the Stoics were determinists (and why Swift is one too) we must look at the Stoic worldview. The important feature of Stoic natural philosophy is its simplicity in explaining how the world works. Stoic philosopher Seneca the Younger (4 BCE–65 CE), writes that only physical things exist, and only physical being can produce change in the world. A blank space will remain a blank space until someone writes on it. Left alone, the inanimate object of the blank page would have no possibility of change. Anything that occurs in the physical world occurs because something has caused it. As the famous Stoic Cicero (106–43 BCE) writes, "things which will be do not spring up spontaneously."[4]

The view of causation is central to the Stoic understanding of fate. For the Stoics, fate is just the result of physical forces. Cicero continues his explanation, "nothing has happened which was not going to be, and likewise nothing is going to be of which nature does not contain causes working to bring that very thing about. This makes it intelligible that fate should be, not the 'fate' of superstition, but that of physics, an everlasting cause of things—why past things happened, why present things are now happening, and why future things will be."[5]

Fate is not something supernatural, but rather a matter of how one physical thing affects another. Everything that happens is the result of a prior occurrence. Let's return to Swift's song "Getaway Car." The meeting between the two people was fated because of the prior course of their lives: "Don't pretend it's such a mystery / Think about the place where you first met me." They had no choice but to meet for a fleeting relationship that could not last because of the events which drove them together in the first place. She's saying that if the end is a surprise, then you have forgotten about our past and how we met. There is no supernatural element. It is not the fault of the stars but simply a matter of one thing causing another—their choices led them to this moment.

"Getaway Car" is about the past, but Swift evokes the future in "Wildest Dreams," writing, "I can see the end as it begins." Later in the song, "When we've had our very last kiss / My last request is / Say you'll remember me," she is describing the inevitable end of the relationship because she understands the present. Her wish is that despite the determined future they should proceed anyway with her ultimate hope that the other person will carry her memory forward. Stoically, Swift is describing an acceptance of fate. There is an acceptance of finality, and yet there is a plea to enjoy it while it lasts—embracing the moment before it ends.

Swift continues this theme of acceptance and enjoyment with "Dress," singing, "And if I get burned at least we were electrified." Similarly, in "Style" she sings, "And I should just tell you to leave / 'Cause I know exactly where it leads / But I watch us go 'round and 'round each time."

Shaking It Off

Stoicism faces a challenge concerning ethical responsibility, because responsibility seems to require the possibility that a person could have acted differently. For example, if your friend steals your vinyl copy of *1989 (Taylor's Version)*, we decide their responsibility based on whether they could have done otherwise. If your friend was forced to steal the album, then we wouldn't say that they were responsible. In "Karma" Swift accusingly writes, "Spider-boy, king of thieves / Weave your little webs of opacity / My pennies made your crown." These lyrics indicate that some individual has stolen money from her through deceit. This person should be held responsible if they could have done otherwise, as the lyrics seem to suggest.

Stoics believe the physical world is the result of causation, but our thoughts are not physical and thus are in our control. So, for Stoicism, we should judge a person, even in a bad situation, by their outlook. An ethical person accepts fate and adjusts their thoughts accordingly. Epictetus writes, "It is not things that disturb men, but their judgments about things.... So whenever we are impeded or disturbed or distressed, let us blame no one but ourselves, that is, our own judgments."[6] Of course, this is difficult. In the face of tragedy, it's hard to sit and think, "such is life."

When someone insults or speaks ill of us, we must remember that their actions are outside of our control. The people who spread gossip or insult us are also beings who are bound by fate. This idea is summed up perfectly in the chorus of "Shake It Off." The players are going to play, the haters are going to hate, and the heartbreakers are going to break our hearts, but in response we "shake it off," not letting the opinions of other people, that we cannot control anyway, affect us negatively.

Swift makes clear the consequences of allowing fate to haunt us. In "Clean," she writes, "You're still all over me / Like a wine-stained dress I can't wear anymore," but she offers hope in the chorus, "Rain came pouring down / When I was drowning, that's when I could finally breathe / And by morning / Gone was any trace of you, I think I am finally clean." Here Swift offers a first-hand account, showing us that accepting fate and taking control of our thoughts can offer us a good life.

The world around us is outside of our control, but, as the Stoics and Taylor Swift remind us, we control how we face this world. Even if we reject Stoic determinism, it is still the case that we do not have control over the actions and opinions of others. They may hate us, break our hearts, play around, and cause us pain. Here, the Stoic conclusion still holds true—our perspective is who we are, ultimately shaping how we live our lives. Stoicism is not about living as hyper-logical, non-emotional beings. It is about not suffering, enduring the whims of fate, and keeping our side of the street clean. Even if we can see the end from the beginning, as in "Wildest Dreams," the experience of life and love in the present is what matters most.[7]

Notes

1. Epictetus 28, *The Enchiridion*, trans. Elizabeth Carter, at https://classics.mit.edu/Epictetus/epicench.html (accessed April 23, 2024).
2. For example, Cicero claims that anger is a mark of "weakness" and not part of a "blessed nature." See Cicero, "On the Nature of the Gods 1.43-9," in A.A. Long and D.N. Sedley eds., *The Hellenistic Philosophers: Volume 1* (Cambridge: Cambridge University Press, 1987), 142.

3. See for example the passages from various Stoic philosophers in chapter 65, "The Passions," in Long and Sedley eds., *The Hellenistic Philosophers: Volume 1*, 410–423.

4. Cicero, "On Divination 1.127 (*SVF* 2.944)," in Long and Sedley eds., *The Hellenistic Philosophers: Volume 1*, 338.

5. Cicero, "On Divination 1.125–126 (*SVF* 2.921)," in Long and Sedley eds., *The Hellenistic Philosophers*, Volume 1, 337.

6. Epictetus, "Manual 5," in Long and Sedley eds., *The Hellenistic Philosophers*, *Volume 1*, 418.

7. Thanks to Laura Hahn for advice on the final draft, and Debbie Martin for song recommendations, initial draft criticisms, and making sure I was holding true to the themes.

27

Mythic Motifs in *The Tortured Poets Department*

"The Story Isn't Mine Anymore"

Georgie Mills

Taylor Swift has repeatedly remarked that she wants the fans to read their own experience into her autobiographical work, and her artistic and marketing choices support this intention. For example, in an Instagram post to promote the *folklore* album, Taylor wrote "Picking up a pen was my way of escaping into fantasy, history, and memory. I've told these stories to the best of my ability with all the love, wonder, and whimsy they deserve. Now it's up to you to pass them down."[1]

By passing along tales this way, Taylor Swift is participating in the centuries-old tradition of oral storytelling. In the time before literacy was widespread, stories were recorded though the process of telling and retelling them. By modernizing ancient motifs from myth and legend, casting herself as the chairman of the tortured poets department, and consciously handing her stories back to the fans, Taylor is changing her role. Rather than the authoritative, autobiographical narrator she once was, Taylor has become, like Homer before her, the caretaker of legends. As a songwriter, she creatively transforms old legends, and then passes them on for fans to retell. Sometimes Taylor uses the third person to describe herself, or the first person to talk from the point of view of someone else. Taylor is always the singer, but she is not always the narrator of the story.[2]

The genre of country music, where Taylor began her career, is characterized partly by storytelling. This element of Taylor's lyricism has stayed with her over the years, through her changes in genre and musical style. *folklore* represented an attempt to participate in the tradition of oral storytelling by creating her own stories and inviting fans to convert them into folklore. *The Tortured Poets Department* builds on this intention, with Taylor picking up ancient folkloric motifs, modernizing them through her own experience, and again, handing them back to her fans.

"The Manuscript," the final track of the double album, states this goal explicitly, ending with the line, "But the story isn't mine anymore." By concluding her album this way, Taylor comments on the way that stories she

Taylor Swift and Philosophy: Essays from the Tortured Philosophers Department, First Edition. Edited by Catherine M. Robb and Georgie Mills.
© 2025 John Wiley & Sons, Inc. Published 2025 by John Wiley & Sons, Inc.

has written previously are transformed by the passion and engagement of the fans. Perhaps without realizing it, she also endorses "the death of the author." This idea, first outlined in a 1967 essay by literary critic Roland Barthes, argues that authorial intent is less important than the reader's interpretation of a work.[3] By invoking this idea, Taylor attempts to turn her autobiography into folklore and epic poetry. Her use and modernization of mythic motifs in *The Tortured Poets Department* adds to this effect, making her an epic poet of the modern age.

"The Black Dog"

Black dog legends are a common motif in the folklore of England and the Celtic nations. Each Celtic nation has its own black dog myth, as do the Channel Islands and many of the counties and regions in England. The myths and stories vary. Some black dogs hunt human beings, while others just want to curl up beside the fire. The spectral hound from Manx folklore, the Moddey Dhoo, is said to haunt Peel Castle on the Isle of Man. While terrifying to behold, this black dog becomes less intimidating if allowed to sit peacefully beside a lit fireplace, and it attacks only when provoked. Haunting castles is a common theme in black dog myths, along with haunting churchyards, forests, and moors. Welsh folklore contains the myth of the Gwyllgi, a black dog who guards St. Donat's Castle in South Wales. Some dogs are an omen of death, some actually cause it. East Anglia has the myth of Black Shuck, a large, red-eyed dog who is thought to be an omen of imminent death.

Though black dog myths are often transferred by word of mouth as part of local folkloric tradition, they have occasionally made their way into literature, with Charlotte Brontë and Arthur Conan Doyle repopularizing black dog myths by including allusions to them in their stories.[4] A modern development in the black dog mythology is its transformation into a metaphor for depression. It's unclear where this use of the black dog as a metaphor began exactly, because some of its uses are ambiguous. For example, Robert Bly's poem "Melancholia" refers to "a black dog near me," but it is unclear if this is a metaphor for depression itself or a way to evoke the image of an omen of death that the black dog represents in folklore or, more likely, both.[5] The black dog as a metaphor for depression is now so ubiquitous in modern parlance that the Black Dog Institute is an organization dedicated to mental health treatment and research that takes its name from this metaphor.

As Swifties know, *The Tortured Poets Department* includes a song titled "The Black Dog." Within the context of the song the narrator's phone location-sharing app indicates that her ex-partner has entered a bar called The Black Dog. In the song the narrator mourns their relationship, and we can interpret this as a modernization of the black dog myths from folklore. The bar is Taylor's Black Shuck, signifying the death of her relationship. The ex-partner walking into the Black Dog seems to break the narrator's heart anew, as in the lyric "And so I watch as you walk / Into some bar called The Black Dog / And pierce new holes in my heart." The listener gets the impression that the narrator, who we assume to be Taylor, takes the action of visiting the bar as confirmation that the relationship is over. We might also see the name of the bar as an allusion to the depression that both she and her ex-partner are experiencing in the aftermath of their breakup, or the depression that they experienced throughout their relationship.

Toward the end of the song, Taylor turns the black dog myth on its head by comparing the narrator's ex-partner to a dog himself, with the lyric "tail between your legs you're leaving." Someone running away with "their tail between their legs" is an idiom used to describe shame or embarrassment by comparing them to a frightened dog. We can see this as a subversion of myths like the Moddey Dhoo. Instead of a fearsome-looking creature who is a lot less terrifying in the light of a warm fire, the ex-partner was a promising love interest who turned out to be cowardly and hurtful upon closer inspection.

"Cassandra"

In ancient mythology, the princess Cassandra was kidnapped from Troy during the Trojan War and brought back to Greece by Agamemnon. Cassandra had both a blessing and a curse: she could see the future, but she would never be believed. According to some legends, this was a curse from Apollo, who had pursued Cassandra and was rejected by her. The mythic Cassandra lived through a war that she knew from the start was doomed to be lost. According to some retellings, she even foresaw her own death, along with Agamemnon's, just as it was about to happen. Cassandra is thus emblematic of the frustrating phenomenon of being right, but not being listened to.

In her song "Cassandra," Taylor sings, "They killed Cassandra first 'cause she feared the worst / And tried to tell the town." This is a creative departure from the traditional mythology, according to which Cassandra was not killed for her warnings, just ignored. Her death eventually came when she was captured by Agamemnon, taken to his home, and then killed by either Aegisthus or Clytemnestra, depending on whose version of the story you are listening to.

We can read Taylor's "Cassandra" in two ways. Either Cassandra is the narrator for most of the song, with Taylor switching between first and third person to tell Cassandra's story from both Cassandra's and Taylor's points of view. Or perhaps Taylor is telling her own story, and mentioning Cassandra for the similarities between them. If we take the latter interpretation, the song tells a story of Taylor speaking honestly about something that later turned out to be true, though nobody believed her at the time. This might explain why her version of Cassandra was killed for her foresight. Taylor may be telling a story of a time when she, or the narrator whose point of view she adopts, feels attacked and vilified for her warnings. She sings "When the truth comes out it's quiet," mirroring the mythic Cassandra who, when her prophecies turn out to be right all along, is rarely acknowledged for her foresight. Notably, Taylor sings, "They say, 'What doesn't kill you makes you aware' / What happens if it becomes who you are?" In this line, Taylor paints a picture of a person so distressed by the experience of not being believed (like Cassandra) that it has become part of their identity. One might even say that the experience hangs from their neck like ...

"The Albatross"

An albatross is a seabird with a large wingspan. A good omen at sea, according to folktales among sailors, albatrosses are seen as the souls of dead sailors, visiting to bring good luck to the living members of their crew. The bird is often white with a black streak down its substantial wings, somewhat resembling Taylor Swift's white gown and black gloves at the 2024 Grammy Award ceremony.

To say that something is like an albatross around your neck is to suggest that something is heavy, burdensome, and impossible to free yourself from. This metaphor comes from Samuel Coleridge's poem *The Rime of the Ancient Mariner* (1797–1798), in which the titular ancient mariner shoots down an albatross unprovoked while at sea.[6] Soon after, the south winds that had carried the ship are gone, and the mariner and his crew are stranded on the calm sea, slowly succumbing to their thirst. The albatross around the mariner's neck serves as a symbolic reminder of his guilt, shame, and callousness. He killed an innocent creature, and his crew are doomed as a consequence. The mariner lives on, while his crew all die. Only when he appreciates the beauty and majesty of the natural world around him is his curse broken, allowing him to return to his homeland.

Taylor plays with this symbol in her song, "The Albatross." Her narration switches between third and first person, singing "She's the albatross" throughout the song until the final chorus, where she changes to "I'm the albatross." We could interpret this song as a retelling of warnings to stay away from the narrator, warnings that the narrator subverts in the final chorus. If we assume the song to be about Taylor herself, she is both described as an albatross as a warning by others, but also as a savior by herself. In the chorus she sings "She's the albatross / She is here to destroy you." Perhaps this is a warning for someone who has wronged her, whose actions are then immortalized in song and will hang around their neck like the mariner's albatross. Or perhaps it is a note of caution for a potential partner who, once involved with Taylor, will be saddled with media attention and fan scrutiny.

In the final repetition of the chorus, Taylor changes the line to "I'm the albatross / I swept in at the rescue." She has turned the order of *The Rime of the Ancient Mariner* around. Instead of going from a friendly helper to a burden and a curse, Taylor's albatross has transformed from the burdensome curse of the mariner to the positive force that the albatross is in folklore more generally—though Taylor still describes the albatross as "terrible danger" during this chorus.

Coleridge's poem transformed the folkloric figure of the albatross from a good omen for sailors into a metaphor for a heavy burden or a guilt-ridden existence. Taylor has taken the sorrowful figure of Coleridge's albatross and transformed the bird back into the good omen of folklore, an agent of rescue. This, along with the music, which sounds light and triumphant during the chorus of "The Albatross," has given us a new turn in the folklore, casting the bird as a symbol of both optimism and danger at the same time.

"The Prophecy"

In Taylor's "The Prophecy," the narrator pleads "Let it once be me / Who do I have to speak to / About if they can redo / The prophecy?" The song expresses concern about being doomed never to have a lasting partnership. But in mythology and folklore, prophecies tend to come true regardless of one's pleading, or one's efforts to evade them. Cassandra's prophecies always came true, and that was part of her curse.

It's a trope in folklore that only fools try to avoid their prophesized fate. Consider the case of Oedipus. Upon hearing that he was prophesized to kill his father and marry his mother, Oedipus left home. But this led to the events in which he killed King Laius, who turned out to be his father, and married Queen Jocasta, who turned out to be his mother. When Oedipus was an infant, Laius and Jocasta heard the prophecy that their son would kill Laius and marry Jocasta. To avoid the prophecy they ordered their infant son to be killed, but the infant survived and did not know his own true identity. So the actions of Laius and Jocasta created the conditions for their son to return as a stranger who did not realize who he was killing and who he was marrying.

Taylor's prophecy, that her narrator's relationship must end, is not one that she goes out of her way to avoid. That she even describes it as a prophecy implies that she thinks its end was somehow inevitable. Nonetheless, she pleads for the prophecy to be changed, and for it to be possible for her to have a happy relationship that lasts. Taylor invokes the mythological trope of prophecy to make the listener feel powerless on behalf of the narrator. It is not her choices that get in the way of her happiness but some "curse." She sings "I got cursed like Eve got bitten." Here, by referring to Eve, Taylor evokes the biblical notion of original sin, a sin inherited from the mythic first woman. The line is in passive voice, Taylor "got" cursed, Eve "got" bitten, implying innocence and a lack of agency on the part of the narrator, who feels powerless to make a relationship work.[7]

Conclusion: "The Manuscript"

In *The Rime of the Ancient Mariner*, the mariner himself, though back in his homeland, is still cursed to retell the story of the albatross at length to anyone he can. He is the narrator of the poem, though Coleridge is the poet. The ancient mariner and Taylor share similarities as narrators. First, their fondness for derailing weddings.[8] Second, Taylor seems cursed, as the mariner is, to tell her story to anyone who will hear it. As someone who enjoys their work and had singing and songwriting as a long-held ambition before their career began, Taylor probably finds this to be a blessing rather than a curse. Nevertheless she has narrated painful and detailed pieces of memory and emotion into song for her fans' enjoyment. By transforming her experiences into folk tales, Taylor transforms herself into narrator rather than subject.

This is especially evident in the final song from *The Tortured Poets Department: The Anthology* (as she called the full double album). In "The Manuscript," Taylor switches between third person and first person. She narrates a story, ostensibly about herself, in the third person, detailing a promising relationship and a painful breakup. Midway through the song, she describes the process of writing something, and then actors hitting their marks. At the very end, she switches to speaking in the first person, describing how she rereads the manuscript every now and then, but the "story isn't mine anymore."

The narratology here tells the story along with the lyrics. By switching from third to first person, Taylor treats herself as the narrator of the story, only acknowledging the autobiographical nature of it in the first-person section at the end, the very section where she states that it no longer belongs to her. She volunteers to be the subject of that story right at the point where it takes place in the imagination of others rather than in her own life. In doing so, she mythologizes herself. Taylor's life is the story to be transmitted through song and fandom, to become folklore.

The Tortured Poets Department combines mythic motifs with autobiographical stories, all while switching narrative voice and person. The entire work closes with the assertion that "the story isn't mine anymore," positioning Taylor as a modern-day Homer, who was himself the legendary origin of an impactful iteration of a collectively owned story. Taylor thus enacts "the death of the author." Fans are invited to read their own interpretations into the stories she tells, and to keep on telling them. There is some irony to this, given her quest to regain ownership of her masters, but there is nothing hypocritical. Taylor wants to own her works, but she wants to share ownership of her stories. She has retold stories that others originated, and in turn she wants others to retell her stories. So Taylor is sincere when she tells us that the story isn't hers anymore. Taylor Swift has found a truly contemporary way to "turn my life into folklore" and in doing so, she has made herself a legend in her own lifetime.

Notes

1. Taylor Swift via Instagram, July 24, 2020.
2. This refers to the "teenage love triangle" from the album *folklore* in which Taylor Swift writes three songs from the perspective of three different characters.
3. Roland Barthes, "Death of the Author," *Aspen* 5–6 (1967).
4. Sir Arthur Conan Doyle, *The Hound of the Baskervilles*, serialized in *The Strand Magazine*, nos. 128–136 (first published in book form, London: George Newnes, 1902). Charlotte Brontë (publishing as Currer Bell), *Jane Eyre* (London: Smith, Elder & Co., 1947).
5. Robert Bly, "Melancholia," in *The Light Around the Body* (New York: Harper & Row, 1967).
6. Samuel Taylor Coleridge, *The Rime of the Ancient Mariner*, in *Lyrical Ballads* (London: J. & A. Arch, 1798).
7. Bonus track "Peter": Though Peter Pan was created by Scottish writer J.M. Barrie, he has so frequently been written into creative retellings of his story that he is acquiring a similar status to mythological figures such as Black Shuck and Cassandra. Barrie wrote several stories featuring Peter, in which he is friends with other folkloric creatures such as fairies and mermaids. His depiction is reminiscent of folkloric creatures such as Puck, also known as Robin Goodfellow, a mischievous associate of the faerie folk. Taylor Swift refers to Peter Pan twice in her discography: "cardigan," from the album *folklore*, contains the line "Try to change the ending / Peter losing Wendy," and in "Peter" from *The Tortured Poets Department,* Taylor follows this through to its conclusion, writing Wendy's point of view as she waits by the window before eventually giving up on the idea that Peter will grow up and come back for her. Fans speculate that Peter in this story represents a real relationship in Taylor's life, but regardless, in retelling this story of Wendy waiting grown up by the window in vain, Taylor has become a transformative contributor to the mythology of Peter Pan.
8. The ancient mariner in Coleridge's poem tells his story to people who are almost late to a wedding and, in telling it, forces them to miss the ceremony. Taylor Swift's song "Speak Now" is about interrupting a wedding to object to the union.

Index of Terms and Names

Index of Taylor Swift's Songs and Albums

Taylor Swift and Philosophy: Essays from the Tortured Philosophers Department, First Edition. Edited by Catherine M. Robb and Georgie Mills.
© 2025 John Wiley & Sons, Inc. Published 2025 by John Wiley & Sons, Inc.